Mac OS X KillerTips

Scott Kelby

MAC OS X KILLER TIPS

**The Mac OS X
Killer Tips Team**

EDITOR
Richard Theriault

TECHNICAL EDITORS
**Chris Main
Barbara Thompson**

PRODUCTION EDITOR
Kim Gabriel

PRODUCTION
**Dave Damstra
Dave Korman**

CAPTURES
Dave Gales

PROOFREADER
Daphne Durkee

COVER DESIGN AND
CREATIVE CONCEPTS
Felix Nelson

The New Riders Team

PUBLISHER
Stephanie Wall

EXECUTIVE EDITOR
Steve Weiss

PRODUCTION MANAGER
Gina Kanouse

SENIOR PROJECT EDITOR
Kristy Hart

PRODUCTION
Gloria Schurick

PROOFREADER
Sheri Cain

PUBLISHED BY
New Riders Publishing

International Standard Book Number: 0-73571-393-6

Library of Congress Catalog Card Number: 2003112022

07 06 05 04   7 6 5 4 3

Interpretation of the printing code: The rightmost double-digit number is the year of the book's printing; the rightmost single-digit number is the number of the book's printing. For example, the printing code 03-1 shows that the first printing of the book occurred in 2003.

Composed in Myriad and Minion by NAPP Publishing

Printed in the United States of America

Trademarks

Warning and Disclaimer

www.newriders.com
www.scottkelbybooks.com

For my amazing wife, Kalebra

"You don't marry someone you can live with.

You marry the person you cannot live without."

—UNKNOWN

ACKNOWLEDGMENTS

Although only one person's name winds up on the spine of this book, it takes a large army of people to put out a book, and without their help, dedication, and tireless efforts, there wouldn't even have been a spine; and to them I'm greatly indebted.

First, I want to thank absolutely just the coolest person I've ever met—my wife, Kalebra. I don't know how I ever got lucky enough to marry her 14 years ago, but it was without a doubt the smartest thing I've ever done, and the greatest blessing God's ever given me. She just flat-out rocks, and at this point, I can't imagine that the crush I've had on her since the first time I met her will ever go away. I love you, Sweetie!

Secondly, I want to thank my son, Jordan. Little Buddy—there's so much of your mom in you, in particular her kind, loving heart, and that's about the best head start anyone could ask for in life. You're the greatest little guy in the world, and thanks so much for making me smile every single day while I was writing this book, and for setting up your iBook next to me so we can "write books together."

I want to thank my team at KW Media Group—they're a unique group of people, with limitless energy and amazing talent, and I'd put them up against anybody in the business. In particular, I want to thank my Creative Director Felix Nelson for his great ideas, cool cover designs, intro artwork, and for his ongoing dedication and consistently amazing attitude. I want to thank my Tech Editor Chris Main for making sure everything works the way it should, and for never letting me slide anything by him. I want to thank the amazing layout master Dave Damstra for making the book look so squeaky clean, my Production Editor Kim Gabriel for making sure everything came together on time, and kudos to my editing and design crew Barbara Thompson, Daphne Durkee, Margie Rosenstein, and Dave Korman.

As always, a special thanks goes to my very good friend Dave Moser for his unwavering commitment to making sure that everything we do is better than what we've done before. He's an insipration to everyone on our team; he helps us go places we couldn't go without him, and I'm honored to have him at the helm.

I'm really delighted to be working once again with my original editor at *Mac Today* magazine, Richard "Dicky" Theriault. He's an absolute joy to work with, and he knows the Mac market, and the people in it, inside and out. His help, input, guidance, and friendship are very important, and warmly appreciated.

I owe a huge debt of gratitude to my good friend Terry White. Terry is a major Mac OS X tip hound (and president of MacGroup-Detroit, one of the very best Macintosh User Groups anywhere), and he was kind enough to share so many of his cool tips and amazing tricks with me; and this book is far better than it would have been without his help. Thank you, man—I owe you big time! Also, many thanks go to Dave Gales who helped me with the screen captures, while being my personal IT dept., idea man, go-to guy, and friend. Your help really means a lot.

I want to thank my friends and business partners Jim Workman and Jean Kendra for their support and enthusiasm for all of my writing projects, and to Pete Kratzenberg for making it all add up. I also want to thank my brother Jeff for letting me constantly "pick his brain," and for his many ideas, input, support, hard work, and most of all for just being such a great brother to me always. And a loving thanks to my dad, Jerry Kelby, for being the father all others are measured by.

Of course, I couldn't do any of it without the help of my wonderful assistant Kathy Siler, and all the "behind-the-scenes" team at KW Media who constantly keep raising the bar.

I want to thank all of my "Mac Buddies" who've taught me so much over the years, including Bill Carroll, Jim Goodman, Dick Theriault, Don Wiggins, Dave Gales, Jim Patterson, Larry Becker, Jim Workman, Jon Gales, Jim Nordquist, and a big thanks to my buddy Rod "Mac Daddy" Harlan (President of the DVPA) for his contribution of some very cool iDVD tips.

Thanks to Steve Weiss, Nancy Ruenzel, Scott Cowlin, and everyone at New Riders and Peachpit Publishing for their ongoing commitment to excellence, and for the honor of letting me be one of their "Voices that Matter."

And most importantly, an extra special thanks to God and His son Jesus Christ for always hearing my prayers, for always being there when I need Him, and for blessing me with a wonderful life I truly love, and such a warm loving family to share it with.

ABOUT THE AUTHOR

Scott Kelby

Scott is Editor-in-Chief and co-founder of *Mac Design Magazine,* Editor-in-Chief of *Photoshop User* magazine, Editor-in-Chief of Nikon's *Capture User,* and president of the National Association of Photoshop Professionals, the trade association for Adobe® Photoshop® users. Scott is also president of KW Media Group, Inc., a Florida-based software training and publishing firm.

Scott is author of the best-selling books, *The Mac OS X Conversion Kit*, *Macintosh: The Naked Truth, Photoshop CS Down & Dirty Tricks, The Photoshop CS Book for Digital Photographers,* and co-author of *Photoshop CS Killer Tips,* from New Riders Publishing. He's a contributing author to the books *Photoshop Effects Magic, Adobe Web Publishing & Design Unleashed, and Maclopedia, the Ultimate Reference on Everything Macintosh* from Hayden Books.

Scott is Training Director for the Adobe Photoshop Seminar Tour, Technical Conference Chair for the Mac Design Conference and PhotoshopWorld, and is a speaker at graphics and photography conferences and events around the world. Scott is also featured in a series of Adobe Photoshop video training tapes and DVDs and has been training Mac users and graphics professionals since 1993.

For more background info, visit www.scottkelby.com.

TABLE OF CONTENTS

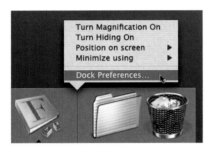

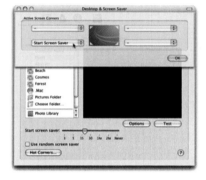

TABLE OF CONTENTS

DT – Wild
Radial Breakaway
Neon

Tri–Cycle
Directrix Expand X
Hue Wheel

TABLE OF CONTENTS

TABLE OF CONTENTS

WARNING:
AS MANY AS 7% OF THE PEOPLE WHO START HERE WILL SUFFER SPONTANEOUS BLINDNESS

Wait a minute. Is this just a scam to get me to read the book's introduction?

Honestly? Yes. That's exactly what it is, so don't worry; 7% of you aren't going to experience spontaneous blindness. It's really more like 4%. I hate to resort to this kind of hyperbole just to get you to read the introduction but because this is a totally different kind of Mac book, it's really important that you fully read the introduction (and it wouldn't hurt if you memorized each paragraph, including punctuation, just in case). Look, it's only like three pages long, and quickly reading it will answer a lot of your questions, help you to get the most out of this book, and lead you to a true and lasting inner peace that only comes from becoming "one" with the introduction. Let us begin.

What exactly is a Killer Tip book?

There are two types of people in this world: (1) the type of people who want to understand everything before they do anything. These are the people who buy a new computer, read the entire instruction manual, inventory all the packing items, and only when they feel certain that they have a full and complete understanding of the entire project before them, do they actually remove the styrofoam cover and pull their new Mac out of the shipping carton. There are no more than 17 of these people using Macs in the world today. This book is not for them.

This book is for (2) the rest of us. People who buy a Mac, tear open the box, set it all up, turn it on, and start messin' around with it. These same people eventually buy computer books, and while casually flipping through them, they stop to read all the sidebar tips first. These are people like you and me. (Well, at least like me, anyway.) I'm an absolute sucker for sidebar tips. I'm hooked on 'em, and whenever I buy a new computer book, the first thing I do is read all those cool little tips scattered throughout the sidebars. Sometimes, they're in boxes with a tinted background (like the one shown on the left), sometimes they're on the side of the page, sometimes at the bottom—it doesn't matter—if it says the word tip, I'm drawn to it like an attorney to a slip-and-fall injury in a Vegas casino.

I finally figured out why I like sidebar tips so much—it's where the "really cool stuff" is. Think about it, if you were writing a computer book and you found some really ingenious technique, some really great undocumented keyboard shortcut, or a closely-guarded inside secret you to wanted to share with your readers—you'd want it to stand out and yell, "Hey, there's a very cool thing right over here!" You're not going to bury it inside paragraphs of techno-text. This is exciting stuff. It's intriguing. It's fun. So, you pull it out from the regular text, slap a border around it, add a tint behind it, and maybe even add a special graphic to

TIP

This is a sidebar tip. Every great Mac book has a few of them. But this book is nothing but them. A whole book of cool sidebar tips. Without the sidebars.

get the reader's attention. It works. The only problem with sidebar tips is—there's just not enough of 'em.

So I got to thinkin', "Wouldn't it be cool if there was a book where the whole book, cover-to-cover, was nothing but those little sidebar tips? No long paragraphs explaining the Hierarchical File System. No detailed descriptions of how to configure a LAN, or 16 ways to partition your hard drive—just the fun stuff—just the tips. Well, that's exactly what this is—a book of nothing but Mac OS X sidebar tips. Without the sidebars.

So what exactly is a "Killer Tip?"

"Double-click on a folder to open it." Technically, that is a tip. It's a very lame tip. It's a boringly obvious tip, and it's definitely not a Killer Tip. If it's a "Killer Tip," it makes you "nod and smile" when you read it, and you'll be nodding and smiling so much in this book, you're going to look like "a bobbing dog" in the rear window of a Buick Park Avenue. (I used a Buick Park Avenue as an example because it has a big enough rear window that you can climb up there yourself to test out my prediction. See, I care.) The goal here is to give you tips that are so cool that after reading just a few, you have to pick up the phone, call your Mac buddies, and totally tune them up with your newfound Mac OS X power.

Now, I have to tell you, the tips in this book are designed for people who are already using Mac OS X, so there's not much beginner stuff in here. However, if you *are* a Mac beginner, I have a special bonus for you—a secret special downloadable chapter of beginner tips that I put together just for you. So technically, the tips in this downloadable beginner's chapter are not "Killer Tips," they're Mac OS X beginner tips written in a Killer Tips style, but hey—they're free, I made them especially for you, and all you have to do is download the PDF chapter from www.scottkelbybooks.com/begtips.html.

Is this book for you?

Is this book for you? Are you kidding? This book is so for you that if you're reading this in a bookstore, and you don't have the money to buy it, you'll shoplift it—risking possible incarceration just to unlock the secrets its coated pages hold. But you won't have to shoplift it, because if you're reading a Macintosh book, you bought a Macintosh computer, and that probably means you've lots of money. So buy at least two copies.

Look, although I don't know you personally, I'm willing to bet you love those little sidebar tips just as much as I do. If you didn't, authors would've stopped adding them to their books years ago. But as much as you love those sidebar tips, you still want something more. That's right—you want visuals. As cool as those sidebar tips are, they're usually just a tiny little box with a couple of lines of text (like the sidebar shown at left). So in this book, I thought I'd expand the explanations just enough to make them more accessible, and then add an accompanying screen capture if (a) it helps make the tip easier to understand, or (b) if the page just looks really boring without them.

Is there any UNIX? It scares me.

Mac OS X is built on UNIX, but don't worry—it pretty much stays out of your way. Here's a way to think of it: The pilots of commercial airliners use engines to fly the plane, right? But if

TIP

When you see a gray tinted box hanging out in the sidebar like this, you can't help but read it, right? That's because you're addicted to gray tinted boxes.

they want to start the engines, they don't climb out on each wing and manually crank them up—they do it from up in the cockpit with a flick of a switch. That's kind of like Mac OS X's relationship with UNIX. You're up front in the cockpit running things, you push Macintosh buttons, and UNIX responds (quite brilliantly, I might add), without you having to get your hands dirty.

The vast majority of people who use Mac OS X will never mess with its UNIX "soul" directly (by "mess with," I mean altering their system by writing UNIX command lines. It's not for the faint of heart, because in some cases, if you make a mistake while coding, you can seriously mess up your Mac). That's why I decided not to include UNIX tips in the book—I didn't want to have a situation where the vast majority of the book's readers would see a UNIX chapter and go, "Oh, that's not for me." I wanted everybody to have the chance to use every single tip, in every single chapter. However, if you're really into the UNIX side of Mac OS X, I didn't want to leave you out altogether, so I put some of my favorite UNIX tips on the book's companion Web site just for you, at www.scottkelbybooks.com/macosxkillertips/scaryunixstuff.html.

Okay, how do I get started?

My books aren't set up like a novel—you can jump in anywhere and start on any page. That's true for all of my books, with the notable exception of *Macintosh: the Naked Truth*, which is about what life is really like being a Mac user in a PC-dominated world. I'm not going to try to plug that book here (ISBN 0-7357-1284-0 from New Riders Publishing. $19.99 found any-where cool Mac books are sold) because that's just tacky (Amazon.com offers discounts on the book—order yours today). Well, with this book, you don't have to start at Chapter 1 and read your way through to the back (although there's nothing wrong with that). Actually, you can start in any chapter and immediately try the tips that interest you the most. Also, don't forget to read each chapter's intro page—it's critical to your understanding of what's in that particular chapter. (That's totally not true, but it took me a long time to write those intros, so I use little lies like that to get you to read them. Sad, isn't it?)

Wait! One last thing!

I want to let you know, before you go any further, that the only three sidebar tip "boxes" in the entire book appear in the sidebars of this introduction. So, don't go looking for them because (as I said) this book is made up of sidebar tips *without* the sidebars. Okay tiger—I'm cuttin' you loose. It's time to go get "tipsy."

> **TIP**
>
> *You're doing it again! Stop looking at these sidebars. See, they're intoxicating—you're drawn to them even after you know it's not really a tip. Okay, here's a real tip: If you like sidebar tips, buy this book.*

window
wonderland

COOL WINDOW TIPS →

I have to be honest with you. I have some major concerns about the subhead for this chapter: "Cool Window Tips."

Window Wonderland

cool window tips

My fear is that you might give it a quick glance and accidentally read it as "Cool Windows Tips" which this chapter, in a Mac OS X book, clearly is not. It fact, this couldn't be a chapter on Microsoft Windows, primarily because I don't know Windows. Well, I know where the Start menu is, and I can launch an application (if it's fairly easy to find) but that's as much as I'm willing to admit (at least without a Congressional subpoena). Besides, how could there be anything cool about Windows? So what is this chapter really about? I was hoping you would know. Hmmmm. This is kind of embarrassing. Okay, I'll take a stab at it—it sounds like it's probably filled with tips on using Finder windows, managing your files within them, and other cool window tips that will amuse your friends and absolutely captivate small children and family pets (except, of course, for fish, which are waiting patiently for you to overfeed them).

   YOU CAN ALWAYS GO BACK

If you have the toolbar hidden, with its all-important Go Back button, you can still go back to the previous window by pressing Command-[(that's the Left Bracket key, which appears diagonally to the left of the Return key on your keyboard).

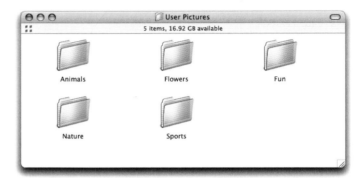

   BURNING A CD RIGHT FROM YOUR FINDER WINDOW

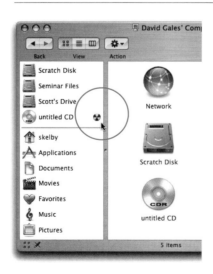

If you've loaded a blank CD (or DVD) into your Mac, it appears in the Sidebar of any open Finder window. A little Burn button appears to the right of the blank CD's name (which is "untitled CD" by default). So now, when you're ready to burn that disc (maybe you're using this disc to back up some files), you can simply press the tiny Burn button that appears right within the Sidebar. Burning doesn't get much more convenient than that.

SEPARATING THE RIFF-RAFF IN YOUR TOOLBAR

I remember the first time I saw a separator bar in someone's toolbar. I thought, "This is the slickest person in the world," or maybe it was, "Gee, I wonder how they got that separator!" I can't remember

which. Either way, they're handy and look cool. To get yours, just Option-Command-click on the little pill-shaped button in the top right of your title bar to bring up the Customize Toolbar dialog. Then, in the collection of icons that appears in the dialog, just drag the Separator icon and drop it right where you want it in the toolbar.

SIDEBAR'S SPACE-SAVING ICON VIEW

If you think the Sidebar takes up a little too much room, you can use its icon view (which displays just the icons of items in the Sidebar, and not their names, which take up most of the space). To get to this space-saving icons-only view, just click-and-drag the gray divider bar (which separates the Sidebar from the folder's contents) to the left, covering the names of the Sidebar items, until it "snaps" to the icons, leaving just the icons visible (and their names neatly hidden). If after doing this, you're not sure which file is which, just place your cursor over one of these Sidebar icons, and its name pops up. If you decide you want the full names visible again, click on the bar again and drag to the right. When you drag past the longest name in the Sidebar list, the divider gently snaps into place.

   GETTING RID OF THE PREVIEW COLUMN

If you've used Mac OS X's Column view, you know that when you click on a file, you get a large preview of that file in a new column type called the Preview column. Click on a graphic—you see its preview. Large! This "feature" annoys the heck out of some people (you know who you are), so to turn off this special column, just view a window in Column view, then press Command-J to bring up the Column View Options. Turn off the checkbox for Show Preview Column and this wonderful (yet occasionally annoying) Preview column disappears.

   CONTROLLING WHAT SHOWS UP IN YOUR SIDEBAR

By default, a whole bunch of "stuff" shows up in your Sidebar, like your hard disks (including any partitions), your iDisk, network volumes, CDs, DVDs, FireWire drives, etc.; plus in the lower section, your Desktop, Home folder, and Applications folders are all there. In fact, there's so much of "their" stuff, there's not much room for "your" stuff. Luckily, you can decide what appears in the Sidebar and what doesn't. Just go under the Finder menu and choose Preferences. When the dialog appears, click on the Sidebar icon (up top) and a list of the default Sidebar items appears. Uncheck any items you don't want cluttering up your Sidebar.

QUICKLY HIDING THE SIDEBAR

If you want to hide the Sidebar (but leave the toolbar still visible) just double-click anywhere within the gray vertical divider bar that separates the Sidebar from the folder's contents. If you're charging by the hour, instead of double-clicking, you can click on the bar, and drag to the left until the Sidebar snaps

shut. To bring the Sidebar back, just double-click on the left side of your Finder window and it springs back open.

   USING "FAVORITES" IN PANTHER

If you're used to how previous versions of Mac OS X handled Favorites, you'll have to get used to a whole new flavor in Panther. First, Apple hid the Favorites folder. (I think they did this because they want you to use the Sidebar for your favorites, rather than the Favorites folder itself.) But, if you want the Favorites folder back, look inside your Home folder, inside your Library folder, where you'll find a Favorites folder. Drag this folder to the Sidebar of any open Finder window. When you do this, the Favorites folder icon changes to the Familiar "red heart" icon, and you can put aliases of your most used folders and files within this Favorites folder. Then, you're only one click away, even in Open/Save dialogs.

   SPEED TIP: FASTER FULL NAME VIEWING IN LIST VIEW

When you're looking for files in either List view or Column view, it's almost certain that some of your files with long names will have some of their letters (or even full words) cut off from view. There is a tip that saves you from having to resize your List or Column view columns—just hold your cursor over the file's truncated name for a few seconds and, eventually, its full name pops up. So what's the problem? The "few seconds" part. Instead, hold the Option key, then put your cursor over the file's name, and its full name appears instantly.

   SPEED TIP: DELETING FILES VIA THE TOOLBAR

Want to delete (trash) a file with extreme prejudice? You can use the old Mac OS 9 shortcut of clicking on the file and pressing Command-Delete, which puts it on the express lane to the Trash, but another thing you can do is add the Delete icon right to your toolbar. Then, you can click on a file, and click the Delete icon for a one-way ticket to the Trash. You do that by going under the View menu and choosing Customize Toolbar. When the dialog appears, you'll see the Delete icon (the red circle with a diagonal line through it). Drag that up to the toolbar and click Done, and now it's right there, ready for the clicking. (Just remember to click on the file you want to delete first before you click the Delete icon.)

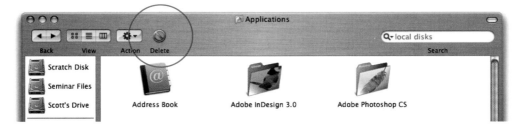

MOVING WINDOWS BEHIND YOUR CURRENT WINDOW

This is a really handy tip for "window overload" while you're working in the Finder. If you're working within a window, you can actually move non-active windows that appear behind it. Just hold the Command key and click-and-drag their title bars to move them (even though you're moving them, it doesn't bring them to front or make them active). Better yet, if you want to minimize or close any of these "windows in the back," you don't even have to hold the Command key: Just move your cursor over their inactive Close, Minimize, or Zoom buttons on the left-hand side of the title bar, and they become active (they appear in their usual red, yellow, and green).

   ## COLUMN VIEW'S HIDDEN POWER

One of the coolest benefits of Column view (the third choice from the left in the toolbar's View icon section) is that, depending on the file, you can see a preview of its contents (at least if it's a photo, MP3 audio file, or a QuickTime movie). This is especially helpful if you're searching for a QuickTime movie, because if you click on a movie while in Column view, a large thumbnail showing the first frame of the movie appears in the far right column. But more importantly, the QuickTime Player controls appear just below the thumbnail. To see the movie, right there in the Column view (without having to launch the full QuickTime Player), just click on the Play button.

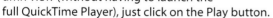

KNOWING YOUR STATUS (ANY TIME, IN ANY WINDOW)

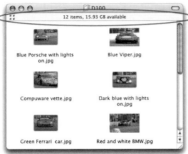

The status bar (the thin little bar that shows how many items are in your window and how much drive space you still have available) was at the top of every Finder window back in Mac OS 9. In earlier versions of Mac OS X (including Jaguar), the status bar was off by default, so you had to turn it on, and then it appeared at the top of your Finder windows. In Panther, you'll find the status bar info displayed at the bottom center of every Finder window by default (well, that's true as long as your toolbar is visible). If that's the case, why is there still a menu command called "Show Status Bar?" That's because, if you hide the toolbar, it hides the status info at the bottom of the window, so you need the old status bar back. It's still off by default, so to turn on the status bar, first open a window, hide the toolbar, then go under the View menu and choose Show Status Bar. (*Note*: If you don't hide the toolbar first, Show Status Bar appears "grayed out.")

ADJUSTING JUST ONE COLUMN IN COLUMN VIEW

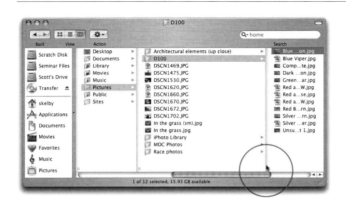

When you're in Column view, you can adjust the width of an individual column by grabbing the column tab (two tiny vertical lines) at the bottom of the divider bar that separates the columns. However, if you want to adjust all the columns at the same time, hold the Option key before you drag the column divider—then when you drag it, all the columns will resize at the same time.

JUMPING FROM COLUMN TO COLUMN

When you're in Column view, you can jump from column to column by pressing the Left and Right Arrow keys on your keyboard.

   IN LOVE WITH COLUMN VIEW? MAKE IT A PERMANENT THING

Since Icon view and List view have been around for over a decade, it's not surprising that many longtime Mac users absolutely fall head-over-heels in love with Mac OS X's lovely new Column view. If you're one of those lovelorn users, you can request that all new windows automatically open in Column view. Just go under the Finder menu, under Preferences, and click on the checkbox for Open New Windows in Column View. This turns every new window into a moment of unbridled passion that knows no bounds. Well, it does for some people anyway.

CHAPTER 1 • Cool Window Tips **13**

   OPENING FOLDERS IN NEW WINDOWS

Personally, I really like the way some things worked back in Mac OS 9. In particular, I liked that when I opened a new folder, a new window opened with the contents of that folder. As you've probably noticed, by default Mac OS X doesn't do that: If you double-click on a folder, that folder's contents are revealed in your current window. Well, if you're like me, you'd like these folders to open in their own separate window (as in previous versions of the Mac OS). So go under the Finder menu, under Preferences, click on the General icon at the top of the dialog, and choose Always Open Folders in a New Window. Ahhh, that's better!

   NEW WINDOWS FOR FOLDERS, PART 2

If you want to make use of Mac OS X's "everything opens in the same window" scheme, but occasionally, you want to open a folder in its own separate window, just hold the Command key and then double-click on the folder. Hold Option-Command, and you can have the new window open, and have the old window close automatically.

   NEW WINDOWS FOR FOLDERS, PART 3

If you're working in a window
while in Icon or List view and
you want folders to open in
their own separate window, just
press Option-Command-T first
(the shortcut for Hide Toolbar).
This hides both the toolbar and
the Sidebar, and by doing so, all
folders that you double-click on
now open in their own separate
window.

   SHOW ME THE WAY TO GO HOME

Since nearly all of your individual
files, with the exception of your
applications, will live in your Home
folder, there's a keyboard shortcut
you should become familiar with
right away. It's Shift-Command-H,
and pressing it while in the Finder
brings your Home window front
and center in a hurry. If speed isn't
an issue (and when is speed not an
issue?), you can also click on the
Home icon in the Sidebar (if you
have the Sidebar visible).

ONE-CLICK TRAIL TO YOUR FILE

This one's a handy holdover from Mac OS 9 (and previous versions of the Mac OS). If you Command-click directly on a window's name (at the top center of your window), a pop-up menu appears that shows its folder hierarchy (which folders your current window resides within).

HIDING THE TOOLBAR WHEN YOU DON'T NEED IT

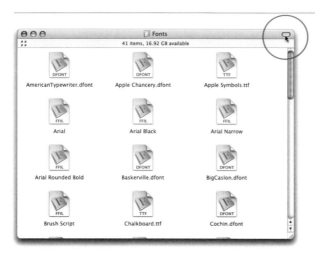

If you don't want the toolbar showing all the time (or ever for that matter), you can hide it by simply clicking on the white pill-shaped button on the top right of the window's title bar (or you can use the keyboard shortcut Option-Command-T).

  MOVING YOUR TOOLBAR ICONS AT WILL

If you decide you want to change the order of the icons in your toolbar, hold the Command key and drag them to where you want them.

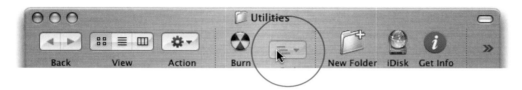

   HOW TO MAKE THE SIDEBAR WORK LIKE THE DOCK

Later in this chapter, I show how you can customize the toolbar using the Customize Toolbar command; but, you can also customize the Sidebar by adding other icons that make it even more powerful. For example, if you use Photoshop a lot, just open the window where your Photoshop application resides, drag the Photoshop icon right over to the Sidebar, and the other icons in the Sidebar slide out of the way. Now, you can use this window kind of like you would the Dock—to launch Photoshop, just click on its icon in the Sidebar, plus like the Dock, you can even drag-and-drop images you want to open right onto the Photoshop icon.

   ADDING ITEMS TO THE SIDEBAR

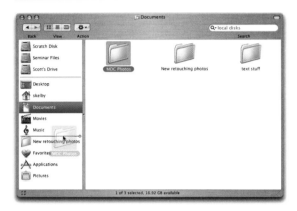

To add a file (folder, or application) to the Sidebar, just click on it and drag it right into the Sidebar (clicking on the file and pressing Command-T also does the trick). If you drag your file, you'll see a thin horizontal blue bar (with a blue circle on the end) appear in the Sidebar at the location where your dragged file (folder, etc.) will appear. If you don't like the location, drag up/down until it's where you want, then release the mouse button to drop it into place. (*Note*: Other than saving a little time, it really doesn't matter where your file originally appears when it lands in the Sidebar, because once it's there, you can just drag it up or down the list.) If you want to remove an item from the Sidebar, just click-and-drag it off the Sidebar and it will be gone in a puff of smoke.

   THE ULTIMATE CUSTOMIZE TOOLBAR SHORTCUT

If you want to customize the items in your toolbar (and there's nothing wrong with that), just Option-Command-click the little white pill-shaped button at the top right of your window's title bar, and the Customize Toolbar dialog appears, right there in your window.

TOO MANY ICONS IN YOUR TOOLBAR? SHRINK 'EM

The toolbar icons are fairly large, taking up considerable space both vertically and horizontally. If you add a few extra icons to the toolbar, the additional icons could wind up being hidden from view. What can you do? Well, you can have the toolbar display just the icons,

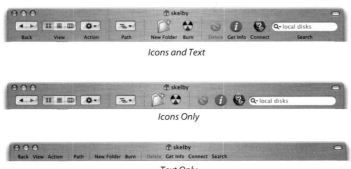

Icons and Text

Icons Only

Text Only

which saves space by removing the text and shrinking the space between the icons. To display the toolbar items by icon, rather than by icon and text, Control-click anywhere in the toolbar and choose Icon Only. If you really want to shrink the toolbar to its bare minimum, try Text Only. For even more space-saving options, try Command-clicking on the white pill-shaped button in the upper right-hand corner of the Finder window. Each time you click, you get a new space-saving look.

⬤ ⬤ ⬤ WHAT ARE THOSE TWO LITTLE GRAY ARROWS IN MY TOOLBAR?

If you've added a number of icons to your toolbar and suddenly they're not there, either of two things has happened: (1) You accidentally reinstalled Mac OS X off the original install disks (that's a joke—no one "accidentally" installs an OS. Well, at least it's very rare). Or (2) what's probably happened is that you shrank the size of your window, and when you do that,

Mac OS X automatically hides the extra toolbar icons and replaces them with those two little gray arrows. Luckily, they're "clickable," so just click on them and a pop-up menu appears giving you access to any hidden toolbar icons. When you expand the window back out, the icons reappear and the little gray arrows go away.

GETTING BACK YOUR TOOLBAR DEFAULTS

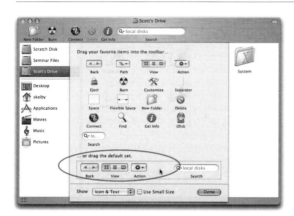

If you've made a total mess of your toolbar, there's no button for returning the icons to the default set, but getting them back there is fairly easy. First, Option-Command-click on the white pill-shaped button at the top right of your window's title bar to bring up the Customize Toolbar dialog. In the bottom left of the Customize Toolbar dialog, you'll see a set called The Default Set. Drag it to the top of the Finder window and it replaces the current icons in your toolbar.

SPEED TIP: REMOVING TOOLBAR ICONS

To remove an icon from the toolbar, you don't have to go digging through the View menu to get the Customize Toolbar dialog. Instead, just hold the Command key, click on the icon, and simply drag it off the toolbar. When you release the mouse button, the icon disappears in a puff of smoke.

THE BAD KEYBOARD SHORTCUT HALL OF FAME: NEW FOLDERS

For about 16 years, the keyboard shortcut for creating a New Folder on a Macintosh was Command-N (and it made perfect sense, because we make so many new folders). Apparently, it was too perfect, because in Mac OS X, Apple changed it. Now, it's Shift-Command-N. Of all the changes in Mac OS X, this one really just doesn't make any sense to me. If you forget, and press the old Command-N, you get a new Finder window, which I find about as useful as fish might find a bicycle. If you want to make the Shift-Command-N keyboard shortcut at least marginally helpful, go under Finder and choose Preferences. In the Finder Prefs dialog, click on the General icon at the top and for New Finder Windows Open, choose Home instead of Computer. At least that way, if you press Command-N, your Home window opens, which you'll use often. If you prefer it to open something else, other choices include any mounted disk, your iDisk, your Documents folder, any other folder you choose; pretty much everything except a stinkin' new folder.

SPEED TIP: CREATING NEW FOLDERS

Okay, so Apple took our beloved "Command-N creates a New Folder" keyboard shortcut from us, but that doesn't keep us from being one click away from a new folder. Just Option-Command-click on the little white pill-shaped button in the top right of a window's title bar to bring up the Customize Toolbar window. Drag the New Folder icon up to your toolbar, and then you're one click away from a new folder any time you need one.

   ### STOPPING THE SCROLLING BLUES

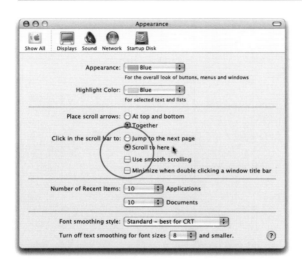

If you don't like sliding the scroll bar up and down in your documents, you can turn on a feature called Scroll to Here, which lets you jump to any position in the scroll bar by just clicking on it (rather than using the scroll handles themselves). To turn this on, go under the Apple menu, under System Preferences, and click on the Appearance icon. When the Appearance pane appears, for the setting called Click in the Scroll Bar To, choose Scroll to Here.

   ### ANOTHER ANTI-SCROLL BAR TIP

Speaking of hating to use the scroll bars, you can always use the Page Up/Page Down keys on your keyboard to move up and down. Hey, think of it this way—your hands are already resting on the keyboard—now you don't have to grab the mouse at all. (*Note*: If you have a PowerBook, hold the "fn" key and then press the Up Arrow key for Page Up and the Down Arrow key for Page Down.)

DON'T LIKE LABELS? TRY COMMENTS INSTEAD

If you're not a big fan of labels (color-coding files and folders by adding a ring of color around their name), you might want to try adding a comment instead. A comment is like your own personal note added to a file or folder. These comments are visible in Finder windows set to List view. To add a comment (your personal note) to a file, just click on the file you want to add a comment to, and then press Command-I. The Info window appears. Click on the right-facing gray triangle to the left of the word Comments to reveal a field for entering your personal notes. Just click in this field and start typing. When you're done, close the window. To see your comments when in List view, you first have to change a preference setting to make the Comments column visible. Make sure you're viewing your window in List view, and then press Command-J to bring up the View Options dialog. In the section called Show Columns, turn on the checkbox for Comments. If you want every window in List view to show comments (not just the currently active window), make sure you check the All Windows button at the top of the dialog.

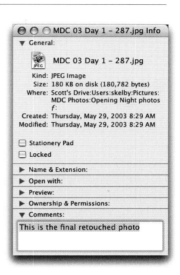

ADDING A PHOTO AS YOUR WINDOW'S BACKGROUND

As long as your Finder window is in Icon view, you can add a photo as its background. You do this by going under the View menu, under Show View Options, and in the Background section (at the bottom of the dialog), choose Picture. Click on the Select button and the standard Open/Save dialog appears where you can choose which image you'd like to have as the background of your window. Click OK and that image then appears. *Note*: This works *only* when viewing the window in Icon view. If you change to List view, the image is no longer visible.

CHAPTER 1 • Cool Window Tips   **23**

   BEATING THE ALPHABETICAL TRAP

Want a particular file to appear at the top of your list when sorting in List view by name? Just type a blank space in front of its name, and it jumps to the top of the list. (In the capture show here, after adding a space before "Third quarter report," the document now appears at the top of the alphabetical list.)

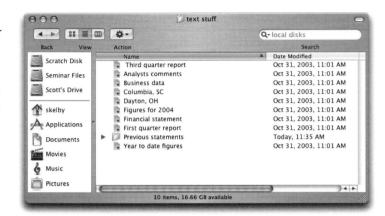

   REARRANGING THE HEADERS IN LIST VIEW

Okay, let's say you're in List view and you decide that you want the Size column to appear right after the Name column. You can make it so. Just click directly on the header named Size and drag it horizontally along the

bar until it appears right after Name. You can do the same with the other headers—move 'em where you want 'em. There's only one you can't move—the Name header. It's stuck in the first position.

SPEED TIP: NAVIGATING WITHOUT THE MOUSE

If you're looking for a faster way to navigate within Finder windows while you're in Icon view, try navigating using just your keyboard. Just as in previous versions of the Mac OS, you can use the Arrow keys on your keyboard to move from icon to icon, but you can also look inside folders by holding the Command key and pressing the Down Arrow key on your keyboard. To go back up a level (for example, close the folder and return to where you were), press Command-Up Arrow.

 JUMPING RIGHT TO THE FILE YOU WANT

Just as in previous versions of the Mac OS, if you're in a Finder window and type in the first letter of the name of the file you want—it jumps to that file. (Well, if that's the only file that starts with that letter. If there are more than one file with the same first letter, try typing the first two letters.) Also, once you select a file, if it's not the one you want, you can jump to the next file (alphabetically) by pressing the Tab key. (*Note*: The Tab key shortcut doesn't work in Column view. Use the Down Arrow key instead.)

   CLOSING MULTIPLE WINDOWS

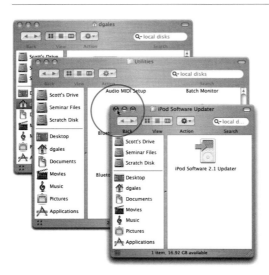

You can close all of your open desktop windows by either Option-clicking on any window's Close button, or pressing Option-Command-W.

   CONTROLLING WHAT HAPPENS WHEN YOU DOUBLE-CLICK A TITLE BAR

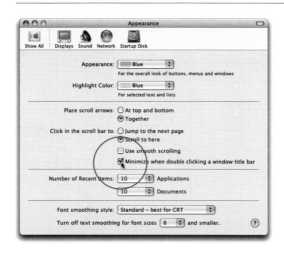

Back in OS 9, you could double-click on a window's title bar, and that window would "roll up," leaving just the window's title bar visible. In OS X, this roll-up feature has been replaced by "minimizing to the Dock," so if you double-click on a window's title bar, it minimizes that window to the Dock. If you want to minimize all of your open windows, Option-double-click on any title bar. As cool as this sounds, this "double-click to minimize" feature drives some people crazy, because they're constantly minimizing windows when they just meant to move them. If that sounds like you, go to the System Preferences, under Appearance, and turn off Minimize when Double Clicking a Window Title Bar.

WINDOW HOUSEKEEPING TIPS

If it looks as if someone tossed a grenade into your Finder window, scattering your icons everywhere with seemingly no rhyme or reason, you need an icon housekeeper. You have two different "housekeeping" choices, but once you make your choice, your windows almost straighten themselves. (1) Make sure your window is in Icon view, and then go under the View menu, choose Show View Options, and click on Snap to Grid. Now, when you move an icon around, it snaps to an invisible grid, which helps keep things organized as you work. (2) If you've got a "Monica Gellar" complex about keeping things in order, instead of choosing Snap to Grid, turn on the checkbox for Keep Arranged By, and select Name from the pop-up menu just below it. This snaps your files and folder icons to a grid alphabetically from left to right, top to bottom neatly in row. Any time you move a file, create a folder, add a new folder, it automatically "straightens itself up." Ahhh, now isn't that better?

   SAVING TIME WHEN CHANGING VIEWS OF MULTIPLE WINDOWS

Back in previous versions of Mac OS, every time you wanted to adjust the View Options for a window, you had to open the View Options dialog. So, if you wanted to adjust 10 windows, you had to open and close View Options 10 times. It was mind-numbing. Now, in Mac OS X, you can leave the View Options dialog box open the whole time, and adjust as many windows as you want. You can click on the window whose settings you want to see in the View Options, make your changes, close that Finder window, then click on the next window and make changes there—all without ever closing the View Options window. The View Options window always stays in front.

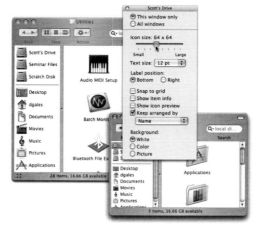

   THE WINDOW NAVIGATION TOOL BORROWED FROM PHOTOSHOP

If you use Photoshop (I've used it a couple times—it seems pretty nice), you're probably familiar with one of its tools called the Hand tool that lets you move the image around by clicking-and-dragging within in the image. Well, believe it or not, Mac OS X has a very similar tool. While in Icon or List view, just hold Option-Command and click within an open space in your window and you can move up/down and left/right in any window that has scroll bars. Freaky, ain't it?

   THE JOY OF SPRING-LOADED FOLDERS

There was a Mac OS 9 feature called spring-loaded folders that longtime Mac users liked pretty well. That is until Apple left it out of the original version of Mac OS X, and then it was as if spring-loaded folders were the most critical single feature ever (in other words—we took it for granted, until it was gone). Luckily, it made its triumphant return in Jaguar, and it works better than ever. It's designed to let you quickly navigate through a number of folders without having to waste time opening them one by one. Here's how to use it: Just drag an icon over a folder, hold it there for a moment, and the folder automatically pops open to reveal its contents. If there's another folder inside that folder, hold it over that one and it too pops open. If you change your mind, just move your icon out of the window, and all the folders automatically close themselves in a hurry. You can control the amount of time (from a short to a long delay) that it takes for a folder to "spring open" by going under the Finder menu and choosing Preferences. (You can also turn this feature off if it bothers you.) If you're not sure how much delay you should choose, try Medium. If you want a particular folder to spring open quicker, just press the Spacebar while your icon is hovering over the folder, and it opens immediately.

HIDING THE ICONS IN COLUMN VIEW

When you're viewing a Finder window in Column view, you might find it looks cleaner (and less intimidating) if you turn off the tiny little icons that appear before each file's name. To do that, make sure you're viewing a window in Column view, then press Command-J to bring up the View Options. In the View Options dialog, turn off the check-box for Show Icons, and the little rascals are hidden from view, leaving you with a cleaner, less cluttered Column view. The downside? With the icons turned off, it's not easy to tell a folder, from

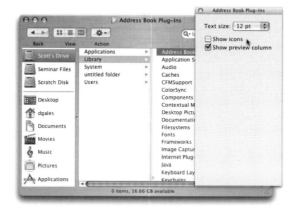

a hard drive, from a file, but it sure is a fun diversion on a boring day. (Actually, this probably should have been in the "Mac OS X Pranks" chapter.)

HOW TO TELL IF SNAP TO GRID IS TURNED ON

If you're wondering whether you have Snap to Grid turned on for a particular window, just look in the bottom left-hand corner of the window. If Snap to Grid is turned on for that particu-lar window, you'll see a tiny grid icon (as shown here). If Keep Arranged By Name is turned on, instead you'll see four tiny evenly spaced folder icons.

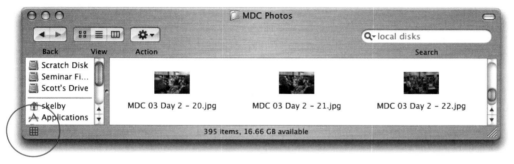

   HOW TO SEE IF YOU CAN WRITE TO A FOLDER

Mac OS X has a level of security called "Permissions" and if a network administrator set up your Mac, chances are there are certain folders you're not allowed to save your files into (it's that whole "power trip" thing). So how do you know if you have permission to write to a particular folder? In Icon or List view, where the icons are pretty large,

it's easy—if you can't write to it, the icon has a red circle with a dash inside of it. However, when you're looking in Column view, since the icons are so small, it's not as obvious, but if you just click on the folder and then look in the bottom left-hand corner of the Finder window (just below the Sidebar) you'll know. If you see a Pencil icon with an "oh no you don't" line through it, you don't have permission to write to that folder. This is why so many network administrators one day wind up having an "accident."

   CREATING YOUR OWN DEFAULTS FOR FINDER WINDOWS

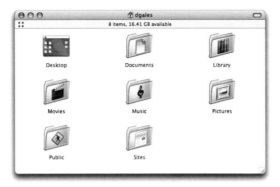

Want to create your own custom default settings for new Finder windows? It's easy: Start by closing every Finder window, then press Command-N (the OS X shortcut for New Finder Window). Set up this window the way you want it (you can choose to show or hide the Sidebar and the toolbar, view by list, the size of the window, even position it on screen where you want all new Finder windows to open). Then, close that window. That's it—you set your prefs. Now, when you open a new Finder window (not a new folder, a new Finder window), it opens using the scheme you just put in place. It's all about you, isn't it? (*Note*: If you set it to open List or Icon view, make sure that the Open New Windows in Column View checkbox in the General Finder Preferences is turned off.)

CUTTING THROUGH THE WINDOW CLUTTER USING EXPOSÉ

It's not only arguably the coolest feature in Panther, it's probably the best thing that happened to any OS since icons. It's called Exposé, and when you invoke it, it instantly (and I mean instantly) shows you miniature versions (thumbnails) of every open window in the Finder and all open applications. That way, you can instantly click and go right to the window you want. Honestly, there's no way to adequately describe this feature, so go try it once and it will instantly (and I mean instantly) make sense. Here's

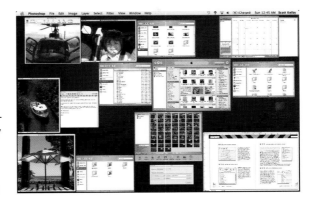

how: Open a few Finder windows, then open a couple documents in an application. Then, press the F9 key, and every window temporarily miniaturizes. Click on the window you want—it comes to the front, and everything else returns to normal. Is that slick or what?

UNCLUTTERING JUST YOUR CURRENT APPLICATION

If you're working within an application (like Photoshop), Exposé works there as well, it's just a different shortcut. For example, if you're working in Photoshop and have eight or nine photos open, their windows are stacked with one overlapping another. Just press F10 and Exposé miniaturizes each of those nine windows within Photoshop so you clearly can see each photo to get right to the photo you want. Using F10 only affects the current application (in this

case, Photoshop), whereas F9 miniaturizes every window in every application, including the Finder. Again, this is one you have to try to really appreciate it, but I must warn you—once you use Exposé, you'll cringe at the thought of using Jaguar ever again. It's that cool.

EXPOSÉ SHOW-OFF TRICK #1

Showing off Exposé to a friend or co-worker who uses a PC is more than a blast, it's your duty, because even Windows XP still has nothing like it. But if you really want to be a major hambone, before you press F9 to invoke Exposé, start a QuickTime movie clip, have a DVD playing, or have iTunes playing a song and click on the visualizer (heck, have all three going at once). When you press F9, the QuickTime clip (DVD, iTunes, etc.) keeps playing even when miniaturized. It's fun to watch their face as it changes from "cool!" to "why doesn't Windows have that?"

EXPOSÉ SHOW-OFF TRICK #2

After you show your friends Exposé, give 'em the "instant replay" to really seal the deal. Hold the Shift key, press F9, and it gives you a slow motion version of the Exposé effect, which reminds your friends yet again of how cool you've become. (By the way, this hold the Shift key slo-mo effect works in other places. Try minimizing a window to the Dock holding the Shift key. Again, totally for show, but "the show must go on!")

GETTING A CLEAN SHOT AT YOUR DESKTOP WITH EXPOSÉ

Okay, besides miniaturizing your Finder and application windows, Exposé has another feature that you may find even more useful—when you press F11, all of your open windows (in every application and the Finder) instantly "get out of the way," giving you a clean view of your desktop. A prefect example of when to use this is when you're working in your e-mail program, and you want to attach a file that's on your desktop. Instead of leaving your Mail app and going to the desktop, just press F11. With everything moved out of the way (as long as you hold F11), click-and-hold on the file you want, then release F11. You're now back in your Mail app, and you can just drop the file in your Mail window as an attachment. Try it once, love it forever!

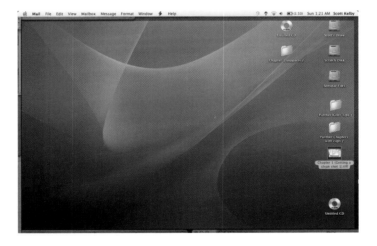

  USING EXPOSÉ WITHOUT PRESSING A BUTTON

You don't have to use F9, F10, or F11 to invoke Exposé. Instead, many people prefer to simply move their cursor to the corner of their screen to have Exposé "do its thing." So, which corner of the screen does which Exposé feat of magic? That's up to you. You set your "hot corners" for each of Exposé's modes by going under the Apple menu, under System Preferences, and choosing Exposé. In the Active Screen Corners area, you'll see a small preview of your screen with a pop-down menu beside

each corner. Just choose which Exposé mode you want assigned to each corner from these pop-down menus. At the bottom of this preference pane is an area where you can also assign different Exposé keyboard shortcuts (rather than the standard F9, F10, or F11 variety).

   THE TWO-BUTTON MOUSE EXPOSÉ EXPERIENCE

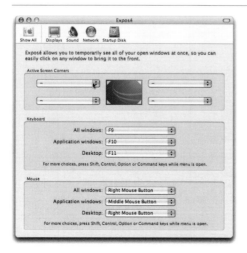

If you're using a two-button mouse, you can access a new world of Exposé functionality that dare not speak its name. For now my friends, you can use the second mouse button to invoke your favorite Exposé mode. Have you got more than two mouse buttons? Four perhaps? (You decadent American!) Then, go under the Apple menu, under System Preferences, and click on Exposé. If your "rich-socialite multi-button mouse" is connected, you'll see a new Mouse section has been added to your Exposé preferences that enables you to assign various Exposé functions to your various buttons.

ACCESSING ONCE-HIDDEN WINDOW FEATURES

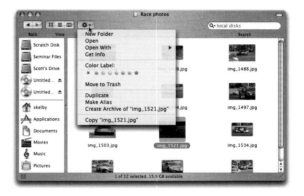

One of the many little tricks Mac OS X "power users" had up their sleeve was that they used contextual pop-up menus to access features and functions that many users didn't even know existed. One reason for its obscurity was that it employed the very least-used of all Macintosh keyboard modifier keys—the Control key. To get to these contextual menus, you'd Control-click on a file, a folder, a window, etc., and up would pop this list of things you could do. (You could also right-click a two- button mouse, but of course, Apple hadn't made a two-button mouse.) Well, Apple must have realized that only a privileged few were taking advantage of these contextual menus, so they added an Action button in the default toolbar of Finder windows. Click on a file, click on this Action button, and you get a contextual menu of "hidden" commands. Feel the power!

   MOVING THAT WINDOW FROM ANY SIDE

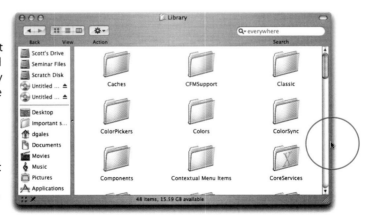

If you've used a previous version of Mac OS X (a non-Panther version), you probably got used to the fact that you could only move a Finder window by clicking on the title bar—there was no place to click and move a window on the sides or bottom. In Panther, one of the advantages of the new brushed metal interface is that it has thin metal sides, so now you can grab a window by the top, sides, or bottom to move it where you want it.

  SWITCHING APPS WITHIN EXPOSÉ

Once you have Exposé invoked (you pressed either F9 or F10), you can toggle through your open applications and Finder windows by pressing the Tab key. Press the Tab key once and the next open application, and its miniaturized windows, comes to front. Press Tab again, it goes to the next open app. Want the previous app? Press Shift-Tab.

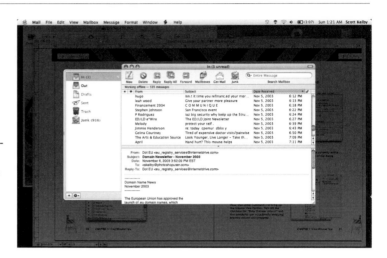

   QUICKLY CYCLE AMONG WINDOW VIEWS

You can quickly cycle among the three window views (Icon, List, or Column) by pressing Command-1, Command-2, and Command-3, respectively (which means, press them with respect).

   NARROWING YOUR TOOLBAR SEARCHES

If you use the Search field that appears in the top-right corner of the Finder window's toolbar, you have a little more control over your search than you might think. For example, if you click-and-hold on the little Magnifying Glass icon that appears at the left of the field, a pop-up menu appears, enabling you to choose exactly where you want to search, potentially speeding up your search by letting you narrow (or expand) where you want the Search field to search.

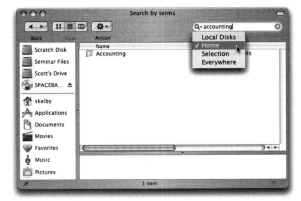

   ONE-CLICK LONG-FILE NAME FIX

If you're working in a window set to Column view, you're going to run into this all the time—files with long names have the end of their names cut off from view, because the column isn't wide enough. That doesn't sound like that big of a problem, until you start working with more

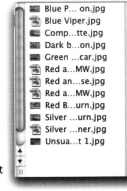 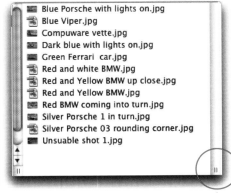

descriptive file names, and you can can't see which file is Blue Porsche with lights on.jpg and which is Blue Viper.jpg because everything from the "Blue" on is cut off. Luckily, there's a quick fix: Just double-click on the little tab at the bottom of the vertical column divider bar, and the column expands just enough so you can see even the longest file name of any file in that column. Option-double-click on the tab, and every column expands to show the longest name in each column. Pretty darn sweet!

    EXPOSÉ BUTTON TIPS

In an earlier tip, I mentioned that you invoke the cool Exposé feature by pressing F9, F10, or F11. But, did you know it's how you press those keys that determines how Exposé works? For example, if you press and release the F9 key, Exposé freezes the thumbnails in place, and continues to freeze them until you either click on a window or press F9 again. This is ideal for when you're not sure which window you want so you need time to look around. However, if you press and hold F9, Exposé only stays active as long as you hold the button down (or until you click a window, whichever comes first), which is perfect for when you just want to look at something quickly, or you know exactly which window you want to jump to.

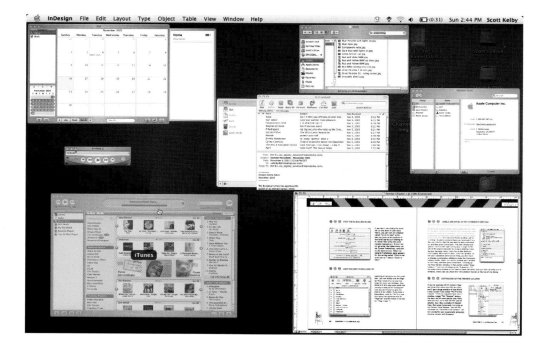

   EXPOSÉ MOUSE TIPS

I mentioned earlier that if you have a multi-button mouse, it opens a new world of Exposé functionality, and I also mentioned (in the previous tip) that Exposé responds to how you press the keys that invoke it. So, here's a cool Exposé tip that lets you switch from one application to another with just one click (rather than two). Click whichever mouse button you assigned to the F9 function (all windows), then keep holding down the mouse button and release it over the window of the application you want to switch to—it's super fast, 'cause it's just one click.

for those about to dock!

DOCKING TIPS

You have to hand it to Apple: When it comes to application launching and switching, with Mac OS X's Dock, they have created

For Those About to Dock!
docking miracles made easy

the Venus de Milo of application launchers and switchers. Okay, that just sounds weird. How about, "…the crème de la crème" of launchers and application switchers? Nah, too "Frasier and Niles." Maybe the adjective isn't the problem—maybe it's the "launcher and application switcher" part—it just doesn't sound sexy enough to describe all the really cool things the Dock lets you do (which we look at in this chapter). Okay, how about this, "…when it comes to doing it, the Dock totally rocks!" Nah, that sounds too "Eminem." Instead, perhaps we should look at the word "Dock" itself. It's clearly a derivative of the popular Latin phrase "One, two, three o-clock, four o-clock, Dock," which, if memory serves me correctly, is inscribed on the torch held high by Lady Liberty in New York Harbor (and Lady Liberty was presented to the United States by French Prime Minister Bill Haley, around five, six, seven o'clock).

THE ONE-CLICK TRICK TO MOVING THE DOCK

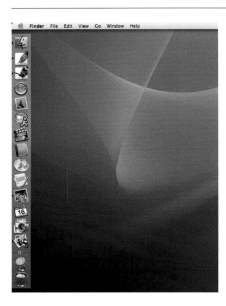

Okay, so you're working in a program like Final Cut Pro or iMovie, which takes up every vertical inch of the screen, and when you go to adjust something near the bottom, the Dock keeps popping up. Oh sure, you could move the Dock to where it's anchored on the left or right side of the screen, but that just feels weird. But what if you could move it temporarily to the left or right, and then get it back to the bottom when you close Final Cut Pro, in just one click? Here's how: Hold the Shift key, click directly on the Dock's divider line (on the far right side of the Dock), and drag the Dock to the left or right side of your screen. Bam! It moves over to the side. Then, once you quit Final Cut, just Shift-click on that divider line and slam it back to the bottom (okay, drag it back to the bottom). A draggable Dock—is that cool or what!

WHAT'S WITH THE QUESTION MARK?

What does it mean if you see a large question mark icon in the Dock? I have no idea. That's why there's a question mark there. No one knows, not even Apple (kidding). What it means is that you deleted the original of whatever

was in the Dock. For example, if you put a Dock icon for Microsoft Word in the Dock, but then deleted Word from your hard drive, the next time you click on that icon in the Dock, you'd see a question mark. So what do you do? Just drag it right off the Dock, and it's gone forever. No questions asked.

CHANGING APPS IN A BIG WAY

In Panther, if you don't feel like moving your cursor all the way down to the Dock to change applications, you can easily rotate an open application to the front by pressing-and-holding Command-Tab. This brings up a large transparent Dock-like window in the center of your screen, with huge icons showing just your open applications. To switch to another application, keep holding the Command key and press either the Tab key, the Arrow keys on your key-board, or click on the icons with your mouse. Also, you can press the Home key to jump to the application on the far left, or the End key to jump to the app on the far right. Want to cruise through the applications in this window in reverse (from right to left)? Just press Shift-Command-Tab. Hey, somebody might want to do this. Really.

DRAGGING FROM THE DOCK, NOT TO IT

In this chapter, we're always talking about dragging files and folders to the Dock, but in Panther, you can now drag from the Dock (out to your desktop or to an open window) by first holding the Command key, then dragging. Want to make an alias of a Dock icon? Just hold Command-Option and drag the docked file to the window you want, and it creates an alias. In fact, most of the things you can do within a window (copying a file, creating an alias, etc.) can be done from the Dock, as long as you start with the Command key.

 ACCESSING SYSTEM PREFERENCES DIRECTLY FROM THE DOCK

Want a quick way to access your System Preferences? (Sure you do.) The next time you have the System Preferences open, don't close or quit; instead, press Command-H to hide the preferences. Now, when you want a particular System Preference, just click-and-hold on the System Preferences icon in the Dock for a moment, and a pop-up list of your System Preferences appears. Choose the one you want from the list, and that panel then appears on screen. Very convenient.

 KEEPING AN EYE ON THINGS, LIVE FROM THE DOCK

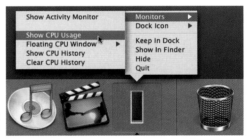

Do you like to know what's going on "under the hood" of your Mac (stuff like your CPU usage, disk activity, memory usage—you know, total geek stuff)? If you do, you can keep an eye on things right from within the Dock using Mac OS X's Activity Monitor. It's found in the Applications folder, under Utilities. Once you find it, drag it into your Dock, then click on it to launch it. Once it's launched, click-and-hold for a moment on its Dock icon. A list pops up, and you see a Dock Icon menu item. This is where you choose which activity you want to monitor from its live Dock icon. Choose it, and a live graph appears in the Dock that's updated dynamically as you work.

THE GIANT APP SWITCHER DOES MORE THAN JUST SWITCH

In a previous tip, I mentioned that holding the Command key, then pressing the Tab key, brings up a giant Dock-like window with huge icons in the center of your screen, where you can cycle through your open apps (using the Tab key, the Arrow keys, or clicking with your mouse). But, there's more to it than that—you can quit any currently running app by cycling to it, then pressing the letter "q" (don't let go of the Command key; keep holding it while you press the letter "q"). Still holding the Command key, press "h" to hide the highlighted app.

THE HIDDEN DOCK PREFERENCES SHORTCUT

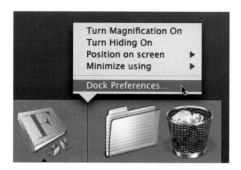

A quick way to get to the Dock's preferences is to go under the Apple menu, under Dock, and choose Dock Preferences, but I think you're ready for the absolute fastest way there is to access the Dock prefs. This tip is so shrouded in Dock secrecy, I don't think even Apple knows it exists (of course they do, but I doubt they'd admit it without administering some sort of "truth serum"). Just Control-click on the divider line on the right side of the Dock and a pop-up list of Dock preferences is right there, just one click away.

   INSTANT DOCK RESIZE

If you want to make the Dock larger or smaller, there's a slider in the Dock preference pane, but you don't have to use it. Ever. That's because you can simply put your cursor right over the divider line on the right side of the Dock (the one that separates your apps from your folders and Trash) and your cursor changes to a horizontal bar with two arrows: one facing up and one facing down. When it does that, just click-and-drag your cursor upward to make the Dock bigger or downward to shrink it.

   FOR THOSE WHO DON'T WANT TO "HIDE"

If the Dock seems to be in your way a lot, but you don't like the whole "hiding-the-Dock" thing, try setting the Dock to its smallest size (so you can barely notice it's there at all). Then, turn on Magnification and set it to a pretty large size, so when you scroll your mouse over the tiny Dock, the icons jump up in size so you can see what's what. You can turn Magnification on by going under the Apple menu, under Dock, and choosing Turn Magnification On.

FREAKY MOVIE DOCK TRICK

This is one of those "show off your Mac" tricks that really amaze people, but outside of that, I haven't found a real use for it. You start by opening a QuickTime movie, hitting the play button, and watching it for a second or two. Then, click the yellow center button in the title bar to shrink the movie to the Dock (it appears down by the Trash). Here's the cool thing: You'll notice the movie continues to play even while in the Dock. You can even hear the audio! Only ants can really enjoy it at this size (in fact, ants love this effect because to them, they're seeing your movie on the "big screen"), but the naked human eye can see the movie, too. I've also tested this by putting my clothes back on, and even when not naked, my human eye can still see it. How cool is that?

YELLOW MINIMIZE BUTTON TOO SMALL? TRY THIS!

Sometimes, hitting that tiny middle yellow button (to minimize your current window to the Dock) is tricky, especially if you're using a Titanium PowerBook or Cinema Display set at its native resolution, in which everything is smaller than a gnat's nose. If you'd like something bigger to aim at than that tiny yellow button, go under the Apple menu, under System Preferences, and click on the Appearance icon, and then click on the checkbox for Minimize when Double Clicking a Window Title Bar. Now, you can just double-click anywhere on the window's title bar and that window immediately minimizes to the Dock, just as if you had clicked the tiny yellow button. Of course, you could skip the clicking altogether and press Command-M, but that just seems like cheating, doesn't it?

   AUTOMATICALLY HIDING THE DOCK

The smaller your screen, the more important the ability to hide the Dock from view becomes (as you might imagine, this is a very popular feature for PowerBook users). Basically, with this feature active, the Dock hides off screen and only reappears when your cursor moves over the area where the Dock used to be. It kind of "pops up" so you can work in the Dock until you move away, and then it hides again. To turn this Dock feature on, go under the Apple menu, under Dock, and choose Turn Hiding On. If you think you might use this function often, you'll probably want to memorize the Turn Hiding On/Off shortcut, which is Option-Command-D.

   EJECTING MEDIA FROM THE DOCK

Although Panther makes ejecting removable media (like CDs, DVDs, and FireWire or USB drives) incredibly easy thanks to the little Eject button that appears beside each media icon in the Sidebar of every Finder window, many longtime Mac OS X users still prefer to use the Dock for ejecting media (it's called "old dog/new tricks" syndrome). If you're one of those (an old dog), you can drag the disc (or drive) icon to the Trash icon in your Dock, and as you approach the Dock, you see the Trash icon change into an Eject button. When you drop your CD/DVD/FireWire drive icon on the Eject button…it erases the contents of your drive. Kidding! Just a joke. Actually, of course, it ejects your disc/CD/DVD or unmounts your FireWire/USB drive.

KEEPING A RUNNING APP IN THE DOCK AFTER YOU QUIT

If you're running an application and you say to yourself, "You know, I use this app a lot," you can keep its icon in the Dock so next time, it's just one click away. Just Control-click on the app's icon in the Dock, and choose Keep In Dock. Of course, there is another way. A cooler way. An "I don't need no stinkin' pop-up menu" way. Just click on the running application's icon, drag it away from the Dock, pause a second, and then drag it right back. It's really no faster, but it makes you look (and feel) less pop-up menu codependent.

   UNLOADING THE DOCK

If you have a few apps running and you like to keep things uncluttered and organized by minimizing document windows to the Dock, it doesn't take long before your Dock gets pretty crowded. If that's the case, here's a tip that might help you bring some welcome space and order back to your Dock: When you're switching from one application to the next, hold the Option key before you click on the new application's icon in the Dock. This hides all the Dock icons for minimized windows from the application you just left, and helps unclutter the Dock. When you switch back to that application later, its minimized windows reappear in the Dock.

   GETTING RIGHT TO THE FILE YOU WANT

If you've parked a folder full of files in the Dock, you don't have to open the folder to get to a particular file. Instead, just click-and-hold on the folder for a moment, and a pop-up list of all the files in that folder appear (that's not the trick). Once that menu opens, on your keyboard, just press the first letter(s) of the file you want and that file is instantly highlighted—all you have to do is press Return to open the file.

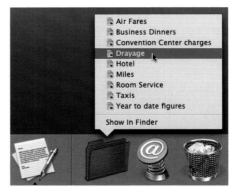

   FOLDERS TO ADD TO YOUR DOCK

Adding folders to your Dock can be a real timesaver, and two of the most popular folders to add to the Dock are your Home folder and your Applications folder. Another thing you might consider, rather than putting your entire Applications folder on your Dock, is to create a new folder and put in it aliases of just the applications and system add-ons (such as the Calculator, etc.) that you really use. Then, you can access these by Control-clicking on the folder in the Dock, and a pop-up list appears that looks a lot like the Apple menu from OS 9.

FORCE QUITTING FROM THE DOCK

If you're running an application in Mac OS X and for some reason, it locks up or crashes (hey, it happens—remember, Apple didn't say applications wouldn't crash in Mac OS X; it said if they did, it wouldn't bring down your whole system), you can easily force quit the application by Control-clicking on its icon

in the Dock, and a pop-up menu appears. Press the Option key, and you see the menu item called Quit change to Force Quit. Click that, and it force quits the application. Also, if you're a longtime Mac user, you might be afraid to force quit an application, because back in Mac OS 9 (and prior to that), force quitting was an absolute last resort in hopes of saving an open document. If you were lucky enough to get force quit to work without locking up the machine (believe me—it was luck—force quitting in Mac OS 9 and earlier usually brought the whole machine down), all you could really do was restart anyway, but at least you got to save your document. Mac OS X is designed to let you force quit then continue to work, so don't be hesitant to use this feature.

   GETTING RID OF EXTRA WINDOWS WHILE YOU WORK

If you have a few Finder windows open, they can be really distracting when you're working in another application—you always see them floating around in the background. Well, you can hide all those messy windows without ever leaving your current application. Just Control-click on the Finder icon in the Dock and choose Hide from the pop-up menu. All those windows are instantly hidden from view. Want to hide everything but those windows? Control-Option-click on the Finder icon and choose Hide Others.

   WHY SOME ICONS WON'T LEAVE THE DOCK

A couple of icons live in the Dock, and Apple thinks that's exactly where they belong, so they won't let you pull them out of the Dock. Apple figures you're always going to need the Finder (and the Trash), and they won't let you remove the icon of any application that is currently running (after all, if they did let you remove the icon, how would you get back to the application? It would just run forever, kind of like a Flying Dutchman). So in short, don't waste your time trying to drag those puppies from the Dock—they're stuck there (for your protection).

   CLOSING A FINDER WINDOW IN THE DOCK

If you've minimized a Finder window to the Dock, you can actually close that window without having to maximize it first (saving untold time and keystrokes). Just click-and-hold on the minimized Finder window in the Dock, and choose Close from the pop-up menu. That's it—it's closed, just as if you had maximized it and clicked on the red Close button.

BRINGING HOME LOST SHEEP: FINDING DOCKED ORIGINALS

Okay, so you see the application's (or document's) icon in the Dock, but you have no earthly idea where the app (or doc) really resides on your hard drive. It's there somewhere, but you really don't know where, and that scares you (well, it scares me anyway). To find where the docked application or document really lives, just Control-click on it in the Dock and choose Show In Finder. The window where it lives immediately appears on screen.

   STOP THE BOUNCING. I BEG YOU!

When you launch an application, its icon begins to bounce incessantly in the Dock, in a distracting vertical Tigger-like motion, until the app is just about open. I love this feature; but then, I enjoy having my cavities drilled. If you enjoy this animation as much as I do, you can turn it off by going to the Apple menu, under Dock, and choosing Dock Preferences. When the Dock preference pane appears, turn off the checkbox (it's on by default) for Animate

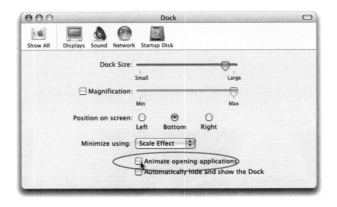

Opening Applications. Turning this off now can save you thousands in therapy down the road.

   FREAKY GENIE EFFECT

There's a little trick you can pull to make the Genie Effect (the little animation that takes place when you minimize a window to the Dock) even freakier (we call it the "freaky genie"). Just hold Shift before you minimize the window and it puts the Genie Effect into a "super slo-mo" mode that looks kinda cool. I say "kinda" because this effect (like the Genie Effect itself) gets old kinda quick, but people who've never seen it before dig it. At least at first.

   MAKING ONE ACTIVE, AND HIDING THE REST

If you want to make just the application you're working on visible and hide all the other running applications, including any open Finder windows, just hold Option-Command, and then click on the application's icon in the Dock. This is much faster than choosing your application, going under your application's menu, and choosing Hide Others.

SNAPPING DOCK SIZES

In a previous tip, I showed how you can resize the Dock by clicking-and-dragging on the divider line, but if you hold the Option key first and then start dragging, the Dock "snaps" to some preset sizes. Who chose these preset sizes? Probably Apple's software engineers, but some feel the presets were secretly designated by high-ranking government officials in yet another attempt to exert more "Big-Brotherly" control over our otherwise mundane lives. Personally, I tend to think it was Apple, but hey, that's just me.

   ## MINIMIZING MULTIPLE WINDOWS AT ONCE

If you have three or four open windows and want to minimize them all to the Dock at once, just hold the Option key and double-click on the title bar of any one of them, and all open windows go to the Dock. Be careful when you do this, because if you have 50 open windows, they're all headed to the Dock in a hurry, and there's no real undo for this. Worse yet, you'll eventually have to pull 50 very tiny icons from the Dock one by one. So make sure that's really what you want to do before you Option-double-click.

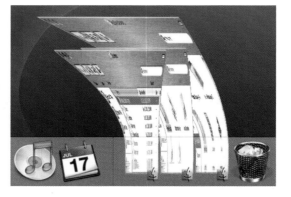

  OPENING DOCUMENTS BY DRAGGING THEM TO THE DOCK

Remember how back in Mac OS 9, if you tore the Application menu off and had it floating around your desktop, you could drag-and-drop documents onto an application listed in the

menu, and it would endeavor to open them? You can do the same thing now in Mac OS X with the Dock—just drag documents directly to an application icon in the Dock, and if it thinks it might be able to open the document, the icon highlights, basically telling you to "let 'er rip!"

   STOPPING THE ICONS FROM MOVING

In the above tip (drag-and-drop to the Dock), I showed how you can drag a document onto an application's icon in the Dock. But sometimes, you may be trying to add the document to a folder in the Dock. When you do this, the Dock thinks you're actually trying to add the document to the

Dock itself, rather than dropping it on the folder, so it kindly slides the icons out of the way to make room for your document. That's incredibly polite (for an operating system anyway), but it can also be incredibly annoying if that's not what you're trying to do. If this happens to you, just hold the Command key as you drag and the icons stay put, which enables you to drop the document into a "non-moving" object.

DRAGGING-AND-DROPPING TO THE APP OF YOUR CHOICE

You can use the Dock to open a document in the application of your choice rather than what OS X

would open it in normally by default. For example, let's say you make a screen capture using the standard Shift-Command-3 shortcut, and the resulting PDF file then appears on your desktop. If you double-click that file, by default, it's going to open in Preview, Mac OS X's app for viewing graphics. But what if you want it to open in Photoshop instead? Well, as long as Photoshop is in your Dock, you can drag the PDF screen capture from your desktop and drop it directly on the Photoshop icon in the Dock, and then Photoshop opens the document.

   FORCING A DOCUMENT ON AN APP

Sometimes, docked apps don't want to open your document, even though they may be able to, so you have to coax (okay, force) them to give it a try. For example, let's say you created a document in WordPerfect for Mac a few years back. If you drag that document to Microsoft Word's icon in the Dock, chances are it won't highlight (which would be the indication it can open that document). If that happens, just hold Option-Command, then drag the document's icon to the Word icon in the Dock, and you can force it to try to open that document.

 FULL-SPEED DOCKING BY LOSING THE GENIE!

The "Genie Effect" that occurs when you send
a document to the Dock sure looks cool, but
things that look cool generally eat up processing
power, and that holds true with the Genie Effect
as well (besides, although the Genie Effect looks
cool the first couple of times you see it, it doesn't
take long before you want to put the genie back
in its bottle for good). To turn off the Genie Effect
and use the faster "Scale Effect," Control-click on
the vertical Dock divider bar, and in the resulting

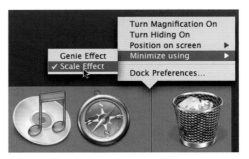

pop-up menu, under Minimize Using, choose Scale Effect. This decreases the burden on the
system resources and keeps things moving at full speed.

ACCIDENTALLY LAUNCHED A PROGRAM? UN-LAUNCH IT.

Because it takes only one click to launch a program
from the Dock, you're just one click away from
launching the wrong application (sadly, I do this all
the time—when I mean to click on one application, I
accidentally click the Dock icon to the right or left of
it). If you do launch a program you wish you hadn't,
immediately click-and-hold on its Dock icon and a
menu appears where you can choose Force Quit. This
stops the launch dead in its tracks.

icon see clearly now

ICON TIPS

Now, you might be tempted to skip this chapter if you think it's just about copying an icon from one file to another (it includes that,

Icon See Clearly Now

sorry...not funny

of course, but it's really much, much more). You might also be tempted to skip this chapter because you're upset that I couldn't come up with a chapter title using a decent song title, movie title, or popular band name that uses the word "icon." Leaving me no choice but to hack up the name of the 1972 hit by Johnny Nash "I Can See Clearly Now," in a desperate moment I wish I could take back. You might skip this chapter if you're the kind of person that just indiscriminately skips chapters, or perhaps you might skip this chapter as a personal form of protest because you believe, like many others, that icons are really part of a much broader government conspiracy to control our lives and eventually take away our right to bear arms. Ahhh, that's what it is. I knew if I kept digging, I'd uncover the real reason. Now, tell me about your mother....

  MAKING .ZIP FILES (COMPRESSED FILES) IN ONE CLICK

One of my favorite Panther features is the ability to create .zip compressed files from within the OS. (Basically, this shrinks the file size, ideal for files you're going to e-mail—smaller file sizes mean faster file transfers.) To create a compressed file, either Control-click on the file, then choose Create Archive (which is Apple-speak for "Make a compressed .zip file"). Or you can click on a file, then go to the Action menu (the button that looks like a gear up in the Finder window's toolbar), and choose Create Archive from there. Either way, it quickly creates a new file with the file extension ".zip." This is the compressed file. You can also compress several different files (like three for example) into one single archive file—just Command-click on all the files you want included, then choose Create Archive of 3 Items from the Action menu. A file is created named "Archive.zip" (that's it!). By the way, if someone sends you a .zip file, don't sweat it—just double-click it and Panther automatically decompresses it.

   SEARCHING BY COLOR LABEL

Besides the visual benefits of having certain files tagged with a color label, there's a hidden benefit: You can search for files by their color. For example, let's say you misplaced an important file for a project you were working on. You can press Command-F to bring up the Find function, and from the Search for Items pop-up menu, choose Label. Then, click on the color for the files you labeled in that project, click the Search button, and it instantly finds and displays all the files with that color. Searching by color—only Apple is cool enough to come up with a search like this!

CREATING YOUR OWN LABEL NAMES

Don't like the names Apple created for the colors used in the Color Labels feature? Then, just create your own by going under the Finder menu and choosing Preferences (or use the keyboard shortcut Command-,). When the Finder Preferences dialog appears, click on the Labels button, and you'll see a field beside each color where you can input custom names. This is great for designating a color for "Hot Projects" or "Backup These Files," or perhaps a project name like "Anderson Catalog" or "Vegas Blackjack Table Scam."

POWER COPY AND PASTE

In previous versions of Mac OS X (and Mac OS 9 for that matter), if you clicked on a file, copied it (Command-C), then opened an application (like Mail) and pasted it (Command-V), it would only paste that file's name, which is just this side of worthless. Now in Panther, in some applications, it pastes the actual file, so you can copy and paste a file from a Finder window or the desktop right into your application. Okay, so what if you do want just the name (which happens from time to time)? Just click directly on the file's name (to highlight it) then press Command-C to copy it. Now, you're copying just the name. It's a power-pasting thing!

   ADDING AUTOMATION THROUGH FOLDER ACTIONS

At the office, I'm on a network and I have a Drop Box where my co-workers (freaks that they are) can send me files. However, for a long time, if a freak put something in my Drop Box, I wouldn't know it unless they called or e-mailed me and told me so. But now any time one of them drops something in my Drop Box, a message dialog appears that says, "Something freaky is in your Drop Box." This is a simple Apple-Script (think of an AppleScript as a built-in automation for your Mac, just like Photoshop Actions add automation to Adobe Photoshop).

Mac OS X includes some cool sample Scripts (Actions), or you can download about a bazillion from the Web for free.

To assign a Script to a folder, start by Control-clicking on that folder, then choose Configure Folder Actions from the pop-up menu that appears. This brings up the Folder Actions Setup dialog. This is where you toggle various Scripts assigned to folders on and off, or even edit Scripts (if you know how to write AppleScripts).

Click the plus-sign button at the bottom left of the dialog to add your folder to the list (this actually brings up a standard Open dialog that shows your folder, so click on your folder in the Open dialog and click Open). Once you do this, a window pops down with a list of built-in sample Scripts you can assign to this folder, and their names give a cryptic description of what they do. Pick the one that sounds like what you want to do (to replicate my "Drop Box warning," choose "add — new item alert.scpt") and click the Attach button (you'll see your newly assigned Script appear in the column on the right of the dialog). You'd think that would do it, but you have to do one more thing because although you assigned a Folder Action to this folder, you have not yet enabled Folder Actions. Click the Enable Folder Actions checkbox at the top-left corner of the dialog. This is a global on/off switch, so any folder to which you've attached Scripts is now "activated."

By the way, once you apply Actions to a folder, you can turn Folder Actions on or off globally by Control-clicking on any folder and choosing Enable Folder Actions or Disable Folder Actions from the pop-up menu. *Note*: You have to Control-click on the folder to access these Folder Action commands; they don't appear in the menu if you click on the folder and then click the Action button in the Finder window. Why? I have no idea.

DRAG-AND-DROP DESKTOP PRINTING

Want the ability to print a document right from your desktop (without opening the application first)? Go under the Apple menu, under System Preferences, and choose Print & Fax. When the preference pane appears, click on the Printing button, then click the Set Up Printers button. Your printer appears in the Printer List dialog. Click on it, then go under the Printers menu (in the menu bar) and choose Create Desktop Printer. A standard Open/Save dialog appears asking you where you want to save it (I save mine on the desktop). Click Save, and an icon for your printer appears on the desktop. To print a document, just drag-and-drop it on this icon. Some documents, such as TextEdit files and PDFs, go straight to the printer. Other files launch their default application and open the Print dialog.

PRINTING FROM THE DESKTOP (WITHOUT A DESKTOP PRINTER)

Don't want a Desktop Printer icon cluttering up your desktop, but you still want to print files from the desktop or a Finder window (kind of greedy, aren't you?) Then try this little trick: Control-click on the file you want to print to bring up a contextual menu. Go under Open With, and choose Printer Setup Utility from the list. (If it doesn't show up there, you have to click on Other, then use a standard Open dialog to navigate to the Printer Setup Utility—it's

inside the Applications folder, within the Utilities folder.) Just choose it, and it either starts printing or takes you directly to the default application's Print dialog.

   SEEING THUMBNAIL IMAGES OF YOUR PHOTOGRAPHIC FILES

Tired of seeing the default icons for your digital photos? Then change just one tiny preference setting, and working with digital photos in Finder windows becomes infinitely easier. The preference is called Show Icon Preview and turning it on automatically replaces the default file icons with thumbnail previews of your photos, so you can see what they look like right in the Finder window. This preview is only available when viewing a Finder window in Icon view, so start by clicking on the View by Icon button in the toolbar. Then, press Command-J to bring up that window's View Options and turn on Show Icon Preview. That's it—now your digital camera images won't have generic icons. Instead, they'll display thumbnail photos of your full-sized images as their icons.

   GETTING TO THE GOODIES FAST

Want fast access to the most commonly used icon-related tasks? Just Control-click directly on an icon and a pop-up menu appears with a list of tasks you're likely to take advantage of at one time or another.

CHANGING A FILE'S ICON

Just as in previous versions of the Mac OS, if you don't like a file's icon, you can change it. (Check out www.iconfactory.com or www.xicons.com. They both have fantastic selections of photo-quality Mac OS X icons ready to download.) To copy an icon from one file to another, just click on the icon you want to copy and press Command-I to bring up its Info window. In the General section, click on the tiny icon to the left of the file's name then press Command-C to copy that icon into memory. Then, go to the file whose icon you'd like to replace, press Command-I to bring up its Info window, click on the existing tiny little icon, then just press Command-V to paste the new icon over the old icon. That's it! Piece of cake. Can of corn. Etc.

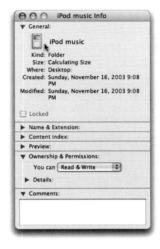

DON'T LIKE YOUR NEW CUSTOM ICON? CHANGE IT BACK

If you've added a custom icon to one of your files and later grow tired of it (custom icons sometimes do get old, just like songs on the radio. You love 'em the first time you hear them, but then after hearing it for about the 200th time, the song you once loved is now so…played), just click on the icon, press Command-I, then press Command-X, and the file's original icon will pop back into place (no radio pun intended).

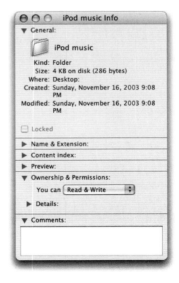

   COPYING AND DELETING AT THE SAME TIME

If you're archiving a file to disk (let's say to an external FireWire drive, for example), you can drag the icon of the file you want to archive directly to that drive and the Mac will write a copy to that drive. However, your original file still lives on your current hard drive. If you want to have that file deleted from your drive as soon as it's copied to another drive, just hold the Command key as you drag your icon, and the Mac does two tasks for you—it copies the file to the new drive, and deletes the original from your drive.

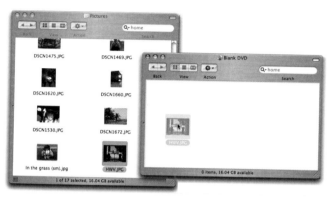

   NEW FOLDER SPEED TIP

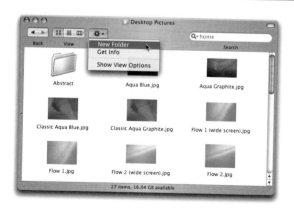

Need another folder to store your files but refuse to use the new keyboard shortcut Shift-Command-N? (I don't blame you.) You have two choices: Either click on the Action button and choose New Folder (as shown here) or just Control-click on an empty space in any Finder window, and then choose New Folder from the pop-up menu.

CLEANING UP WINDOWS ONE ICON AT A TIME

Want to bring some order back to your icons? Just hold the Command key while dragging any icon, and when you release the mouse button, it automatically snaps to an invisible alignment grid, helping, once again, to keep your icons tidy and organized. See, Mac OS X cares. Another way to "clean up," icon-by-icon, is to click on the icon you want aligned, and then choose Clean Up Selection from the View menu.

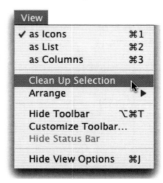

ICON ORGANIZING TIPS

I cover these in more detail in the chapter on window tips, but I was afraid you might come here instead, looking for ways to organize your icons, so I'll quickly recap them in this one tip:

- To have your icons snap to an invisible alignment grid (and help keep them organized in rows), press Command-J and in the View Options dialog, choose Snap to Grid.
- If you don't have Snap to Grid on and you want a particular icon to snap to the grid, just hold the Command key while you drag the icon.
- To have your icons sorted alphabetically in rows, go under the View menu, go to Arrange, and then choose By Name from the pop-up list.

DUPLICATING FILES THE FAST WAY

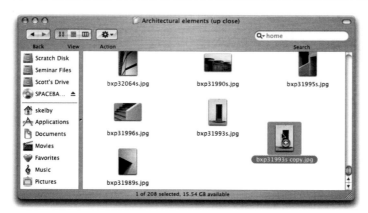

Want to copy a file? Piece of cake—just hold the Option key, click on the file's icon, and drag yourself a copy. This makes an exact duplicate of the entire file, and it's even courteous enough to add the word "copy" to the end of the file name. How's that for service?

ICON SUPERSIZING TIP

They're your icons; choose your favorite size. You can control the size that your icons appear when viewing a window in Icon view by pressing Command-J, which brings up the View Options dialog. You'll find a slider there where you can size your icons to your heart's content, and there's a pop-up menu for choosing the text size. You can also choose whether this icon size is just for the current window, or make it across the board in every window, by choosing All windows.

   INSTANTLY FINDING THE ORIGINAL FOR ANY ALIAS

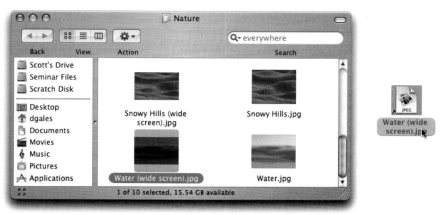

Since an alias is just a copy of the file's icon (not the actual file itself), you may need to find the original at times. To do that, just click on the alias and press Command-R; the "real" file appears on screen in its Finder window.

   CREATING ALIASES WITHOUT THE WORD ALIAS

Do you find it as annoying as I do that Mac OS X adds the word "alias" every time you create an alias? (I know, previous versions of the Mac OS did that as well, and it annoyed me there, too.) Well, you can bypass the "adding-the-word-alias" uglies altogether by holding the Option and Command keys, and dragging the original file outside the Finder window it's currently in (I usually just drag mine to the desktop). This creates an alias without the word "alias" attached. (*Note*: Don't worry, you'll still know it's an alias, because its icon will have a tiny arrow at the bottom left-hand corner.)

COLOR CODING YOUR FILES USING LABELS

One of Mac OS 9's most popular Finder features has made its way to Mac OS X in Panther. It's called Labels and it lets you color code your files for easy visual recognition (for example, you could label all your work files green, home files blue, etc.). To assign a color label to a file, click on the file, then click on the Action button in the toolbar, and in the pop-up menu that appears, under the Color Label section, go directly to the color you want (you can also Control-click on a file and access the Color Labels there). *Note*: Adding a color label doesn't actually change the color of a file's icon; instead, it puts a color bar around the file's name.

 SELECTING MULTIPLE ICONS IN COLUMN OR LIST VIEW

If you're in List or Column view and you want to select a series of icons, just click once on the top icon, hold the Shift key, and click on the last icon in the series that you want selected. Instantly, all the other icons between the first and last are selected. Command-click to remove any selected icon that you want out of your "group."

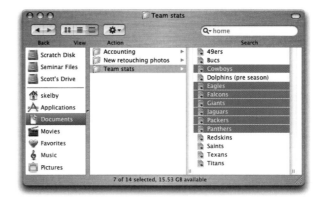

SEEING YOUR FILE'S HIDDEN INFO

Want more info on your files than the standard Icon view provides (after all, it just gives you the file's name in Icon view)? Then, turn on Show Item Info. This adds an extra line of information below many files and folders that can be very useful. For example, now not only do you get a folder's name, but just below the name (in unobtrusive light-blue, 9-point type), you'll see how many items are in that folder. If the file is a QuickTime movie, the item info shows you the length of the movie. MP3 files show how long the song is, etc. To turn "Item Info" on for your current Finder window, press Command-J to bring up its View Options. Then, turn on the checkbox for Show Item Info. If you want to show the item info for every window (globally), then choose the All Windows button at the top of the dialog.

EJECTING DISCS FROM THE SIDEBAR

When you insert some kind of removable media into your Mac (removable media is geek-speak for CDs, DVDs, FireWire or USB drives, digital camera memory cards, etc.), a micro-icon (I'm not sure that's what they're really called) appears to the right of its name in the Sidebar of your Finder window. These are actually buttons, and they're there to save you time and trouble. For example, next to removable drives, that little icon is an Eject button. Click it, and it ejects that drive or CD, or whatever (this beats the heck out of dragging the disc down to the Eject button in the Dock). If you insert a blank CD or DVD, you'll see a little "nuclear" warning sign. This is a Burn button that lets you burn (write) info to that disc.

SELECTING NONCONTIGUOUS ICONS IN COLUMN OR LIST VIEW

If the headline for this tip doesn't sound both fun and fascinating, really, what does? It's actually not as boring as it sounds. In List or Column view, to select more than one icon at a time that aren't contiguous, just hold the Command key and click on each icon. Click on any open space in the window or press Escape to deselect. In Icon view, you still Shift-click to add multiple icons to your selection.

MOVING ICON NAMES TO THE SIDE: IT'S UNNATURAL

You do *not* want to mess with this, because an icon's name is supposed to appear beneath the icon. It has been this way since the beginning of Mac-time, and moving the name to the right of the icon, rather than the time-honored tradition of appearing below it, is just plain sick. It's twisted, odd, and unnatural. It's not only weird and perverse, it's perverse and weird. Nevertheless, here's how to do it: Just open a Finder window, click on the Icon view button in the toolbar, then press Command-J to bring up the View Options. Under Label Position, choose Right, and the name of each icon appears to the right of the icon (Yeecch!). However, "Right is wrong!" Just so you know.

SUPER-FAST FILE RENAMING IN COLUMN VIEW

What's the quickest way to rename an icon while in Column view? In my opinion, it's this: Select it, then press the Return key. The naming field becomes highlighted, then you can type in a new name. Press Return to lock in your change. If speed's not your game, and you would just prefer a nice wide-open field for renaming your icons, just click on the icon you want to rename. Then, press Command-I to bring up its Info window. Then, choose Name & Extension in the Info window, and

you'll have an entire field to enter the name of your dreams.

NAMING SHORTCUTS

If you're naming a number of files with similar names (such as Fishing Trip 1, Fishing Trip 2, Fishing Trip 3, etc.), you can save time by highlighting the words "Fishing Trip" and pressing Command-C to copy those words to the Clipboard. Then, when you come to the next icon you want to rename, just press Return to highlight the name field, press Command-V to paste in the words "Fishing Trip," then press the Right Arrow key and enter the number for this file (like 4), and so on. You can also copy and paste a name

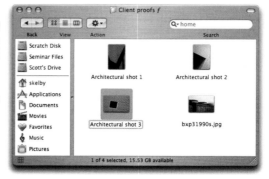

from one folder to another, as long as these two identically named folders don't wind up in the same folder. That's a big no-no and you will be severely disciplined if that should happen (or at least a mean warning dialog will appear).

   ADDING WORDS TO THE END OF FILE NAMES

If you want to add to an existing file's name (for example, if you had a Photoshop file named "cruise collage" and you wanted to add the words "summer 2004" to the end), in Icon View, just click on the name directly below the icon to highlight the name (in List or Column view, click on the name then press Return to highlight the name), then press the Right Arrow key to jump to the end of the existing name. Then, all you have to do is type in "summer 2004". Press the Enter key to lock in your new name. *Note*: To add characters at the beginning of the name, do the same routine, just press the Left Arrow instead.

   DON'T START YOUR FILE NAMES WITH...

You can use most any alpha or numeric characters when naming your files in the Save Sheet in Mac OS X; but it's just a little sticky about one particular character that it really doesn't want you to use in your file's name. Okay, it's more than a little sticky—it flat out won't let you do it.

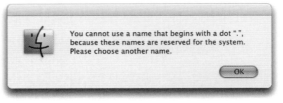

It's the ":" (colon) character. It also won't let you *start* a filename with a period (.) which it calls a "dot." You can use a period in the middle or end of your filename, just not at the beginning. So that's the scoop—Mac OS X selfishly hogs the colon (that doesn't sound nice) and it won't let you start with a dot. Other than that—let 'er rip! However, according to Apple, some applications won't let you use "/" (the Slash key) when naming a file. So, I guess that leaves out naming a file "/from Guns & Roses." Pity.

EJECTING A BLANK DISC

If you insert a blank CD or DVD into your Mac, when you look in the Finder window Sidebar, you'll see a Burn button next to your blank disc—not an Eject button like with other removable media. So, how do you eject the disc from there? Just click on the Burn button. Yes, this brings up the Burn dialog, but on the left side of this dialog is a big ol' Eject button you can click to eject this blank media.

show me
the way

NAVIGATION
TIPS

The title of this chapter, "Show Me the Way," is an obvious tribute to musician Peter Frampton. I feel that I owe him this tribute because one day

Show Me the Way
navigating your new world

I received an e-mail from a reader of one of my other books leading me to a Web site about Peter Frampton. On the site, Peter names his favorite movies, books, albums, etc., and among his favorite books, he listed my book Photoshop Down & Dirty Tricks. *Of course, being a Frampton fan myself, I was really tickled, and learning this has changed my life in immeasurable ways. For example, if Peter Frampton (who is currently touring, by the way) is appearing in concert at any nearby venue, I can just drop by the box office, pay the admission price, and they'll give me a ticket to his upcoming performance. Not only that, but if I go to the local record store and try to buy any Peter Frampton CD (including his classic "Frampton Comes Alive" double-album set), they'll let me. No questions asked. All I have to present is my ID and credit card. How cool is that?*

  GETTING TO YOUR MOST-USED FILES AND FOLDERS FAST

Do you find yourself going to the same folders over and over again? (Of course you do, we all do, we just don't admit it at parties.) Well, if this sounds like you, you can place these most-used folders right in the Sidebar so you can access them anytime (including from right within the Open/Save dialog). To add a folder to the Sidebar, just click on it, then press Command-T (the old Favorites shortcut from previous versions of the Mac OS X). Although technically there's still a Favorites folder (I talked about it in Chapter 1), it doesn't really help much, because (1) there is no longer a keyboard shortcut to move a file into your Favorites folder, and (2) you can no longer designate a folder to be a "Favorite" from within Open/Save dialog boxes, like you could in previous versions. Basically, Apple wants you to use the Sidebar to keep your most-used files and folders—that way, you can access them from Open/Save dialogs.

   STEALING A FILE'S NAME, THEN SAVING RIGHT OVER IT

If you're saving a file, you can use the name of an existing file by just clicking on it in the Save dialog navigation window. Even if the file is grayed out, you can still click on it, and when you do, its name appears as your new file name at the top of the Save dialog. This is a huge timesaver. When you click OK, it asks you if you want to replace it with the file you're saving. If you're saving a different version of a file, and all you want to do is add a version number (like "Brochure Inside Cover 2"), all you'd have to do is click on the existing file named "Brochure Inside Cover" in the Save dialog, and that name would then appear as your new file name, then just type in a 2.

MENU SPEED TIP

Getting right to the menu item you want fast can save loads of time (since we spend so much time digging around in menus all day). That's why you'll love this tip. The next time you're in a pop-down menu, instead of mousing down to the item you want to select, just press the first letter of the command you want and that command becomes selected. For example, to select the Customize Toolbar command, click once on the View menu, press "c", then press Return. That's speed menus, baby! By the way, if two commands start with the same letter, type in the first two letters.

   FINDING THE HIDDEN "GO TO" FIELD

In previous versions of Mac OS X, there was a "Go to" field at the bottom of the Open dialog where you could jump directly to the folder you wanted by typing in its location. In Panther, that field no longer appears in the Open dialog, but luckily, it's not gone forever—it's just one simple keystroke away. When you're in the Open dialog, just press the "/" (slash) key on your keyboard and the Go to the Folder dialog pops down from the top of the Open dialog, ready for you to type in the path to your folder. *Note*: This doesn't work in all applications, so if typing the slash doesn't bring up the Go to the Folder dialog, just press Shift-Command-G and that'll do the trick.

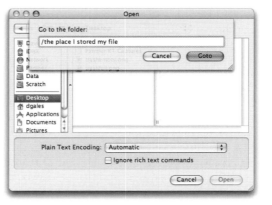

   SPEED TIP: TAKE OUT THE PAPERS AND THE TRASH

Want to empty the Trash without making a trip up to the Finder menu first? Just Control-click on the Trash icon in the Dock and choose Empty Trash. Of course, you could also press Shift-Command-Delete, but how much fun is that? Incidentally, if you want to get

something in the Trash in a hurry, just click on it, press Command-Delete, and that file jumps into the Trash lickety-split!

   GET INFO'S SECRET SECOND PERSONALITY

While Command-I brings up the regular Info dialog, pressing Option-Command-I brings up a second version with a special hidden feature (you'll know it's the second version because its corners are squared, rather than rounded, and there's no Minimize or Zoom button). This second version stays live when you click on different files—giving you their file info as well (the regular version just deselects when you click on a different file, so you have to press Command-I all over again to get info on that file). This is great for quickly comparing things like file sizes or modified dates, because you can just click from file to file, and the file info is instantly displayed. Another nice speed benefit is that when you use Option-Command-I to open Get Info, you can also use that same shortcut to close it instead of clicking on the red close button. (The standard Command-W shortcut closes the "first personality" Command-I Get Info window.)

ERASING FILES FOR GOOD!

People are getting pretty freaky about the security of the files on their drives. Especially since they learned that even though they "trashed" some of their most personal and sensitive files and thought they were gone forever, they're still recoverable. And not just recoverable by the FBI lab, but by your average junior-high student. That's why Apple created a secure version of the Empty Trash command called—big surprise—Secure Empty Trash. Without going into too much techno-geek-speak, it deletes your file and writes over the drive space where it once lived so many times that agents from top-secret government agencies that we're not even supposed to know exist couldn't resurrect those files. In short, use Secure Empty Trash when you really want your files gone for good.

LOOKING INSIDE MULTIPLE FOLDERS AUTOMATICALLY

Need to see what's inside more than one folder while in List view? Do it the fast way—Command-click on all the folders you want to expand, then press Command-Right Arrow. All the folders expand at once. If the file you're looking for isn't there, just press Command-Left Arrow (you can do that, because your folders are still highlighted) to quickly collapse them all.

BETTER THAN THE OLD CONTROL STRIP—IT'S MENU EXTRAS!

The Control Strip, thankfully, is gone and has been replaced by something infinitely better—Menu Extras. These tiny black icons appear in the menu bar, just to the left of your menu clock; and not only do they tell you what's going on, they actually work (at least if you click on them, anyway) kind of similar to how the Control Strip worked, but without the annoyance of the Control Strip. (Are you getting the feeling that I didn't like the Control Strip?) Just click on the Menu Extras to access their controls. For example, click on the one that looks like a speaker, and a volume-control slider pops down, just like a menu, where you can control your system volume. You add Menu Extras in the System Preferences of each control you want to add. For example, you can add the Displays Menu Extra by going to the Displays preference and choosing the Show Displays in Menu Bar checkbox.

REARRANGING THE MENU EXTRAS

Want to change the order of the Menu Extras in your menu bar? Just hold the Command key and drag the icons into the order you want them. It gives you a real feeling of power. Well, a feeling of power over tiny icons anyway.

REMOVING MENU EXTRAS FROM YOUR MENU BAR

To remove a Menu Extra, just hold the Command key and click-and-drag the Menu Extra right off the bar. It doesn't get much easier than that.

   THE ACCIDENTAL-DELETE PROTECTION DEVICE

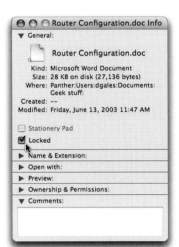

In previous versions of the Mac OS, you could protect an important file from accidentally being deleted (trashed) by clicking on the Locked checkbox in the Info window. The problem was you could still put the file in the Trash, and if you held the Option key while emptying the Trash, you could still delete it. Talk about a half-assed security device. Well, in Mac OS X, you apply the lock the same way (click on the file, press Command-I to bring up the Info window, and click on Locked); but the improvement comes in that Mac OS X will not even let you drag that file to the Trash in the first place. Instead, you get a warning dialog telling you basically, "Sorry, punk." Hey, serves you right for trying to delete a file you thought was important.

SAVING TO THE DESKTOP IN A FLASH

When you're in the Save As dialog and you want to save a file to the desktop, just press Command-D and the "Where" pop-up menu switches to Desktop, so all you have to do is name your file and click OK. Another alternative to saving in the Documents folder (like the OS really wants you to), is to save the file directly to your Home folder by pressing Shift-Command-H and Home appears as your Save destination.

   HIDDEN COLUMN VIEW NAVIGATION TIP

Here's somewhat of a weird problem (and a simple fix): Let's say you have your Favorites folder in your Sidebar, and you click on it to get to some of your favorite files. If you're viewing all this in Column view, the first column winds up being the contents of your Favorites. You can't scroll to a column farther back (like to your Library folder, which holds your Favorites folder or to your Home folder, or Users folder, etc.) Well, you can't unless you know this hidden little tip: Just hold the Command key and press the Up Arrow key on your keyboard. Each time you press it, it moves you back farther, so instead of hitting "the wall" when you're in the Favorites column, now you can keep going as far as you want.

SAVING WHERE YOU WANT TO

When the Save As dialog appears, it appears in a "simple" mode by default, asking only what you want to name the file, and there's a simple pop-up menu for where you want to save it (again, it assumes you want to save everything in the Documents folder). However, if you want (or need) to go digging through your drive to find (or create) a folder that isn't in the pop-up menu, just click on the small blue button with the down-facing arrow next to the name field to expand the Save As dialog to include a Column view of your hard drive.

   PUTTING FREQUENTLY USED FILES IN YOUR TOOLBAR

Okay, you know the Sidebar stores frequently used files and folders, but it can get full pretty fast. If yours gets "packed," try parking some of your most-used files right on the toolbar at the top of your Finder window. Here's how: Click-and-drag the file up to the toolbar. Hold it there for just a second, and a thin rectangle appears, letting you know to release the mouse button. When you do, the file appears in the toolbar, where it's always just one click away. If you decide to remove it one day, just hold the Command key and drag it off the toolbar.

   CREATING YOUR OWN KEYBOARD SHORTCUTS

Keyboard shortcuts are such huge time-savers, but sadly, not all Finder commands have them. But they can, because in Panther, you can create your own. Here's how: Go under the Apple menu, to System Preferences, and choose Keyboard & Mouse. When the dialog appears, click on the Keyboard Shortcuts tab, then click the + (plus) sign at the bottom left of the dialog. A dialog appears. Choose Finder from the pop-up list, then type in the exact name of the menu command you want to add a shortcut for. Then, type in the shortcut you want to use, and click the Add button. It's that simple.

   THE SAVE DIALOG SAVES ITSELF

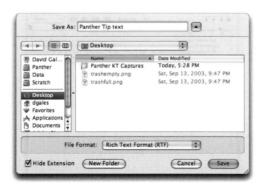

The Save dialog has an excellent memory, because not only does it remember the recent folders that you saved to, but it also remembers if you expanded it into Column view or stretched out the size. The next time you open that application and go to save a file, it remembers that you like Column view and how large you made the dialog. It treats it as if you're setting "Save dialog" defaults for that application.

 AUTOMATICALLY ADDING FILE EXTENSIONS

Sharing your files with someone using a PC? Make sure you name the file "Don't you wish you had a Mac.txt" or something like that (kidding). Actually, if you're sharing files with a PC, you can ask Mac OS X to automatically add the three-letter file extension to your file name every time you save a file. Just go to the Finder menu, choose Preferences, click on the Advanced icon, and select the Show All File Extensions checkbox.

 HOW TO BE SELECTIVE WITH EXTENSIONS

In Mac OS X, every file has a three-letter file extension (like PC files do), but by default, Mac OS X hides those three-letter extensions. In the previous tip, I showed you how to make those three-letter extensions visible all the time, but what if you just want to see the three-letter extensions for an individual file or two? If you want to see these extensions (perhaps if you're designing Web graphics and want your files to have the .gif and .jpg file extensions visible), you can do that when you save each file. In the Save dialog, you'll notice a checkbox called

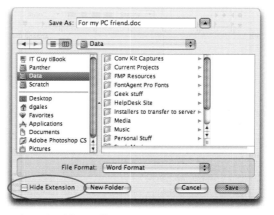

Hide Extension, which is on by default. Just turn that checkbox off, and the appropriate file extension is added to the file. In some applications, you may see a checkbox for Append Extension instead. In this case, make sure the checkbox is on to show the extension.

SPEEDING THROUGH YOUR SYSTEM PREFERENCES

When you're in the System Preferences dialog, there's a superfast way to quickly get to the individual preference pane you want. Just type the first letter of the preference, then hit the Spacebar. This not only selects the preference, it opens that pane as well. This, my friends, is one juicy speed trick!

SAVING TIME IN THE "GO TO THE FOLDER" DIALOG

Once you enter a path in the Go to the Folder dialog of a Cocoa app, that last path stays in memory (thanks to Panther's auto-complete feature), so if you want to get back to that same folder, don't press the "/" (slash) key when you're in the Open dialog. Instead, press Shift-Command-G; that way, when the Go to the Folder dialog appears, the last path you entered is already input for you, saving you the trouble.

BECOMING THE ULTIMATE MENU MASTER

Want to really speed things up? How about jumping right to the Apple menu without even clicking the mouse? Just press Control-F2 and the Apple menu pops down. Oh, but there's more! Now that you're in the Apple menu, press the Right Arrow key on your keyboard to move to the other menus (Finder, File, Edit, View, etc.) and the Left Arrow to move back. Once you get to the menu you want, use the tip I mentioned earlier: Type in the first letter of the command you want and it jumps right there, then press Return to choose that command (and you did it all without ever touching the mouse).

   A FASTER WAY TO GET YOUR SYSTEM INFO

If, for some reason, you run into some serious problems with your Mac (hey, it could happen), you might have to tell Apple tech support, a repair tech, or a Macintosh consultant some technical information about your particular hardware and system software configurations. Luckily, all that information is found by launching Apple's System Profiler. The only bad news is it's buried deep within your Applications folder, inside your Utilities folder. Here's the tip: There's a quicker way to get to the Apple System Profiler. Just go under the Apple menu and choose About This Mac. When the dialog appears, click on the button at the bottom called More Info and it launches the Apple System Profiler for you.

   FINDING SYSTEM PREFERENCES FAST BY SORTING ALPHABETICALLY

If you've been using Mac OS X for a while, you've no doubt noticed that the System Preferences window puts all the individual preferences in horizontal rows, sorted by four categories (Personal, Hardware, Internet & Network, and System). That's great, if you know exactly which category to look under, but if you're new to Mac OS X, you might prefer a feature introduced in Jaguar—sorting the preferences alphabetically, rather than by category. That way, if you need the Universal Access preferences, you already know that alphabetically it's probably located near the end of the list. To sort your System Preferences alphabetically, first open the System Preferences window, go under the View menu, and choose Organize Alphabetically. If you later decide you'd like your categories back, choose Organize by Categories in the View menu.

   SHORTCUT TO HIDE YOUR APPS

This simple keyboard shortcut is one of my favorite features. When you're in the Finder, you can hide all of your running applications from view by pressing Option-Command-H (the shortcut for Hide Others, which is found under the Finder menu). Ahhhhh, to me, that alone was worth the upgrade price (okay, it was almost worth the upgrade price).

she drives me crazy

ANNOYING LITTLE THINGS

Mac OS X is an amazing operating system. Yet, it can also be an annoying operating system. So, depending on what you're doing

She Drives Me Crazy

how to stop annoying things

*with it—it's either annoyingly amazing, or amazingly annoying. Okay, I'm not really being fair, because in reality, it's not the operating system itself that's annoying. It's things **in** the operating system—aspects of it (if you will) that are annoying. And not just a little annoying—we're talking "put you in a tower with a high-powered rifle and night-vision goggles"-type annoying, and this chapter is about how to quickly make some of the most egregious annoyances go away. But make no mistake about it—Mac OS X isn't the first Apple operating system to include wildly annoying features. Remember Balloon Help—Apple's attempt at coming up with a better form of on-screen help, which could have been devised only by the Prince of Darkness himself (not Darth Vader—El Diablo!)? There's a hint, just a hint, of that type of stuff in Mac OS X, but this chapter helps you exorcise those demons fast!*

   THE WORKAROUND FOR REAL MULTIPLE USER ACCESS

If you have multiple users sharing the same Mac (and with Panther's Fast User switching, it's a breeze), you're going to run into a snag when you share files between users. If you've created a file and you want the other user (or users) on your Mac to be able to open and view this file—no problem—just put it in the Shared folder. However, they don't have permission to edit or delete this original file (it's built that way by default). But what if you *want* them to be able to edit and delete? Or what if you're the only person using your Mac, but you've set up multiple users so your Mac is configured differently for different tasks—you can edit or delete your own files in the Shared folder. So, how do you get around this? Just attach an external drive (like a FireWire or USB drive), then when it mounts on your desktop, click on it, then press Command-I to bring up the Info window. Go to the Ownership and Permissions panel and choose Ignore Ownership on the Volume. Now, anything you put on this external drive will be available to all users. Also, if you don't want to use an external drive, you can do the same thing by partitioning your startup drive using Apple's Disk Utility.

   STOPPING CLASSIC FROM LAUNCHING WITHOUT PERMISSION

If you're just making the migration from Mac OS 9 to Mac OS X, one day, you'll be doing a search for a file you created last year. You'll find it, then double-click on it, and since it was created in a "Classic application" on your old machine, it boots Mac OS X's Classic mode and launches your old Mac OS 9 application. My bet is, you don't want to open that application in Classic (unless you absolutely have to). That's why you might want to have your Mac ask, "Do you really want to start Classic?" To turn on this helpful warning, go under the System Preferences, under Classic, click on the Start/Stop button and choose Warn Before Starting Classic.

STOPPING THE QUICKTIME PLAYER BLUES #1

Okay, let's say that you're not a big fan of Panther's built-in auto-software updating. So much so that you've gone to the System Preferences panel, under Software Update, and actually turned it off. You'd think that you've seen the last of the Software Update alert dialogs, right? Nope. If you open a movie or an audio clip in the QuickTime Player, by default, it automatically goes and checks for QuickTime updates. To turn off this QuickTime auto-software updating, go to the System Preferences, under Quick-Time, and click on the Update button. Then, uncheck the checkbox named Check for Updates Automatically.

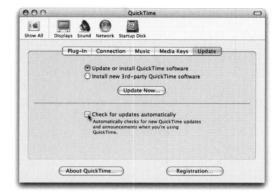

STOPPING QUICKTIME PLAYER BLUES #2

This one may be even more annoying than the first. It's called "Hot Picks," and if you like pop-up window and banner ads, you'll love this. If you launch the QuickTime Player while you have an Internet connection, before you can do anything else, it goes to the Web, downloads a little advertising clip (usually for a new album, or movie), and plays it in your QuickTime Player. The good news is, you can turn this annoying "ad feed" off. Just launch the QuickTime Player, then go under the QuickTime menu, under Preferences, then Player Preferences, and under Hot Picks, turn off Show Hot Picks Movie Automatically. Ahhhh, now isn't that better?

   STOPPING THE SOFTWARE AUTO-UPDATING MENACE

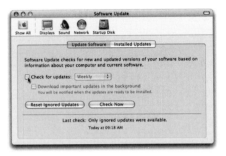

The idea is great—whenever Apple releases even the tiniest update to your system software or any of the iApps, a window pops up to tell you that it's been released, and it even offers to download the software for you. The problem? It always, always opens at the wrong time: when you're on deadline, when you're five minutes from leaving the office—really, any time you don't want it to pop up—it pops up. Personally, I'd rather decide to update at my leisure (once a week or so) rather than when my system feels it needs a fix. To turn off this auto-updating menace, go under the Apple menu to System Preferences. Click on the Software Update icon, and where it says "Update Software," make sure to turn off Check for Updates. Or, you can choose to be interrupted at the wrong time only once a month (from the pop-up menu). Either way, "Another one bites the dust!"

   STOP ASKING ME WHAT TO DO!

There's a feature in Mac OS X that's both a blessing and a curse (it's a blessing if it does what you want, but otherwise…). For example, when you insert a blank CD, it brings up a dialog asking what you want to do with it. Chances are, you do the same thing over and over (prepare it for burning, launch Toast, launch iTunes, etc.), but it keeps asking you, again and again, every time you insert a CD. It's just this side of maddening. You can change Mac OS X's list of "When you insert this, I'm opening that…" by going under the Apple menu, under System Preferences, and choosing CDs & DVDs. There, you find a plain-English list of pop-up menus that lets you stop opening any applications that you don't want, and you can choose which apps, if any, you do want opened. Most importantly, Mac OS X stops asking you what to do.

IT WON'T LET ME ERASE A DISK!

In all previous versions of Mac OS, when you wanted to erase a disk, you just went under the Special menu and chose Erase Disk. But in Mac OS X, there's no Special menu. (Apple might counter that all the menus are special—they're not.) Now to erase a disk, you have to launch Disk Utility (inside your Utilities folder on your hard drive). When you launch Disk Utility, just click on the tab for Erase and you're there!

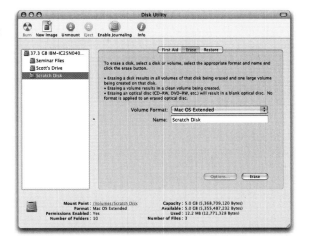

HOW TO STOP MAGNIFYING YOUR DOCK

This may be a very embarrassing subject for some of you, so I'll try to handle it with the utmost sensitivity. If you have a very small Dock (and you know who you are), the Magnification feature is almost a necessity. However, if you leave your Dock icons at their default size (which many people do), magnification can be wildly annoying and since the icons are so large to begin with, magnification is totally unnecessary. When my wife first saw large Dock icons being magnified even more, the first thing she said was, "Is there a way to turn that awful thing off?" There is: Control-click on the Dock's vertical divider bar (on the far right side of the Dock) and from the pop-up menu that appears, choose Turn Magnification Off.

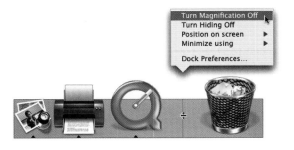

   TURNING OFF THE "EMPTY TRASH" WARNING

There's nothing like executing a simple command, and having the OS ask, "Are you sure you want to do this?" By default, every time you go to empty the Trash, it asks this annoying question (and it has for years upon years). Disabling the Empty Trash warning is a little different in Mac OS X than it was in previous versions. Now, you go under the Finder menu, under Preferences, and click on the Advanced icon. Then, uncheck the checkbox for Show Warning Before Emptying the Trash.

   DELETING LOCKED FILES

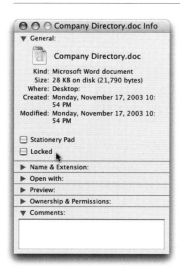

Mac OS X is much tougher about your trying to delete a locked file. In fact, you can't pull that "drop it in the Trash, hold the Option key, and choose Empty Trash" routine, because Mac OS X won't even let you put it in the Trash in the first place. You have to unlock it manually by clicking on the file and pressing Command-I to bring up the Info window. Then, uncheck the checkbox for Locked. Now, it's yours for the trashing.

PUTTING THE GENIE BACK IN THE BOTTLE

Certainly, the Genie Effect (which is that genie-like special effect that occurs by default when you minimize a window to the Dock) would be a nominee for the "Mac OS X Annoying Hall of Fame." Luckily, putting this Genie back in its bottle is easy—just go under the Apple menu, under System Preferences, and when the prefs dialog appears, click on Dock. In the Dock preference pane, in the pop-up menu for Minimize Using, choose Scale Effect rather than Genie, and that should put a cork in it (so to speak).

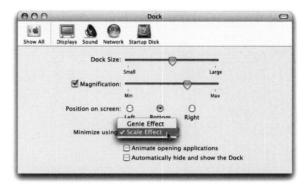

   STOP ASKING ME FOR MY PASSWORD

Are you like me? No. Then how about this: Are you like me in the sense that you're the only person that works on your Mac? Maybe it's your Mac at home, and not a single soul but you uses your machine (meaning, of course, your spouse, your kids, and the cat all have their own Macs). Then, you don't need an administrator to tell you what you can and can't add to your own single, solitary machine, right? It's just you. And you're a good person. Then when you install Mac OS X, and it asks you for an administrator password, don't put one in. Leave it blank, and that way, you'll never have to remember your password. Oh sure, it'll try to tell you that you may have a security problem (the cat might try to sneak a virus onto your machine), but if you're the only one who will ever install a program on that machine, wouldn't you love to just click the OK button when the annoying password dialog pops up the next time you want to install a program?

HIDING THE ANNOYING MICROPHONE DISC THINGY

I cover this tip elsewhere in this book, but since this is so annoying, I knew you'd be looking for it in this chapter, too. When you
open an application that supports Mac OS X's built-in Speech
control (like Chess, for example), it brings up what I call "the
incredibly annoying round microphone thingy." It floats around,
taking up space, and if you're not using Speech control (which
most of us aren't), it's just plain annoying. If you are actually using Speech control, it's still annoying (necessary perhaps, but still
annoying). To get it out of sight, double-click on the top half of it,
and it tucks itself into the Dock while you work.

MAKING THE ANNOYING ALERT SOUND LESS ANNOYING

Do you find the default alert sound annoying?
Oh yeah, after a few days, its very sound
sends blood trickling down my ear (okay,
that's a bit of an exaggeration, but only a
bit). You can change it to a different sound,
but that would stop just short of what it
really needs—to be much quieter (unless,
of course, you're using your Mac on a noisy
factory floor). To change sounds and lower
the Alert volume, go under the System
Preferences and click on the Sound icon.
When it appears, click on the Alerts tab,
and then you can hear each alert tone by
clicking on it. Find the one that makes you
shudder the least and then, most importantly,
use the Alert volume slider to set it at a

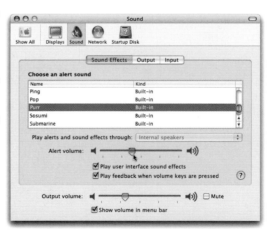

volume that doesn't take your head off every time you make a little mistake. Ahhhh. That's
better, isn't it?

HOW TO STOP AN APPLICATION FROM LAUNCHING

If you've accidentally launched an application that you didn't want to launch (this can happen quite frequently, especially if you're drunk), you can stop that launch dead in its tracks by pressing Shift-Option-Command-Esc. (Just in case you were wondering, we used Adobe InDesign to lay out this book, and their splash screen looks so cool, I thought I'd show it here.)

SAVING TIME WHEN LAUNCHING PROGRAMS—NEVER QUIT!

Isn't it annoying how long it takes applications to launch? The fix: Don't quit your applications. Because Mac OS X manages its memory so well, you can leave the applications you use most open all the time—there's no major advantage to quitting after you're done working in them (like there was back in Mac OS 9). They just don't take up the resources, or put much of a strain on your computer, so quitting them doesn't really help. (*Note:* This is for Mac OS X apps only—not Classic Apps.) Many experts also recommend that you don't shut down your Mac; rather just put it to sleep, because the UNIX core of Mac OS X was designed to run all day and all night, and shutting it down just isn't necessary (unless, of course, you live where I do in Florida, where the next thunderstorm is usually just a few hours away, especially in summer, in which case not only do I shut down, I run around my house unplugging everything in sight).

DISABLING SCREEN SAVER HOT CORNERS

Does your Screen Saver keep turning on when you rest your cursor in one of the corners of your screen? Well, this used to drive me crazy. (I say used to, because I used this tip to fix it.) What's happening is that one of your corners has been designated as a "Hot Corner" (at least as far as Mac OS X's screen saver is concerned), and whenever your cursor winds up there for more than a second or two, it starts Mac OS X's built-in screen saver. To make this "hot corner" stuff go away, go to the System Preferences and click on the Desktop & Screen Saver icon. When its pane appears, click on the Screen Saver tab, then click on the Hot Corners button to bring up the Hot Corners panel. When it appears, you'll see four pop-up

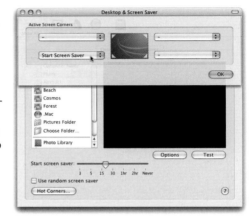

menus, each representing one corner of your screen. If one or more of these pop-up menus says Start Screen Saver, that indicates a hot corner. To turn off a hot corner, click on the pop-up menu and choose " — " from the menu to make that corner go "cold." The full screen is now yours to enjoy uninterrupted.

SLEEP LESS—WORK MORE

Have you plugged your PowerBook or iBook into an A/C outlet, but it's still going to sleep on you every 5 or 10 minutes? Honestly, that drives me nuts, and if you're like me, once you plug in, you'll want to go to the System Preferences and click on the Energy Saver icon. When its pane appears, click on the Sleep Tab (if you don't see the tab, click on the Show Details button on the bottom right), and then drag the slider over to a reasonable amount of time (like 30 minutes or more). That way, if you do call it a night and forget to put your PowerBook to sleep, Energy Saver eventually kicks in.

STOP THE BOUNCING. I BEG YOU!

When you launch an application, its icon begins to bounce incessantly in the Dock in a distracting vertical Tigger-like motion until the app is just about open. I love this feature; but then, I enjoy having my cavities drilled. If you enjoy this animation as much as I do, you can turn it off by going to the Apple menu, under Dock, and choosing Dock Preferences. When the Dock preferences pane appears, turn off the checkbox (it's on by default) for Animate Opening Applications. Turning this off now can save you thousands in therapy costs down the road.

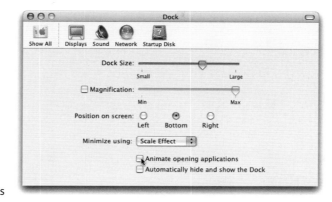

SHUTTING DOWN WITHOUT THE WARNING

When you choose Shut Down from the Apple menu, a dialog appears asking if you really want to shut down. Yes, it's annoying. To make the bad dialog go away, just hold the Option key before you choose Shut Down, and it just shuts down (without insulting your intelligence by asking you if what you chose is really what you want to do).

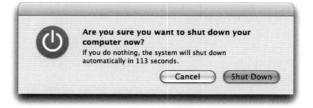

hooked on classics

CLASSIC TIPS

Apple really pulled off an amazing feat by nesting a version of Mac OS 9 right within *Mac OS X so you can still run applications*

Hooked on Classics
tips for using the classic environment

that haven't yet been updated to run in Mac OS X. When you think about it, it's really brilliant. Once you use it, you'll find that it runs those applications surprisingly well. Once you begin to use it often, it won't be long before you hate the Classic Environment with every fiber of your being. Just seeing the Classic Environment start-up bar can set into motion a vexing combination of facial tics, with an uncontrollable urge to shout obscenities that make no sense whatsoever (stuff like, "Eat my mandible, you shoe-wearing turquoise trailer-hitch"). In short, you quickly start to dedicate every waking hour, and all your available resources to never, ever, having to use the Classic Environment. But, until you reach that ultimate nirvana, where all of your applications run in an operating system actually released in the 21st century, here are some tips to keep your temporary bouts of Tourette's Syndrome in check while working in Classic.

   RECOGNIZING A CLASSIC APP

Sure, once the application is fully launched and its icon appears in the Dock, you can usually tell if it's a Classic app and not a Mac OS X app by its jaggy icon. But if you'd rather know before you go though the Classic launch cycle, just click on the app's icon and press Command-I. When the Info window appears, look at the Kind field. If it's a Classic app, it says so right here.

   STARTING CLASSIC MODE AUTOMATICALLY EVERY TIME

If you use Classic mode apps every day (and I feel bad for you if you have to), you might want Mac OS X to launch Classic mode automatically whenever you start up your Mac. You can do that by going under the Apple menu, under System Preferences, and clicking on the Classic icon. When its pane appears, click on the Start/Stop tab, then click the checkbox for Start Classic When You Login, which is a very un-Apple-like way of saying, "When I start my computer, go ahead and start Classic, too." I've always felt that someone who used to work at Microsoft came up with that checkbox description, but I can't prove it.

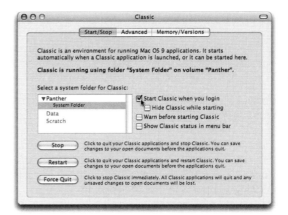

ACCESSING CLASSIC CONTROL PANELS IN PANTHER

In Panther, you can now have access to Classic's Control Panels (and the other items in the OS 9 Apple menu) from right within OS X. Under Panther's Apple menu, choose System Preferences, then click on the Classic icon. In the Classic preferences, click on Show Classic Status in Menu Bar, then close the preferences. This puts a tiny "9" icon in your OS X menu bar. Click on it, and a pop-down menu appears that gives you direct access to Classic's Apple Menu Items and Control Panels. You can also start, stop, and restart Classic from here. Before, you had to go to System Preferences for that.

   THE COOLEST THING ABOUT CLASSIC?

My buddy Terry called me one day and said, "If there's anything cool about Classic mode, and I'm not sure there is, but if there is, I've found it." He told me to launch Classic and look down in the Dock. When you first launch Classic, the OS 9 logo appears in the Dock during startup, then it goes away once it's up and running. The cool thing is what Apple added to the logo in Panther. As Classic boots, the large "9" in its Dock icon acts as a status bar—it starts off in gray and fills with gold as the loading progresses. I have to agree with Terry—if there's anything cool about Classic—this is it.

   OPENING MAC OS X APPS IN CLASSIC MODE

A number of applications (Apple calls them "Carbonized" apps) will run in either Mac OS X or Classic mode (such as Adobe Photoshop 7.0), but by default, they're going to launch in Mac OS X (and why not? OS X is a much better operating system). However, there may be instances where you want the application to launch in Classic mode (for example, if you can't get a printer or scanner to work in Mac OS X, you might need to have the application open in Classic so you can access printing/scanning). To launch a Mac OS X app in Classic mode, just click on the application's icon and press Command-I. When the Info window appears, you see a checkbox for Open in the Classic Environment. Click on the checkbox, close the window, launch the application, and it opens in Classic. Don't forget that you've done this little wizardry, or it will always open in Classic, so go back and "uncheck" that box when you're ready to relaunch it in Mac OS X.

   GIVING CLASSIC APPS MAC OS X MEMORY POWER!

If you've used Mac OS 9 for a while, you already know how to assign memory to individual applications, and you do it the same way today in Classic. You just click on the Classic app's icon, press Command-I, and up pops the Info window. Click the right-facing gray triangle at the left of the word "Memory" to expand that pane. Enter the amount of memory you'd like the app to have in the Preferred Size field. (For best performance, make sure it's more than the amount shown as its Suggested Size. In fact, to really take advantage of Mac OS X's new memory management, you need to increase this amount by quite a bit, so go memory-hog-wild.)

ONE-CLICK DESKTOP REBUILDING

If you've been using the Mac for years, no doubt you're familiar with the concept of "rebuilding the desktop" in Mac OS 9. It's one of those things you do once a month, whether you need it or not, to keep everything running smoothly, to keep your icons looking right, plus a host of other good things. You used to rebuild the desktop by holding Option-Command while booting your computer, but now you don't have to (especially since holding Option-Command while booting in Mac OS X won't rebuild your Classic desktop). Now, it's easier than ever. Just go under the Apple menu, choose System Preferences, and

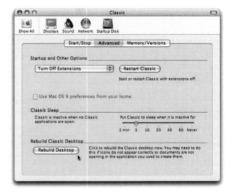

click on the Classic icon. When its pane appears, click on the Advanced tab, and the advanced features pane appears with a Rebuild Desktop button (at the bottom of the pane). Just click it, and it does its thing. You don't even have to restart Classic—just click the button. In fact, you don't even have to launch Classic to rebuild the desktop.

   THE SUPER-SECRET HIDDEN MEMORY CONTROLLER

Senate military subcommittees don't have secrets as well-hidden as Apple hides this controller. If you want to throw a little more memory to Classic mode (you're running a bunch of Classic apps and need the head-room), go under the Apple menu, choose System Prefereneces, click on the Classic icon, then click on the Memory/Versions button. Look in the bottom-right corner. Do you see a button? (Not a checkbox—a button). No? Then, click on the Start/Stop button, hold the Option key, and click on the Memory/Versions button again. Holy cow—look at that. A secret Adjust Memory button appears (shown here).

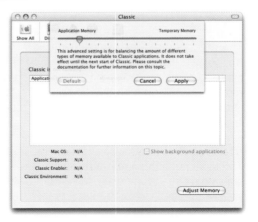

Click it and a secret panel pops down (also shown here). Drag the slider toward Temporary Memory to send more memory Classic's way.

   GETTING RID OF JAGGY DOCK ICONS

Mac OS X doesn't put an icon in the Dock to let you know that an application is running in Classic mode, but it does give you a hint; it makes the icon for your Classic application look really ratty and jaggy. Well, you might not notice how ratty these icons look if you have your Dock icons set to a fairly small size. But if they're large, or you give them a glance when you roll your cursor over them and they're magnified, you'll notice that those Classic icons look totally ratty at those larger sizes (while your cool OS X icons look great at any size). The way around this? Even though those old apps run in Classic mode, you can still copy-and-paste OS X-style icons over their original icons (so at least you won't have to live with the jaggies). You can download some of these icons from various Web sites, such as www.iconfactory.com or www.xicons.com, where they've got loads of Mac OS X-savvy icons. To copy an icon, click on it in the Finder and press Command-I. When the Info window pops up, press Command-C to copy the icon. Then, go to the Applications (Mac OS 9) folder, click on the app whose jaggy icon drives you nuts, click on the still-open Info window to make it active, and press Command-V to paste your new icon right over the old one. Now, the next time you run this Classic app, take a look in your Dock and a wonderfully clean icon appears there. Ahhhh, that's better.

   NOT ALL CLASSIC CONTROL PANELS WORK

If you're a longtime Mac user, you're used to working with Mac OS 9's Control Panels, and that's why I want to warn you not to get upset when you choose them in Classic mode and many of their functions appear grayed out. That's because those functions are now handled by Mac OS X, and shouldn't be addressed by both OSs. (Is that a word? OSs? Or is it OSes, or OS's? Better yet, does anyone really care?) For example, you don't want to set the time in Classic and then have a different time, off by a few seconds perhaps, in Mac OS X mode. So, for your own sanity, some of these Control Panel items are grayed out.

CAN'T REMEMBER WHETHER CLASSIC IS RUNNING?

If you can't remember whether Classic is running or not, just go under the Apple menu (or to the Dock), under System Preferences, and click on the Classic icon. In the pane that appears, if the Classic Environment is running, you see the message "Classic is running."

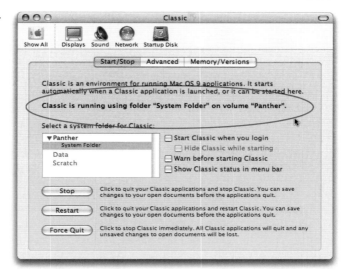

 SWITCHING APPS IN CLASSIC

If you want to switch between applications while running the Classic environment, you do it the same way you would back before Mac OS X—click on the application's name in the upper right-hand corner of your screen, and choose the currently running application you want to switch to from the pop-up menu. The cool thing is, any Mac OS X applications will be listed there too, so you can choose to switch to either Classic or Mac OS X applications from this pop-up menu.

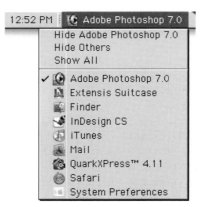

   WANT MORE THAN ONE CLASSIC SYSTEM FOLDER? GO FOR IT!

Back before Mac OS X, having more than one System folder was akin to driving on the freeway totally blindfolded—big problems are right around the corner. It was something you just didn't do, and if a Mac consultant found more than one system on your machine, they would berate you till you were on the ground in the fetal position. But now, everything's different. If you want one trimmed-down system for running a couple of Classic apps, but then want the option of booting a separate OS 9.2 system packed with every Control Panel and Extension known to man, it's totally cool. There's

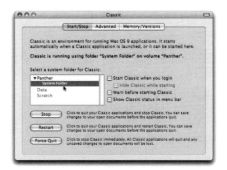

just one thing you really have to do to keep things running smoothly: Make sure that these other systems either reside on a totally separate hard drive, or partition your drive so the other system appears on a different partition. Once that's done, go under the Apple menu, under System Preferences, and click on the Classic icon. In the Start/Stop pane, you'll see a list of drives from which you can boot (under the heading Select a Startup Volume for Classic). Choose the drive that has the system you want to use, then click the Start button.

   IF OS X WANTS TO ADD STUFF TO CLASSIC, LET IT

The first time you launch Classic mode, a warning dialog may appear telling you that Classic Needs to Update Files in "System Folder" on "Whatever the Name of Your Hard Drive Is."

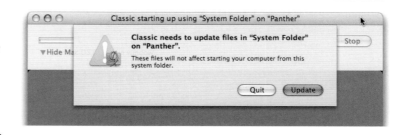

It gives you two choices: Quit or Update. This freaks a lot of people out, because it sounds as if they themselves are responsible for determining which these are, and installing them. But if you click Update, Mac OS does all the dirty work for you, and your only involvement in this process is clicking that Update button to start the process (which only takes a few seconds). So, in short, it's okay to press the Update button.

STOPPING A CLASSIC LAUNCH

There's nothing more aggravating than accidentally launching the Classic Environment and having to sit there waiting for the whole thing to load, just so you can quit. If that happens, you can press the "Stop" button, but you'll get a scary-looking warning dialog trying to convince you not to stop now,

but to wait until the whole thing launches, then switch to Mac OS X, go under the Apple menu to access the System Preferences and quit it there. Yeah, I've got time to do that. After you do this once or twice (sat through the whole aggravating process, etc.), you finally start hitting the Stop button. It stops immediately, and although you're flying in the face of a very scary warning dialog, you'll be glad to know many people have been doing this for quite a while, and they have still gone on to lead successful and productive lives. In short, we hit that Stop button any time we accidentally launch Classic.

   SLEEPY JUICE

Once you launch Classic, there's no real reason to quit it, except maybe to free up some memory; but, if you have to restart Classic, you have to wait for the whole darn thing to load again. Instead of doing that, you can put Classic to sleep. Putting Classic to sleep is like putting a PowerBook to sleep—it's still launched, but it's kind of in the background, and barely taking up any valuable system resources. To put Classic to sleep, go under the Apple menu, under System Preferences, or click System Preferences in the dock, then click on the Classic icon. When the Classic pane appears, click on the Advanced pane, and you see a slider

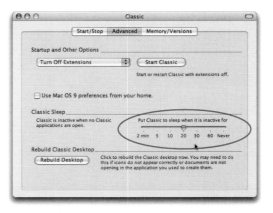

where you can reduce the time before it sleeps to two minutes. (I know, where's the "sleep now" button?) Close any open Classic apps, and in a couple of minutes, Classic finally nods off. To wake it up, just scream at your computer. If that doesn't work, just open a Classic application. It takes a few seconds to wake up (just like waking up a PowerBook in OS 9.2), but it beats the heck out of launching Classic all over again.

   SKIPPING MAC OS X ALTOGETHER: STARTING IN MAC OS 9

If you need to start up in Mac OS 9.2 (rather than starting in Mac OS X as usual), go under the Apple menu or to the Dock, choose System Preferences, and choose Startup Disk. You have a choice of starting up with either OS 9 or Mac OS X. Click on OS 9, then click on the Restart button, and it's like pushing a button to a time warp. At least that's the way you'll feel after running Mac OS X with its beautiful aqua look and feel. When you launch Mac OS 9.2, it feels so, well…old-fashioned.

   WHERE IS THE CLASSIC FINDER/DESKTOP?

Because of the way Mac OS X works, you can't see the Classic Finder/ Desktop. The only way to see it again is to have your Mac ignore Mac OS X's Finder altogether by restarting your Mac in Mac OS 9.2. You do this in the System Preferences under Startup Disk.

SAVING BEFORE YOU QUIT CLASSIC

If you've got half a dozen Classic applications open with one or two documents in each, what happens if you Quit Classic mode? All is well, as long as you quit in a civilized way by switching to the Mac OS X Finder (use the Finder icon in the Dock), going under the Apple menu, and choosing System Preferences. Click on the Classic icon, and in the pane that appears, just press the Stop button. Classic mode quits, but it gives you a chance to save any open, unsaved documents running in Classic. However, if you choose Quit and Classic doesn't quit, you can choose Force Quit from the Apple menu (or press Option-Command-Esc); but doing that quits all applications and closes all open documents without saving them first, so think twice about force quitting Classic.

   ## GETTING CLASSIC TO START UP FASTER

Do you want the Classic Environment to start up faster? (I know, that may be the stupidest question of the year. Really, who doesn't want Classic mode to start faster?) Then, all you have to do is disable any extraneous Extensions and Control Panels you may have had running when you upgraded to Mac OS X. (If you brought a brand-new machine with Mac OS X pre-loaded, you may not run into this problem as much.) To disable any extra Extensions and Control Panels, choose System Preferences under the Apple Menu, and click on the Classic icon. In the Classic pane, click on the Advanced tab. In the pop-up menu in the Startup Options section at the top, choose Open Extensions Manager, and then click on the Restart Classic button right next to the pop-up. As Classic is starting up, the Extensions Manager appears (just like the old days, eh?), and you can then choose which of these goodies you can live without. Not sure which ones you can pitch? Try using the Base set (just the Extensions that are necessary to start the system) from the pop-up menu.

   CAN'T REMEMBER THE CLASSIC KEYBOARD SHORTCUT?

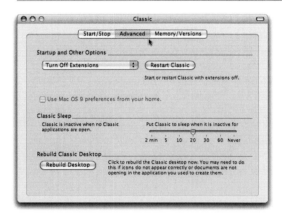

Can't remember all the little keyboard shortcuts to "tweak" Classic mode? Neither can I. That's probably why Apple replaced most of those Classic keyboard short-cuts—at least the ones you were used to when you launched Mac OS 9 anyway—with one-click buttons and pop-up menus. You can find these under the Apple menu, under System Preferences, under Classic. When the Classic pane appears, click on the Advanced tab, and you'll see options for little shortcuts (such as bringing up the Extensions Manager during startup, rebuilding your desktop, etc.).

   RESTARTING MANUALLY TO PURGE MEMORY

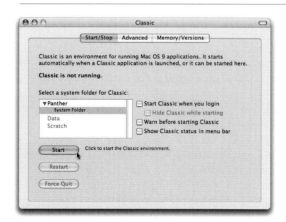

If the Classic Environment quits on you (hey, it happens), just re-launch it by going under the Apple menu, to System Preferences, and clicking on the Classic icon. In the pane that appears, click on the Start button. Doing it this way purges the memory automatically and helps keep the problem from recurring.

RESTARTING CLASSIC WITH KEYBOARD SHORTCUTS

Remember all the keyboard shortcuts you could use when you were starting up your Mac in OS 9 for such things as starting with the Extensions off or rebuilding your desktop? Well, these shortcuts are still there for the Classic environment, but it's not as simple as just holding the keys anymore. Here's how: Go under the Apple menu, under System Preferences, and click on the Classic icon. When the pane appears, click on the Advanced tab, and in the pop-up menu under Startup and Other Options, choose Use Key Combination, and then simply type in the keyboard shortcut you want to use (for example, the Shift key

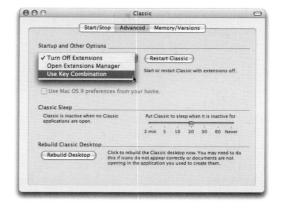

to start with Extensions off). Now, click on the Restart Classic button right next to the pop-up. Classic restarts as if you were physically holding these keys. *Note:* These shortcuts work only when you start Classic the slow way—from the Classic pane itself.

ONE-CLICK CLASSIC MODE

Apple decided not to put the Classic mode icon in the Dock while you're running Classic mode apps. Maybe it's because they didn't want early Mac OS X adopters to realize how many times they'd have to be running apps in Classic

mode (hey, it's just a guess), but nonetheless, it's not there. However, some people (mostly freaks) like to have the Classic icon appear in the Dock (okay, it's not just freaks; but it's mostly freaks). If you're one of "those" people (you know who you are), you can add the Classic icon to your Dock by double-clicking on your hard drive icon, then look inside the folder named "System" (the one with the "X" on it, not the one named System Folder with a 9 on it), then look inside the Library folder, and inside that, you'll find a folder named CoreServices. In this folder is a file named Classic Startup. Drag this icon onto the Dock and then if you feel like taking a "time tunnel" back to the past, you're only one click away.

   RUNNING APPS THAT WON'T RUN IN CLASSIC

If you haven't already, you'll almost certainly run across an application that simply won't run in Classic mode or Mac OS X. You know it won't because you get a little warning dialog telling you, "The application is not supported." When that happens, you'll have to change your Startup System to Mac OS 9.2 and restart. This is just one of those cases where Mac OS

X's Classic emulator just isn't enough. Luckily, these instances are few and far between, but now at least when you run across one, you'll know what to do, eh?

   FORCE QUITTING CLASSIC MODE

If, for some reason, Classic just won't quit when you choose Stop from the Classic preferences (found in the System Preferences by clicking on the Classic icon), you can press Option-Command-Esc. This brings up the Force Quit Applications pane, and you'll see an item in the list named Classic Environment. Click on that, then click the Force Quit button, which forces Classic to quit.

JUMPING TO CLASSIC MODE WHEN YOU CHARGE BY THE HOUR

You probably already know that the fastest way to get into Classic mode is to double-click on a document created in a Classic application. Mac OS X automatically launches Classic mode for you, launches the application, and opens your document (hey, if you didn't know that, there's another tip!). But if you don't want to do it the fast way, there is another slower, more "billable-hours" way: Go under the Apple menu, under System Preferences, and click on the Classic icon. Its pane appears, where you can click on the button labeled Start.

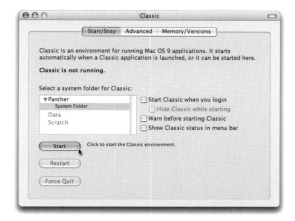

CLASSIC SPEED TIP: TURN OFF THE FUNKY SOUNDS

Mac OS 9 offered you the ability to add a "soundtrack" to your Mac life. If you clicked on something, it made a sound. Open a window—another sound. Scrolled through a window—more sounds. They were cute at first, but most users turned them off after just a few days. Those who chose to leave them on had to be institutionalized after hearing these sounds for just a few weeks. Well, now there's a new reason to turn them off—it slows things down. To turn off the annoying soundtrack, while in Classic, go under the

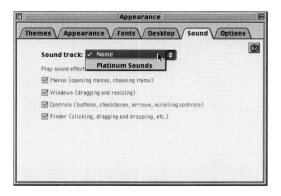

Apple menu, under Control Panels, and choose Appearance. Click on the Sound Tab, and from the Sound Track pop-up menu, choose None.

fly like
an eagle

SPEED TIPS

If I could show you some Mac OS X speed tips that would make you faster and more productive at Mac OS X than you ever

Fly Like an Eagle
mac os x speed tips

dreamed possible, how much would you be willing to pay? 50 bucks? 75 bucks? 100 bucks? Easily. So basically, by paying a list price of only $29.99 for this book, I figure you're ahead by at least $20.05 (if you said 50 bucks) and possibly as much as $70.05 (if you said 100 bucks). Well, if you think about it, although many of the tips in this book makes you faster, only this particular chapter is on speed tips, so in reality, you were willing to pay between $50 and $100 for just the tips in the this chapter; technically, you should've paid extra for the other chapters. Now granted, they won't all make you faster, so I'm willing to give you a discount—$10 a chapter—so add $120 (there are 12 other chapters) onto the $70.05 you already owe, making your total value around $190.05. Now, if you ordered this book from Amazon.com, and got 30% off the list price, you're just flat taking advantage of the situation, and to make up for it, I expect you to feel a level of guilt that is commensurate with the value actually received.

IS THAT TASK DONE YET? THE DOCK KNOWS

Let's say you're working in a power-crunching app like Photoshop, and you go to apply a filter to a high-res image, and it's going to take a minute or two to process your command. You're going to

get a progress bar so you can see how long the process is going to take, right? Well, thanks to Mac OS X's way-cool Dock, you can switch out of Photoshop and work on something else, and the Dock lets you know when the filter is applied. How? Well, when a progress bar appears in Photoshop, the Dock automatically adds a tiny little progress bar to the bottom of the Photoshop icon in the Dock so you can keep an eye on the progress, even when you're doing something else (like checking your mail, shopping online, or writing a letter).

SYSTEM PREFERENCES SUPER-SPEED SHORTCUT

This is one of my favorite Panther tips, because once you learn it, it saves time every day. When you've got the System Preferences dialog open, to jump directly to the preference pane you want (you notice I said jump to "the pane," not just its icon), press the first letter of the preference you want, then press the Spacebar. That instantly opens that preference pane. This is another one of those "try it once, use it forever" tips.

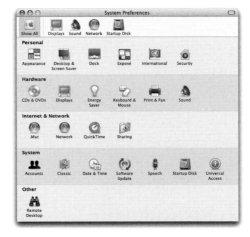

SAVING TIME IN SAVE AS

Here's a fairly wild Mac OS X tip for saving a file. (This is a great one to show at parties. Well, at least parties where there are lots of Mac-heads.) If you're going to save a document and you can see the folder on your drive where you want to save it (it's in a Finder window or on your desktop), in the Save As dialog, expand the Column view by clicking on the blue button with the down-facing triangle next to the name field. Then, you can actually drag-and-drop the folder that you want to save your document in from the desktop or Finder window to one of the columns in your Save As

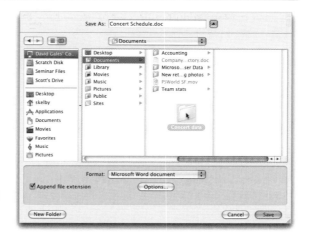

dialog. This is one of those things you have to try once yourself, but once you do, you'll use it again and again to save time when saving documents.

   DESKTOP PRINTING? HOW ABOUT "SIDEBAR PRINTING?"

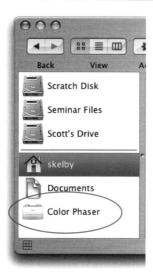

Earlier in this book, you learned how to create a Desktop Printer in Panther (in the Print & Fax preferences, click on Set Up Printers, and when the Printer List dialog appears, click on the printer you want as a Desktop Printer, then press Shift-Command-D). However, once you create a Desktop Printer, you can really make things convenient by clicking on the Desktop Printer and pressing Command-T, which adds this Desktop Printer to your Sidebar, so now you can drag-and-drop from your current window right onto the printer in the Sidebar. The mind reels.

LEAVING BREADCRUMBS WITH THE PATH BUTTON

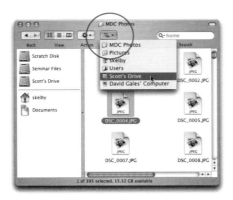

You've already learned that you can find the trail of folders to the currently active window by Command-clicking on the window's title bar, but if you find yourself doing this a lot, you might prefer a one-click method instead. In Panther, you can actually add a Path button to the toolbar by Option-Command-clicking on the white pill-shaped button in the upper right-hand corner of your Finder window to bring up the Customize Toolbar panel. Drag the Path icon (it's second from the top left) up to your window's toolbar, then click Done. Now, when you want to see, or jump back to, a previous window in your path, just click the new Path button.

FIND SPEED TIP: FIND IT AND CLOSE THE RESULTS WINDOW FAST!

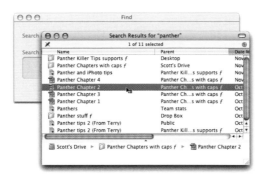

If you use Mac OS X's built-in Find function to find and open a file, you can save yourself time by having the Find function automatically close the Search Results window for you as soon as your document opens. All you have to do is hold the Option key as you double-click on the file to launch it, and the Search Results window closes immediately, saving you from having to close it manually later.

OPENING SIDEBAR ITEMS IN THEIR OWN WINDOW

My buddy Terry White just iChatted me with this cool Panther tip: If you click on an icon in your Sidebar, it just opens in the current window, but if you Command-click on an item in the Sidebar, it leaves the current window alone, and opens that item in its own separate window. Option-click on a Sidebar item, and it closes the old window while opening a new one. Very handy stuff.

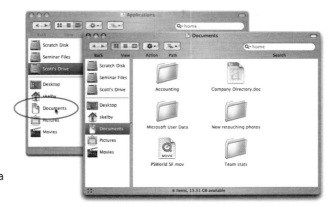

   NEED THE FIRST AVAILABLE PRINTER?

If you've got a print job on your hands and you need it as soon as possible, but all the printers on your network are often busy, you can pool these printers together so your document automatically prints to the first available printer. Just go to the Printer Setup Utility (in the Applications folder, within the Utilities folder), then Command-click on all the printers you want to pool together, then go under the Printers menu and choose Pool Printers. A dialog opens where you can name your pool (the default name is "Printer Pool"), and it shows a list of printers that are in that pool. You can click-and-drag the printers into the order that you want and then click Create, which adds a new printer in your Printer List called Printer Pool. Choose that as your printer, and then when you choose Print, Mac OS X starts looking for the first available printer.

   JUMPING TO THE FIND FIELD FAST

Want the fastest way in town to jump to the Find field that appears within the Finder window's toolbar? Just press Option-Command-F, and you'll see your cursor blinking in the field, ready for you to type in your search term. That's fast, baby!

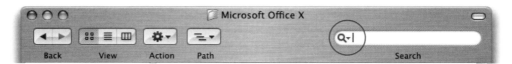

   CHANGING WHICH APP OPENS WHICH DOC

If you have a file, let's say it's a graphic file in PICT format, by default, it opens in Preview, right? And you probably know that you can go into the file's Info window and reassign that file to open in a different application; but there's an easier way. Just click on the PICT file, go under the File menu, and choose Open With and choose the app you want to open that particular file (I would choose Photoshop, but hey, that's just me). If you decide you always want that file to open in a different app (such as Photoshop) hold the Option key first, and when you go under the File menu, you'll see that the menu item named Open With has changed to Always Open With.

SPEED NAVIGATING IN THE SAVE AS DIALOG

Want to speed things up by using the keyboard to get around in the Save As dialog? There's just one thing you have to do first—press the Tab key. That removes the highlighting from the name field, and changes the focus on the Sidebar (notice the blue highlight rectangle around the Sidebar shown here). Once the Sidebar is highlighted, you can use the Up/Down Arrow keys to move up and down the Sidebar. Press Tab again, and the Column (or list) View becomes highlighted, and you can use the Arrow keys on your keyboard to quickly get right where you want to be. When you get there, press the Tab key again to highlight the Name field so you can name your file, and then hit the Return key to "make it so!"

   LAUNCHING WITHOUT THE DOCK

Don't feel like going all the way down to the Dock to launch programs? Don't sweat it—you can use any Finder window's Sidebar as your own personal Dock alternative. Just open your Applications folder, click on the application you want in your Sidebar, then press Command-T. Now, you can launch that app with one click, directly from the Sidebar. Plus, you can drag-and-drop files you want to open right on the application's icon in the Sidebar.

   DESKTOP BACKGROUND QUICK CHANGE

If you change your desktop patterns frequently, you'll love this tip that saves you a trip to the Apple menu. Just Control-click anywhere on your desktop, and a pop-up menu appears. Choose Change Desktop Background and the Desktop preference pane appears, ready for you to choose a new background.

   QUICK QUITTING SPEED TIP

You can quickly quit any program without actually going to that program. Hold the Command key and press the Tab key until the program's icon appears highlighted in the Dock-like window that appears in the middle of your screen, and then press the letter "q" and it quits. (Okay, this is kind of cheating: Since you already have Command held down, you don't have to press it again, and you're really pressing Command-Q.)

WAIT! I DIDN'T MEAN TO DRAG THAT!

I've done this a million times (okay, not a million, but at least 640,000 times)—I've been in a Finder window, and I started dragging a file or folder to another folder somewhere else in the window and then I realized that I either (a) grabbed the wrong icon, (b) changed my mind, or (c) changed my mind when I realized I grabbed the wrong icon. If you let go of the mouse button—it just drops the file right where you are. So, the next time this happens to you—don't let go of the mouse (at least not yet anyway)—simply change directions and drag the file up to the Finder window's toolbar and release the mouse button there. Mac OS X dutifully puts your icon right back where it came from—no harm done. (*Note*: If you hesitate too long before you release the mouse button over the toolbar, you'll wind up putting the file in the toolbar of the Finder window. Also, if you drag it too far and drop it on the title bar, it will move it to that folder.)

   DOCUMENT ALIASES—THE FAST WAY

Want to quickly create an alias for the document or folder you're working on? Just press Option-Command and then click-and-hold on the tiny icon that appears to the left of the document's name in its title bar and drag that little icon to your desktop. (By the way, that "tiny little icon" is technically called the "proxy icon," but that's just so…technical-sounding.)

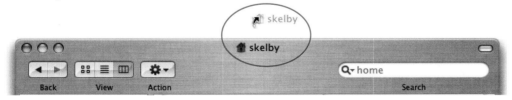

   MOVING A FILE OUT OF A FOLDER IN LIST VIEW

Let's say you're in List view, and the file you want is inside a folder you see in the list (hey, this is going pretty good so far). You can expand the folder to get to the file you need, but to get that file out of the folder that it's currently in and place it in the original window (before you expanded the folder), you have two options: (1) just drag the icon straight up to the headers along the top of the columns and a little line of whatever color you've chosen for your

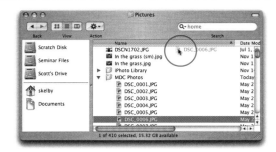

highlight appears along the bottom of the column headers to let you know "you're there." Release the mouse button, and your file now appears as a separate item, outside the folder, with the other items in the list. Or (2) drag-and-drop the file on the title bar of the Finder window, which works the same as dragging it to the column headers.

   GETTING THAT FIRST ICON FAST

If you've opened a Finder window in Icon view and want to select the first document (alphabetically), just press Tab and it instantly becomes highlighted. If you want the last file (alphabetically) in the window, press Shift-Tab.

QUICK SHUT DOWN/SLEEP/RESTART

If you want to shut down, and I mean in a hurry (like if you work at Apple and you see Steve Jobs coming down the hall toward your desk and he doesn't look like he's in a terribly good mood), and you have a keyboard with a power button, just press that power button, then hit Return. Here's what that does: A dialog appears asking if you want to Shut Down (high-

lighted), Restart, Sleep, or Cancel (in case Steve takes a sharp turn right outside your office and heads for the rest room). This is a particularly handy tip for people who (a) use PowerBooks or iBooks, or (b) work on the fourth floor at Apple's headquarters. Ah—you have an Apple Pro keyboard and it doesn't have a power button? No sweat. The upper-right key on the keypad is the Eject key, with a triangle above a bar as its symbol. It's meant for your CD-ROM drive, but press Control-Eject and you get the same shut down dialog. By the way, once the dialog appears, you don't actually have to use the mouse: Typing R(estart), S(leep), or Esc (Cancel) works the same as clicking that button, and hitting Return or Enter activates the highlighted Shut Down button. It's mega quick.

   SPEEDING THINGS UP WITH A TWO-BUTTON MOUSE

Tired of Control-clicking? Maybe it's time to buy a two-button mouse. (What!!!! A Mac with a two-button mouse?) I guess Apple figured at some point we'd get tired of Control-clicking, so in Mac OS X, if you connect a two-button USB mouse to your Mac, the second button automatically becomes the "Control-click" function (just like a PC's right-click). From that point on, every time in this book when it tells you to Control-click (like on application icons in the Dock), instead you can just right-click.

   FOUND MORE THAN ONE? OPEN 'EM ALL AT ONCE!

If you're searching for files using Mac OS X's built-in Find command (Command-F), and it turns up more than one right answer (in other words, you found three files you want to open, rather than just one), you can open all three at once. Just Command-click on the files you want to open (right within the Search Results window), then press Command-O, and all the files opens, one right after the other.

   CREATING YOUR OWN KEYBOARD SHORTCUTS

One thing in Panther that doesn't get enough press, but kicks butt in the productivity department is that you can now create your own custom keyboard shortcuts. Here's how: Go under the Apple menu to System Preferences, then click on the Keyboard & Mouse icon. In the pane that appears, click on the Keyboard Shortcut button. Then, click the + (plus) sign button at the bottom of the list of existing shortcuts to add your own. The pop-up menu at the top of the dialog that opens lets you choose whether this shortcut works across all applications, or in just an individual app (or just the Finder, if you like). In the Menu Title field, enter the

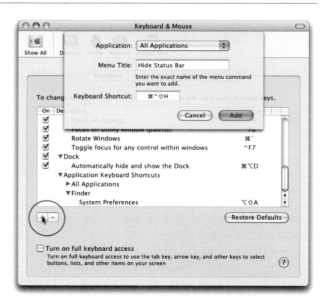

EXACT name of the menu item you want a shortcut for, then type in the shortcut you want to use and click Add. It's that easy. (*Note*: Make sure the application that you're making the shortcut for isn't open.)

CAN'T FIND IT? MAYBE YOU NEED TO INDEX

If you're trying to find a file by searching the contents of your files (rather than just by file name) and you can't find a file that you're certain is on your drive, you should probably have Mac OS X re-index your drive. You do this by clicking on the drive you want to be indexed, and then press Command-I to bring up its Info window. Click on the right-facing triangle next to Content Index to expand its pane, and then click on the button called Index Now. You can also do the same thing with a folder—such as your Documents folder perhaps: Index it if you're having a hard time finding a file that you're certain is in there. (*Note*: Indexing can take quite a while, especially the first time, or for a large hard drive.)

A SECRET TO FASTER SEARCHES USING FIND

If you find yourself searching a particular folder fairly often (like your Music folder for MP3s or your Documents folder), you can set up the Find function so it searches only in that folder. Here's how: Press Command-F to bring up Find, then from the Search In pop-up menu, choose Specific Places. This brings up a window showing where the Find function will search. Now, back in the Finder, navigate to the folder you want to add to this list, drag-and-drop that folder right into the Find's Specific Places window, and that folder is added to the list. Uncheck any other drives/ folders and only the checked folders are searched, giving you lightning-fast searches.

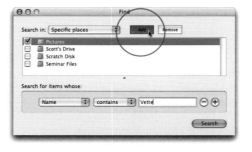

TWO SECONDS TO SLEEP

Want the fastest way to put your Mac right into a deep, sleepy-bear hibernation-like sleep (no whirling fan, no dialogs, no sound—nuthin'—just fast, glorious sleep). Just press Command-Option, then hold the Eject button for about 2 seconds and Zzzzzzzzzzzzzz. It doesn't get much faster than that.

   DO YOU WANT ONE WINDOW UP FRONT, OR ALL OF THEM?

Remember how back in the old days of Mac OS 9 and earlier, if you were working in one application and clicked on the window of another open application, all the open win-

dows of that app in the background all popped up front? Well, even if you don't remember, that's the way it worked. In Mac OS X, Apple changed the way windows and apps stack, and now if you're working in an app and click on a document window from another app, just that window comes to front, leaving the rest behind (weird, I know). If that weirds you out, instead of clicking on a document window, just click on that application's icon in the Dock, and all of its windows are brought to front, just like "the old days."

● **LAUNCHING YOUR FAVORITE APPS AUTOMATICALLY**

If you use the same applications every day (and most people do), you can have Mac OS X open these for you automatically, as soon as you log in. Here's how: Go under the Apple menu (or to the Dock) to System Preferences. In the System Preferences pane, click on the Accounts icon, then in the Accounts pane, click on the Startup Items button. To choose which applications you want to launch automatically when you log in, click on the + (plus) sign below the list, then navigate to the application you want to add, then click the Add button. Repeat for any additional applications. Cool option: You can set it up so the application launches but then stays hid-

den from view until you click on it in the Dock. To invoke this way-cool feature, click on the Hide checkbox next to the application's name when you choose it in the Startup Items dialog.

● ● **HOW TO KNOW IF YOU'VE SAVED THAT DOCUMENT**

Have you saved the document you're working on? Can't remember? Don't worry, in many cases (depending on the application), Mac OS X remembers for you, and even lets you know it hasn't been saved by placing a black dot in the center of the red "close" button up in the title bar of your docu-ment. If you see the dot, it hasn't been saved. If after

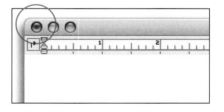

you've saved the document, you go on to make any other changes (even just typing a word or two, etc.), the dot reappears, telling you changes have been made since the last save. Pretty smart (at least for an operating system).

cool &
the gang

WAY COOL

TIPS

I know, I know, it's supposed to be "Kool & the Gang" (with a "K") not "Cool & the Gang" with a "C." Okay, Mr./Ms. Smarty Pants—

Cool & the Gang
way cool tips

you know so much about the band, which one is "Kool"? The lead singer? Wrong! That's JT. Kool is actually the bass player—the guy who originally formed the band. Okay, now what was their first million-selling single? "Ladies Night"? "Celebration"? "Too Hot"? "Fresh"? Nice try. It was "Jungle Boogie." Geez, I don't know where you got all this attitude, because apparently aside from spelling their name, you really don't know that much about the band. Now, what does all this have to do with Mac OS X? Plenty. For example, let's say you're invited to a party, and the host asks you to prepare an '80s dance mix using iTunes. Well, it's the night of the party, the front door opens and who walks in? That's right—Kool & the Gang (hey, it could happen). You walk up to JT and say, "Hey Kool, it's great to meet you," and everybody looks at you like you walked up to Darius Rucker and said "Hi, Hootie!" Anyway, here's a "Celebration" of tips that were "too hot" to be contained in any other chapters. (I know—they're lame puns, I don't care—I'm using 'em.)

   SCREEN CAPTURE OF JUST ONE WINDOW

If you want to take a screen capture of just one window, there's a little-known keyboard shortcut you should get to know. Just press Shift-Command-Spacebar-4 (in that order) and your cursor changes into a large camera. Click this camera cursor on the window you want to capture, and it creates a capture of just that window, which appears on your desktop as Picture 1.

   SHORTCUT TO YOUR APPLICATIONS

You probably can't put every application you'll ever use in your Dock, or you'll have one incredibly long microscopic Dock. A popular way around this is to drag your Applications folder to the the right of the gray divider bar in the Dock (the left side is for apps only). Not only is this a great idea—in Panther, it's even more useful. Here's why: Once your Applications folder is in the Dock, if you Control-click on the folder's icon, a list of the apps inside pops up—then, just press the first letter of the application you want to launch, and it becomes highlighted and now all you have to do is click.

DO YOU MISS THE OLD TRASHCAN?

This is one of my favorite tips in the whole book, because I'm a longtime Mac user and darn it, I admit it—I miss having the Trash at the bottom-right corner of my screen. If you miss it there too, here's how to get your own (even though there are four steps, it's absolutely simple to do):

STEP ONE: Go to your desktop and create a new folder by pressing Shift-Command-N. Make an alias of this new folder by pressing Command-L, then name this alias folder "Trash" (you can now delete the original folder—you don't need it anymore).

STEP TWO: Click on the alias folder and press Command-I to bring up its Info window. Click on the Select New Original button, and the Select New Original dialog appears. Press Shift-Command-G to bring up the Go to the Folder dialog. Type in this: /users/yournamehere/.trash (of course, don't type "yournamehere," instead, put your user name in there. If you don't know what it is, look inside your Mac's Users folder and look at what the Home icon is named). Press the Go button and it takes you to the invisible

Trash file on your drive. Now, click the Open button to make that folder become an alias of your Trash. You're almost there.

STEP THREE: Click on the Trash icon in the Dock to open its window. Then, press Command-I to open the Trash's Info window, click on the tiny Trashcan icon, then press Command-C to copy the Trash icon.

STEP FOUR: Go back to your Trash folder icon on your desktop, click on it, press Command-I to bring up its Info window, click on the tiny folder icon, then press Command-V to paste the Trash icon over the folder icon. All that's left to do now is drag your new Trash alias down to the bottom right-hand corner of your screen, and you've done it!

   FROM EPS TO PDF IN NO TIME FLAT

This Panther trick is pretty much just for graphic designers who work with EPS images from applications like Adobe Illustrator, CorelDraw for Mac, Freehand, and Photoshop. If you want to convert your EPS image instantly into a PDF (ideal for e-mailing), just drag it onto Apple's Preview ap-

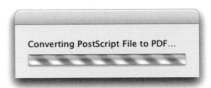

plication icon in your Dock (or in your Applications folder), and OS X automatically converts your PostScript file to a PDF on the fly. When you choose Save, it saves as a PDF.

   TWEAKING YOUR VIDEO IN QUICKTIME PRO

If you have Apple's QuickTime Pro installed (rather than just the standard QuickTime Player), you have more video-tweaking controls than you might have thought. Open a movie, then press Command-K, and a host of Video Controls appear at the bottom of your QuickTime screen, including controls for Brightness, Color, Tint, and Contrast. To increase any of these values, just click right on the horizontal bar and drag. To move to the next setting, click the tiny gray up/down arrows to the right of the adjustment's name. When you're done, save your movie and your changes are saved right along with it.

APPLYING FILTERS TO YOUR PHOTOS

In Panther, you can edit the tonal values in your photos by applying filters to them at the printing stage. To do this, just open a photo in Preview (or any Cocoa app, like TextEdit), and choose Print from the File menu. In the Print dialog, click on the Copies & Pages pop-up menu, and choose ColorSync. When you do this, a new set of pop-up menus appears, and when you click on the pop-up menu for Quartz Filter, a list of tonal filters appears, which you can apply by choosing them from the list. But how do you know how these filters will really look when applied to your photo? Just choose Add Filters from the Quartz Filter pop-up menu and a large Preview window appears. Click the checkbox, then when you click on various filters, you'll see an instant on-screen preview.

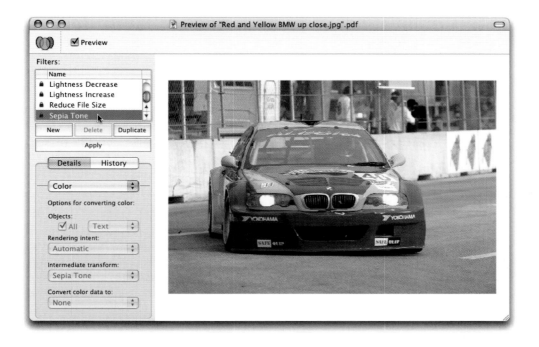

PLAYING MP3S FROM THE INFO WINDOW

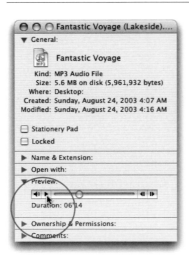

If you downloaded an MP3 file, you can play it without opening iTunes or any other MP3 player for that matter. Just press Command-I to bring up the file's Info window, then click on the right-facing gray triangle to the left of the word Preview to bring up the Preview pane. A QuickTime-like thin horizontal bar appears. Press the Play button and the song plays from right there, within the Info window.

CRANKING THE JAMS BEYOND REASON!

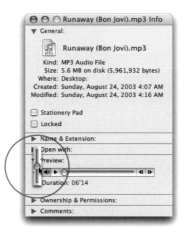

I just showed how you can actually play an MP3 file (or audio file) right from within the Info dialog by choosing Preview from the pop-up menu. Well, the first part of this tip makes that feature more usable, but the second part tears the roof off the sucka (so to speak). First, if you use the Up/Down arrow keys while playing an MP3 file in this fashion, it changes the volume (which is handy, but it isn't the killer part of this tip). The killer part is to add the Shift key, keep pressing the Up Arrow key, and (get this) it actually cranks your volume way past the maximum loudness of your current system setting. Try this once and you'll find yourself "cranking the jams" more often than not!

THE PANTHER TRICK FOR GETTING TO YOUR FAVORITES

Although Apple no longer lists Favorites in the Go menu in Open/Save dialogs, and the Command-T shortcut no longer adds files to the Favorites folder, your Favorites folder is still in Panther. (It's in your Home folder, in your Library folder, but I recommend dragging it to your sidebar.) But, here's a trick that helps make using the old Favorites folder easier. Go under the Finder menu and choose Preferences. Click on the General icon, and for New Finder Windows Open, choose Other from the pop-up menu, then navigate to your Home folder inside your Library, and click on Favorites. By doing this, if you press Command-N, it now opens your Favorites folder, rather than a new Finder window, and you can then Option-Command-drag items into your Favorites folder (which makes an alias of them, just like the old Favorites folder).

MAKING ONE PRINTER YOUR DEFAULT PRINTER

In previous versions of Mac OS X, your default printer was whichever printer you used last. This kinda stunk, because if you used the same printer most every day, but changed to a different printer to print even just one document, the next time you'd go to print, that's the printer you got. Well, that's the way it was until Panther. Now, you can designate one printer to always be your default printer, and even if you switch

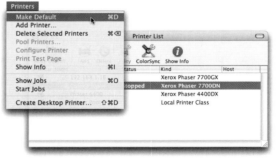

to another printer temporarily, the next time you come back, your default printer is right there waiting for you. To assign a printer as your default, go under the Apple menu and choose System Preferences. Click on the Print & Fax icon, then click on the Setup Printers button. When the Printer List appears, click on the printer you want as your default, then go up to the Printers menu and choose Make Default. That's it!

   ### CREATING ACROBAT PDFS ON THE FLY

By now, you're probably familiar with Adobe's Acrobat PDF technology, which enables you to create a file in most any application and share that file with other users on other platforms. Well, even if you don't own Adobe's full Acrobat application, Mac OS X can build a PDF file for you—so you can share your document with, well…just about anybody.

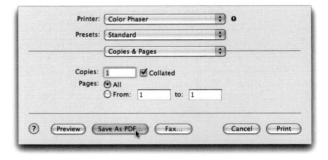

Here's how: When you're in the application and you're ready to save as a PDF, press Command-P (the standard Print shortcut) and in the Print dialog, click on the Save As PDF button at the bottom of the window. A dialog appears asking you to name your file and decide where to save it. Click Save and Mac OS X instantly creates the PDF for you. Does that rock, or what?

   ### MAKING WEB PHOTOS OPEN IN PHOTOSHOP

If you download any photos from the Web, chances are they're compressed JPEG files, and if you double-click on them, by default, they open in Apple's Preview application. If, like me, you'd prefer that all JPEG images open in Adobe Photoshop, here's what do to: Download a photo from the Web, click on it, press Command-I to bring up its Info window. Click the right-facing gray arrow to the left of the words "Open With" to expand this pane. From the Open With pop-up menu, look for Adobe Photoshop CS. If you don't see it, just choose Other, and then navigate to it. After you choose Photoshop, click the Change All button in the "Open With" pane. From now on, all JPEG photos will open in Adobe Photoshop CS, rather than in Preview. Cool, eh?

CREATING FULL-SCREEN SLIDE SHOWS

The next time you're forcing someone to look at digital photos of your recent hernia operation on your Mac, don't open them one by one in Picture Viewer—that's brutal. It's bad enough that you're making them look at the photos of your procedure; you should at least give 'em a show using Mac OS X's built-in slide-show projector (okay, it's not a projector in the Bell & Howell sense, but it creates a pretty slick slide show right on your screen). Here's how to create your own, and before you know it, your friends will see you coming and immediately run for cover:

STEP ONE: Go under the Apple menu, under System Preferences, and when the dialog appears, click on the Desktop & Screen Saver icon. When the panel appears, click on the Screen Saver tab, and in the list of screen effects choices on the left side of the screen, click on Choose Folder.

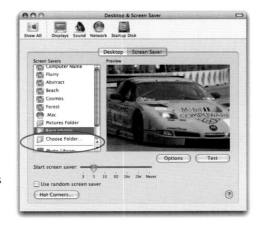

STEP TWO: In the Open dialog that appears, navigate your way to the folder of photos you want to use for your slide show and click the Choose button. This adds your folder of photos to the list of screen savers on the left side of the Screen Saver preferences panel.

STEP THREE: By default, the Screen Saver uses the Ken Burns effect on your photos, but if you'd like to choose your own display options, click on the Options button that appears below the large preview window. In a few moments, you'll see a preview of your slide show right there in the dialog, but if you want "the big time full-screen test," press the Test button.

STEP FOUR: Last, you need to know how to turn this slide show on once you've exited System Preferences. Click on the Hot Corners tab, and you see a checkbox in each of four corners of the screen (well, it's a large icon of your screen). Choose a corner, and then close System Preferences. When you're ready to start your slide show, just drag your cursor to that corner of your screen, wait just a moment, and your slide show will appear. To stop it, just press any key.

   OPENING THE CD TRAY BY MAGIC (ON OLDER MACHINES)

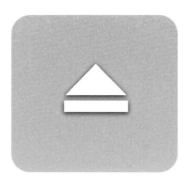

If you're running Mac OS X on an older machine (by older, I mean it's not one of the newer units which have a button for popping out your CD tray on the keyboard), you may not be out of luck—try holding the F12 key down for a few seconds (which invokes the Eject CD command), and your keyboard tray should pop out. I say it "should" pop out, because I haven't tried it on every machine with every keyboard, so instead, let's say, "I hope it will pop out," or "I feel pretty good about it popping out," or perhaps even, "I bet it pops out."

   FORCE QUITTING KEYBOARD SHORTCUT

Need yet another way to force quit a running application (hey, force quitting is all the rage in Mac OS X)? Try the ol' Option-Command-Esc key routine. That brings up a list of applications you can force quit, and by golly, your current one is already highlighted and ready to quit. If force quitting is what you really want to do, just click the glowing Force Quit button and it does its best to bring your application to its knees. *Note:* If an application's name appears in the list in red, that means it's not responding (it's locked up), so force quitting is about your only option anyway, eh?

  ## QUICK SET: WARNING BEEP SOUND

Here's a hidden little tip for changing the volume of your alert beep right from the Desktop. The pop-down volume control (Menu Extra) on the top right of your menu bar controls the overall system volume; but if you hold the Option key, the pop-down slider now controls the volume of just your system's alert "beep."

   ## DIDN'T MEAN TO MOVE IT? SEND IT BACK WHERE IT CAME FROM

Did you just move a folder you didn't mean to move? Worse yet, did you drop a file into a folder and didn't mean to do it? Just Undo it—before you do anything else press Command-Z and the file returns to where it was before you moved it.

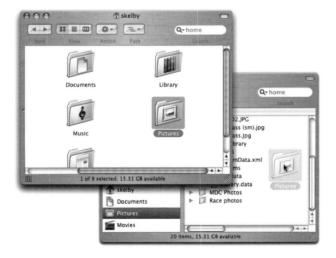

DON'T FEEL LIKE OPENING PHOTOSHOP?

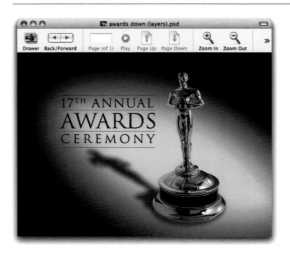

If you need to take a quick look at a Photoshop file, but don't feel like launching Photoshop, just drag the icon to the Preview application icon in the Dock, and Preview opens the Photoshop file. If the Photoshop file is layered, it even displays all the visible layers.

BUILT-IN TEXT STYLE SHEETS

If you have formatted some type (let's say it's in the font Times New Roman, at 18 point, and it's both bold and italic) in a Cocoa app like TextEdit or Stickies, and you want to apply those same type attributes to another block of text that has completely different font formatting (let's say the other text is Helvetica, 12-point regular), try this: Highlight some of the text that has the formatting you want and press Option-Command-C. Then, highlight the text that you'd like to have these attributes (the Helvetica 12-point), and press Option-Command-V. The highlighted text takes on your originally copied font attributes (Times New Roman, 18-point, bold, and italic)—kind of like a Style Sheet in QuarkXPress, InDesign, or PageMaker. (*Note:* For Stickies, the shortcut is Command-3 to copy and Command-4 to paste.)

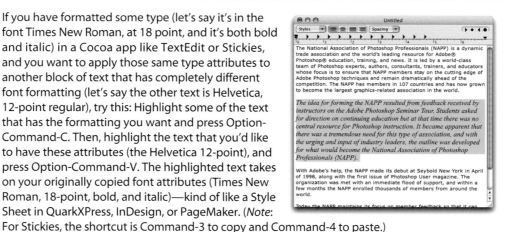

MENUS WITHOUT THE MOUSE

Check this out—you can actually navigate through your menus without turning on the Full Keyboard Access System Preference. Here's how: Just click once on a menu (don't click-and-hold), then just press the Up/Down Arrow keys and watch what happens—you can now navigate up and down that menu—and if you press the Left/Right Arrow keys, you can jump to any of the menus in your menu bar. By the way, this doesn't work in Classic Mode. (Did I even have to say that?)

   KEEPING YOUR PRIVATE DATA PRIVATE

If you have sensitive information on your computer, you're probably most vulnerable to "peekers" when your computer is up and running (like at the office) but you step away for a moment to grab a quick cup of Starbuck's Peppermint Mocha Frappuccino Blended java (or maybe you just go to the bathroom. Either way, for a few minutes, it's "open season" for anyone with a curious mind). If that's a concern, you can keep those prying eyes away by going under the Apple menu, choosing System Preferences, and clicking on the Security icon. When the FileVault preference pane appears, turn on the checkbox for Require Password to Wake

this Computer from Sleep or Screen Saver. Of course, before you do this, make darn sure you know your password.

  CHANGING YOUR DEFAULT DESKTOP PICTURE

The ubiquitous blue desktop background that is the default for Mac OS X is named "Aqua Blue.jpg" and it's found in the main Library folder, in the folder called Desktop Pictures. Want to create your own default desktop background? Drag this image into Photoshop, erase the blue background, and create the image you want for your desktop background (or drag an existing file into this document). Then, replace the "Aqua Blue.jpg" in your Desktop Pictures folder with this new Photoshop file.

   QUICK SWITCH TO OS X

You already know about using the Startup Disk pane of System Preferences to choose OS 9 or OS X for your next startup. Well, if you have both OS 9 and OS X on the same disk (or in different partitions on the same disk), you can skip those steps when switching from OS 9 to OS X. Just restart, holding down the "X" key, and you boot directly into OS X. Very cool. Sorry— it doesn't work going the other way.

THE SECRET SCREEN CAPTURE SHORTCUT

Okay, you probably already know the ol' Shift-Command-3 shortcut for taking a screen capture of your entire screen, and you may even know about Shift-Command-4, which gives you a crosshair cursor so you can choose which area of the screen you want to capture. But perhaps the coolest, most-secret hidden capture short-cut is Shift-Control-Command-3 (or 4), which, instead of creating a file on your desktop, copies the capture into your Clipboard memory, so you can paste it where you want. (I use this to paste screen captures right into Photoshop.)

   THE SILENCE OF THE BEEPS

If you have a keyboard that has volume controls right on the keyboard (like most PowerBooks), you're probably used to hearing a little "confirmation" beep each time you press one of these volume controls. If those little beeps get on your nerves (who needs more things beep-ing at them?), just hold the Shift key and this silences the beeps as you press the volume keys. If you want to turn these sounds off permanently, go under the Apple Menu, under System Preferences, then choose Sound. Click on the Sound Effects tab, then uncheck Play Feedback when Volume Keys Are Pressed.

   CHANGING THE HANDS OF TIME

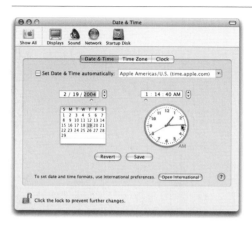

This tip is just for fun, because honestly, it's not tremendously practical, but it looks pretty cool. The next time you're changing the time by using your System Preferences Date & Time pane, and one of your friends or coworkers is watching you, instead of typing in the desired time, just grab the hour and minute hands of the preview clock and move them to set your time. Again, it serves no real purpose, but every time I set my clock like this with someone looking, they're always amazed by it. Unless they're Swiss, of course.

   GETTING FONTS TO LOOK THEIR BEST ON YOUR SCREEN

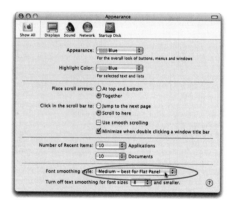

Mac OS X already does a special brand of font smoothing (a form of anti-aliasing) to make your fonts look crisp and clean on screen. However, you can tweak how it smooths your fonts to give you the best possible look depending on which type of monitor (flat panel, CRT, etc.) you use with your Mac. To choose which style of font smoothing works best for your monitor, go under the Apple menu, under System Preferences, and click on the Appearances icon. In the Appearances panel, in the bottom section, choose the type of font smoothing that matches the type of monitor you're using from the Font Smoothing Style pop-up menu.

STOPPING EXPLORER FROM LAUNCHING

If you've switched over to Safari as your Web browser, how come sometimes when you click on a Web link, it launches Microsoft Internet Explorer instead? It's because although you launch Safari manually, Mac OS X has Internet Explorer listed as your default Browser. To set Safari as your default Web browser, launch Safari, then go under the Safari menu and choose Preferences. Click on the General icon, then change the default browser (in the pop-up menu) to Safari.

COLORSYNC SHOWOFF TRICK

I'm sure there's an important reason for this feature; I just can't figure out what it is. But it sure looks cool, and therefore, it's a perfect tool for showing off to your PC friends (which may be the real reason it's in Panther in the first place). Here's how it works: Look inside your Application folder, inside your Utilities folder, and double-click on ColorSync Utility. When the ColorSync panel appears, click on the Profiles icon, then click the gray triangle beside System to display a list of profiles. Click on Generic RGB and to the right, a Lab Plot color graphic appears. Here's the show-off part—it's a 3D object—click your

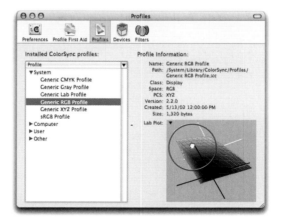

cursor right on it, drag upward, and the object rotates in 3D. Totally cool. Totally useless. I love it!

   GETTING A SUPER SMALL FONT PANEL

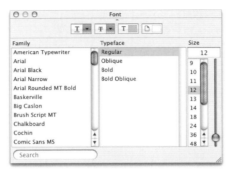

Regular

Same Dialog, Super Small

If you don't need all the typographic features of Apple's Font panel (the Font panel that appears in Cocoa apps, like TextEdit), you can use a much smaller version. Just click-and-drag the bottom-right corner of the regular Font panel and it automatically reconfigures itself into a much smaller one-row panel, with just three pop-up menus (rather than windows), giving you access to the most-used Font panel functions. When you think about it, it's pretty amazing that the Font panel can morph into an entirely different scheme (from scrollable windows into pop-up menus) on the fly. Even if you don't use the Font panel, it's worth trying it once just to see this amazing technology at work.

   GETTING RID OF THAT ANNOYING FILE EXTENSION DIALOG FAST!

If you've saved a file and later realize it needs to have a three-letter file extension (like .jpg or .gif for the Web), when you go and add those to the file's name, Mac OS X gives you a warning dialog asking you if you're sure you want to make this change. If you meant to add the extension (and frankly, I'd

be surprised if you were adding it to a file by accident. Whoops—my fingers fell on the keys and accidentally added .jpg to my Photoshop image), you can make this dialog disappear just as fast as it appeared by pressing the Esc key as soon as it makes its annoying appearance.

USING YOUR IPHOTO LIBRARY AS DESKTOP PATTERNS

You're not stuck using Apple's default sets of desktop backgrounds, because now you can use any photo in your iPhoto library as a desktop pattern. Just Control-click anywhere on your desktop background and choose Change Desktop Backgrounds from the pop-up menu that appears. In the Desktop & Screen Saver preferences panel, near the bottom of the left column (where all the default sets of photos are), click on Photo Library. The photos in your iPhoto library now appear in the main window, and you can click on any one to instantly make it your desktop background.

   BURNING CDS FROM THE DOCK

If you're burning CDs from files on your desktop, here's a tip that'll speed things up. Once you insert your blank CD, and drag the files you want onto the disc, you can burn that CD right from the Dock.

Just click on the blank CD and as soon as you start dragging it, the Dock's Trashcan icon has changed into a large "Burn" icon. Just drag the disc onto that icon and it starts-a-burnin'.

   Font Book: **COMPARING FONTS SIDE BY SIDE**

If you're trying to make a decision on which font to choose, and it's down to just a few choices, here's a great way to do some side-by-side comparisons. In the Font list, double-click on the first font you want to compare. This brings up a preview of the font in its own separate floating window. Then, double-click on the next font, and its preview appears in another floating window, so you can position them side-by-side and see which you like better. You can open as many different font preview windows as you need to help you find just the right font. Also, once the floating preview window is open, you can choose different font weights and variations from the pop-up menu at the top of the window.

   Font Book: **FINDING ALL OF YOUR BOLD FONTS FAST**

If you've ever been working on a project, and you know you need a bold font for the headline, but you're not exactly sure which bold font you should use, this tip is for you. Just type Bold into the Search field in the top-right corner of the Font Book window. This instantly gives you a list of every font that has a bold variant, and you can use the Up/Down arrow keys on your keyboard to get a quick look at how each bold font looks. Of course, this isn't just for bold fonts, you could search for all italic fonts, or script fonts, or…you get the idea.

Font Book: CREATING YOUR OWN CUSTOM PREVIEW TEXT

By default, the Font Panel preview text shows "ABCDEFGHIJKLMNO…etc." and although seeing your fonts previewed like this can be helpful, it pales in comparision to seeing the font previewed using your own real text from the project you're working on. Here's how to make that happen: Go to the font you want, then press Command-3 (the shortcut for Custom Preview). Now, you can click on the text in the Preview window and type in your own text (as shown here). Even cooler: You can copy-and-paste text right from your project (from InDesign or QuarkXPress) straight into the Custom Preview panel. Nice!

   Font Book: FONT FIELD SIZING TIP

If you want to see your font in various sizes, you could use the slider on the far right side of the Preview window, but it moves so quickly, and so freely (it's not stopping at the common sizes used in page-layout applications) that you find yourself using the pop-down font menu more. If you do, here's a tip on how to speed things up a bit. To choose your size quickly, just click in the Size field, then use the Up/Down arrow keys on your keyboard to quickly jump to the size you want. Here's where it might throw you—unlike the slider, the font doesn't change size as you change sizes in the list, so what you have to do is choose your size, then click anywhere within the Preview window and your font resizes to your chosen value.

   Font Book: **FIXING FONT PROBLEMS**

If there's one thing that messes with an application's (or a system's) head, it's font conflicts (duplicate copies of the same fonts installed on your hard drive). Thankfully, Font Book kicks this problem in the butt. If Font Book detects a duplicate font, it puts a little bullet point in front of the font's name. Then, it's up to you to choose which version you really want to keep open (you shouldn't have both open). Click on the version you want, go under Font Book's Edit menu, and choose Resolve Duplicates, and it automatically turns off the duplicate, leaving you free and clear to enjoy a single-font family life.

   Font Book: **ONE-CLICK FONT INSTALLS**

If you've downloaded a font from the Web (there are boatloads of free fonts available on the Web), getting that font installed is now about as painless as double-clicking. In fact, it's exactly as painless as double-clicking because that's all you have to do. Double-click on the downloaded font; it launches Font Book and opens the font. Sweet!

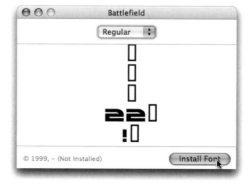

Font Book: SEEING ONLY THE FONTS YOU WANT TO SEE

If you're like most people, you probably use only a handful of fonts on a daily basis—your favorite, workhorse, use-all-the-time fonts. But even though you use only a few, you still have this long list of fonts, including a bunch Apple throws in

(many of which I still, to this day, have never used). Wouldn't it be wonderful to have a font list of just the fonts you use, and not all the other filler fonts? It's easy. Just go to Font Book, click on the All Fonts category, then Command-click on every font you don't use (you'll probably click on most of them). Then, click the Disable button at the bottom of the center panel. A dialog tells you that you've turned off multiple fonts. Click Disable, and your font list just got much shorter. (*Note*: You didn't delete the fonts, you just turned them off from view.)

   Font Book: GETTING THE INSIDE SCOOP ON YOUR FONT

Believe it or not, Font Book knows more than it's letting on about your fonts. To find out the full inside info on a particular font, double-click the little dot that appears beneath the font's preview panel but above the font's name (if that seems like too much trouble, just press Command-I). This brings up an Info pane that spills the beans about that font, including the name of the foundry that created it, when it was created, the font type (Postscript, Truetype, etc.), and more.

cheap trick

OS X PRANKS →

Although this is clearly the shortest chapter in the book, it may be the most (a) fun, (b) cruel, or (c) a delightful combination of

Cheap Trick

mac os x pranks

the two. (The difference between "fun" and "cruel" is the difference between "reading the pranks" and "perpetrating them.") The original outline for this book didn't have a "pranks" chapter at all, but as I was writing tips for the other chapters, I'd sometimes think, "Boy, if you didn't know about this, and somebody who did know it wanted to mess with you, they could pretty much bring your Mac life crashing down around you." I imagined this could create a new brand of Mac heroes—people who would pull these pranks in secret on the machines of unsuspecting co-workers, then show up later to offer to "take a look at the problem," and with a few clicks, fix it—winning the respect and admiration of the victim and other co-workers.

I feel pretty safe in sharing these pranks, because I know you're not the type of person to use or abuse these little gems. Right? Right? Hello…

  CREATING A TERRIFYING FAKE DIALOG

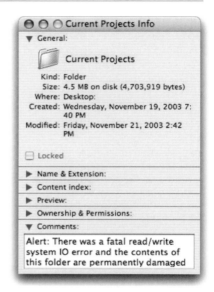

Annoyance Factor 7: Picture this: Your co-worker comes back from lunch, double-clicks on the folder that holds the project she's been working on for three weeks, and a dialog appears telling her "Alert: There was a fatal read/write system IO error and the contents of this folder are permanently damaged and cannot be restored." Sound like fun? It's easy to pull off, because the ability to create your own custom message that appears when a folder is opened is built right into Panther. Here's how it works: First, click on the folder and then press Command-I to bring up the Info window. Then, click on the right-facing gray triangle next to Comments. In the Comments field, write a scary-sounding warning. (Feel free to use the one above, or make up your own. Messages mentioning how a virus has attacked the folder also work nicely.) Close the Comments pane, close the Info window, then Control-click on the folder, and from the pop-up menu, choose Configure Folder Actions.

In the Folder Actions Setup dialog, click the + (plus) sign in the bottom left-hand corner of the dialog. A standard Open dialog appears; navigate your way to the person's folder and click Open. When you do this, a window pops down

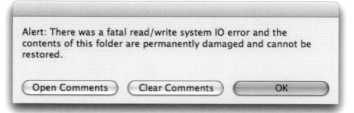

prompting you to Choose a script to attach. Choose the script "open – show comments in dialog.scpt" and click the Attach button. One last thing, turn on the Enable Folder Actions checkbox at the top of the Folder Actions Setup dialog (if it's not already on) then close the dialog, sit back, and let the fun begin. By the way, I might add one more line to the Comments field if you want this prank to last a little longer. Add "Pressing 'Open Comments' will delete this folder—Pressing 'Clear Comments' will perform a Secure Empty Trash as well." It adds a nice touch, dontchathink?

HIDING, WELL…EVERYTHING!

Annoyance Factor 6: This is a great trick to pull on people who keep lots of stuff on their desktops. First, hide all open windows, then press Shift-Command-3 to take a screen shot of their entire desktop. Go to the System Preferences and choose Desktop & Screen Saver. Click on the Desktop button, then drag your screen capture into the preview well at the top left of the pane to make the screen capture their desktop. Close the System Preferences. Next, create a folder on the desktop and drag everything on the desktop into that folder, and drag this folder into the Home folder (for safekeeping). Then, go under the Finder Preferences, click on the General icon,

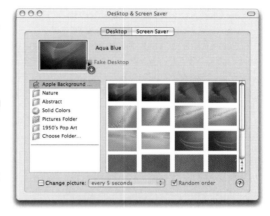

and where it says Show These Items on the Desktop, uncheck Hard Disks, CDs, and Connected Servers. When they return, they can't click on anything (except the menu bar)—all the icons, folders, hard disks, etc., appear frozen because they're seeing the desktop capture. Even if they figure out that it's a desktop pattern, when they remove it, their drives are still missing. This is one sweet prank.

   LOCKING THEM OUT OF THEIR OWN MACHINE

Annoyance Factor 5: This is a good one to pull on someone who is a single user (they're not sharing their machine with other users) and thus they're not used to logging in each day with a user name. Go under the System Preferences, click on the Desktop & Screen Savers icon, click on the Screen Saver button, and slide the Start Screen Saver slider to, say, 3 minutes. Now (this is the key to the whole thing), go to the Security preference pane and check the box next to Require Password to Wake This Computer from Sleep or Screen Saver. Now, every time the computer sits idle for three minutes, it requires them to enter their user password—if they can even remember what it is. Ahh, it's the simple things in life.

   UNCOLORING THEIR WORLD

Annoyance Factor 4–7: This has a variable amount of annoyance—from mild to strong—because you have options. Start by going under the Apple menu, choose System Preferences, and click the Universal Access icon, then click on the Seeing button. You're staring at three fairly solid pranks: (1) Click the large Switch to White on Black, which gives their entire computer the "negative" look shown here. (2) Perhaps even better is the button to the right of that: Set Display to Gray-scale, which removes all color from everything. Very effective, and Universal Access is the last place they'll look—they'll spend hours looking in Display Preferences and/or ColorSync. (3) Drag the Enhance Contrast slide to the right, which makes it look like their monitor is starting to die.

   SOMETHING JUST DOESN'T ADD UP

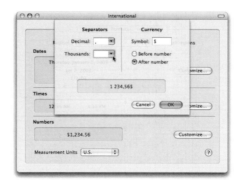

Annoyance Factor 3: This is more of a "warm-up" prank designed to get your "victim" just a little off balance before you get into the juicier stuff later in this chapter. Go under the Apple Menu, under System Preferences, and click on the International icon. When the pane opens, click the Format button, then click the Customize button in the Numbers section to bring up the window shown here. Now the fun part: Under Currency, click on the After Number radio button. This moves the dollar symbol ($) after the number (changing $1,200.45 into 1,200.45$). Then, in the Separators section, change the Decimal pop-up menu from a period to a comma and the Thousands Separator to Space (which changes $1,200.45 into 1 200,45$). They may track this down fairly quickly, but then again….

JAMMING THE DOCK

Annoyance Factor 10: This is just one of those things that make people crazy, because without getting your hands dirty, there's really no quick way to undo the damage, and it takes a long time and a lot of keystrokes to get things back to the way they were. Start by looking through the victim's hard drive until you find a folder with lots of items (any folder with 50 or more items qualifies, but think, "the more, the merrier!"). Press Command-A to select all, and drag them all to the right side of the Dock. Repeat this in as many folders as you like, until your victim has hundreds (if not thousands) of items in their Dock. (A good place to start looking for folders with a lot of items is inside their Home folder, inside the Library folder, inside the Caches folder, inside the iPhoto Cache folder. That's at least 126 items right off the bat—dying to be dragged to some poor soul's Dock.) Not only does this make the Dock microscopic in size, but there's only one way (short of some serious under-the-hood system tweaks) to get these items back out of the Dock—dragging them out one-by-one. A full reinstall is probably faster. This is something you should probably save for your last day at your current job, for obvious reasons.

   THE CASE OF THE MISSING HARD DISK

Annoyance Factor 7: It's the simple things in life that make it worth living. Like removing someone's hard disk icon from the desktop. To do this, go to the Finder menu, under Preferences, click on the General icon, and under Show These Items on the Desktop, uncheck the box for Hard Disks. The next time they start up, their hard drive won't appear on their desktop. Let the subsequent freak-out begin.

   TAKING AWAY THEIR PRIVILEGES

Annoyance Factor 2–8 (depending on whether they're on a network): This is a great prank to play on a single user who's not connected to a network, because they won't have any experience with setting folder privileges. Go to their Documents folder, click on it, and press Command-I to bring up the Info window. Click on the right-facing gray triangle to the left of Ownership & Permissions, then click on the one next to Details. From the Owner/Access pop-up menu, choose Read Only and then click on the Apply to Enclosed Items button. This makes the contents of their Document folder (where documents are saved by default) pretty much locked. They can't drag files into it, they can't delete files within it, they can't even save an open document into their own Documents folder (how ironic is that?). They can basically only read files within it, and that's about it. When they try to do most anything else, they'll get a nasty warning informing them that they don't have privileges to do what they're trying to do. People seem to really get annoyed with that. If you're in a really bad mood, maybe set the Owner/Access permission to No Access, or Write only.

   UNEXPLAINED LAUNCH MYSTERIES

Annoyance Factor 6: If you know which applications your victim uses most, the fun is about to begin. Click on a document from one of those applications. For example, let's say that they use TextEdit quite a bit. Look on their drive for a TextEdit file. Click on one of those documents, and then press Command-I to bring up the file's Info. In the Info window, click on the right-facing gray triangle to the left of Open With to reveal the Open With pane. When that pane appears, click on the pop-up menu and you'll see a list of applications that you can use to open the TextEdit file. Choose a different application than TextEdit. Try something like Adobe Illustrator CS (if you've got it), or if not, you can try something as tame as Safari (which comes with OS X). Then, click on the Change All button, and finally, close the window. The next time they double-click a TextEdit file, it won't launch TextEdit—instead, it launches Illustrator (or Safari). Annoying? You bet. Try changing any Photoshop files to open in Preview or, worse yet, have them open in Graphic Converter. There's just no limit to the fun.

SHIFT-BEEP. OPTION-BEEP. COMMAND-BEEP. BEEP-BEEP!

Annoyance Factor 7: Would it drive you crazy if suddenly every time you pressed Shift, Option, Command, or Control it would make an annoying typewriter sound and then giant icons (that represent those modifier keys) appeared on the upper right side of your desktop? Sure it would. Wouldn't it be funny if that suddenly happened to a friend's or co-worker's machine? Sure it would. Go under their System Preferences, click on the Universal Access icon, click on the Keyboard button, and turn on Sticky Keys. Will they know where to go to turn the sound and giant icons off? I doubt it. One of two things will happen: (1) They learn to live with it, or (2) they'll do a reinstall.

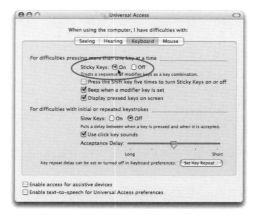

   SAYING GOOD-BYE TO MAC OS X

Annoyance Factor 5: Go under the System Preferences, under Startup Disk, and change their system to start up using Mac OS 9.2, and then shut down their machine. Next time they start up their Mac, it skips Mac OS X altogether and opens in System 9.2. Restarting their system won't help; it'll boot into 9.2 again and again until they figure out how to change their startup disk to 10 using 9.2's Control Panels. Or—if they know to hold down the X key while starting up. This boots in OS X. You gotta love that.

   APPLICATION ICON MADNESS

Annoyance Factor 9: Imagine if you clicked on an application and instead of launching the application, it just opened an empty Finder window. This would get mighty frustrating, wouldn't it? This type of thing would basically bring a person's work to a halt, wouldn't it? Sound good? Here's what to do:

STEP ONE: Create a new blank folder on the desktop and name it "gotcha!"

STEP TWO: Go to their Applications folder, open a folder for one of their major applications (something like FileMaker Pro), and click on the FileMaker Pro application icon. Press Command-I, and when the Info window opens, click on the icon in the top left-hand corner and press Command-C to copy the FileMaker Pro icon.

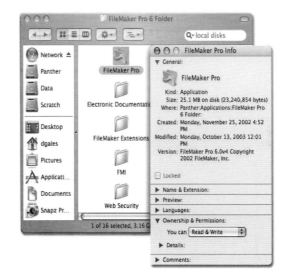

STEP THREE: Drag just the FileMaker Pro application icon into your Gotcha! folder.

STEP FOUR: Go back to their Applications folder and open their FileMaker Pro folder. Press Shift-Command-N to create a new blank folder within their FileMaker Pro folder.

STEP FIVE: Click on the new folder and press Command-I. When the Info window opens, click on the folder icon and press Command-V to paste the FileMaker Pro application icon onto this blank folder. Rename this folder FileMaker Pro.

STEP SIX: Go to the Dock and remove the FileMaker Pro icon (if it's there). Repeat this process for the rest of their major apps, and every time they launch an app, all they'll get is an empty Finder window. Once they're in tears, you can lead them to the Gotcha! folder—for a small fee.

IF I COULD TURN BACK TIME

Annoyance Factor 6:
I left this simple yet maliciously effective prank till last because it can really screw up people's lives, even beyond reinstalling their OS. Go to the System Preferences and click on the Date & Time icon. Make sure that the Set Date & Time Automatically checkbox is turned off and then simply click back one year in the calendar, and for at least a day or so, every e-mail they send to anyone (their boss, a big client, etc.) winds up at the bottom of the recipient's inbox, making them think

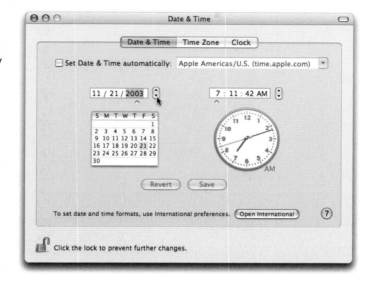

the victim never sent the e-mail at all. This is the kind of thing that gets people fired, loses big accounts, and makes otherwise happy couples break up; so use this only on people who pull Mac OS pranks on you with an annoyance factor of 6 or higher. Serves 'em right.

takin' care of business

BUSINESS APPLICATIONS

I know what you're thinking: Does Address Book really count as a business application? I mean, if you're using it to store personal

Takin' Care of Business
business apps that come with mac os x

contacts (like your bookie, your pharmacist, your bail bondsman, etc.), it's really not a business application, true. But, if you gave your bookie some Darvocet you got from your pharmacist to pay off a bad debt, but then he got busted and looked to you to bail him out (which is a surprisingly common turn of events), then it's all business, baby. Yeah, what about TextEdit? Hey, the thing's nearly Microsoft Word 5.1, gimme a break—total business. Unless of course, you wind up using TextEdit to methodically detail your plans for a multi-million dollar gold heist. Then, it's a fun caper-planning application. Well, it is until you're caught, and your bookie has to come down to the jailhouse and bail you out; and by that time, he's had to pawn your iBook to raise your bail money, and now all you have is a spiral bound notebook and a piece of chalk. Address Book doesn't seem so bad now, does it, Bunky?

Mail: FITTING MORE IN YOUR MAIL DRAWER

If you have a lot of mailboxes, your Mail Drawer can get pretty crowded. If that happens, just Control-click within the Drawer and choose Use Small Mailbox Icons from the pop-up menu that appears. These smaller icons create much more room, enabling you to fit more in your Drawer (so to speak).

   Mail: QUICKLY BACKING UP YOUR E-MAILS

If you want to archive (or backup) your e-mails (I often back mine up to a FireWire drive just in case things go south), here's an easy way: Make your Mail Drawer visible (choose Show Mailboxes under the View menu), then click the little gray right-facing triangle to the left of your Inbox icon. This expands the Inbox listing your e-mail accounts. Just click on the e-mail address you want to archive, and either drag it right out onto to the desktop, or if the hard drive or server you want to back up to is visible, drag it right there for an instant backup.

Mail: CONTROLLING YOUR MAIL SEARCH

If you're searching for a particular piece of mail (aren't we all? I'm still searching for that one from Publishers Clearing House), you can either expand or narrow your search by choosing search options. You access these by clicking on the tiny down-facing triangle just to the right of the Magnifying Glass icon within the Search field. A pop-down menu appears where you can choose how wide (or narrow) a search you want to initiate.

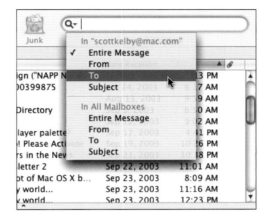

Mail: ACCESSING MAIL COMMANDS FROM THE DOCK

If your Mail app is running, but you're working in another application, you can save time by accessing a number of Mail's commands right from the Dock by just Control-clicking on Mail's Dock icon. A pop-up list of commands appears, including shortcuts for checking your mail and composing new messages.

Mail: YOU'VE GOT MAIL? LOOK IN THE DOCK

You'll see another example of how cool Mac OS X's Dock is the first time you use the built-in Mail program (simply called "Mail"). As mail comes in, the number of messages you have in your Inbox is displayed right on the Mail icon itself in the Dock.

Mail: CUSTOMIZING MAIL'S TOOLBAR

This is another place you can customize the toolbar, and probably one of the most useful because most people will only take advantage of a few tools, so why clutter the toolbar with tools you won't ever use, right? As usual, Control-clicking on the toolbar brings up a contextual menu where you can choose the size you want for your icons, and whether you want them displayed as icons and text, or just icons or just text (and which size you want for both). If you Command-click on the white pill-shaped button in the upper right-hand corner of the title bar, you step through the various toolbar icon/text configurations. Hold Option-Command and click the same button, and the all-important Customize Toolbar sheet appears.

Mail: HOW TO MAKE YOUR MAIL DRAWER SWITCH SIDES

You know how the Mail Drawer (the little panel that holds your In, Out, Drafts,
etc.) sticks out from the right side of
your Mail window? Well, here's a little
tip on getting it to "switch sides." In
your Inbox, click on a mail message
and simply drag it off the left-hand side
of the Mail window. The little panel immediately jumps to that side to "catch"
your e-mail (providing, of course, that
there's enough room on your screen
for it to pop out on the left side. If you
have your mail window butted up

against the left side of your monitor, it may not have room to pop out. So, if you drag the message out and the drawer doesn't pop out, drag your window to the right until there's enough
room for it). If you decide later you want to switch back to the right side, just drag an e-mail
message off the right side, and the drawer jumps over to that side to catch it.

   Mail: QUICK WAY TO ADD WORDS TO YOUR DICTIONARY

If you're typing a message in Mail and run across a word
that should be in your Spell Checker's dictionary (such as
your name, your company's name, etc.), you can quickly
add it to your Mail dictionary (then, it will recognize the
name in the future instead of flagging it as misspelled).
Here's how: When you come to a word you want added
to your dictionary (such as the name "Kelby," which
seemingly should be in every dictionary, but sadly is not),
Control-click on the word and choose Learn Spelling from
the pop-up menu. Now it's added, and it will no longer
be flagged as not recognized (unless you misspell it).

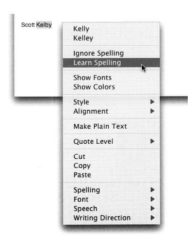

   Mail: **THREADING SHORTCUT**

If you have your e-mails organized by threads (under the View menu), there's a nice, simple keyboard shortcut for opening and closing the threads. Just click on the thread to highlight it, then press the Right Arrow key on your keyboard to open the thread, and the Left Arrow key to close it.

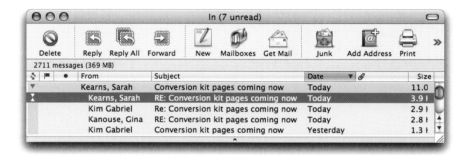

   Mail: **E-MAIL ATTACHMENTS MADE EASY**

I mentioned this in the Dock chapter, but since you might go looking for Mail-related stuff here, I thought I'd repeat it here too: If you want to attach a file to an e-mail message, you can drag the file directly to Mail's icon in your Dock. This opens Mail and creates a brand-new e-mail message window with that file already attached. Sweet! Better yet, even if you drag multiple attachments, they all attach to just one e-mail message (rather than creating one message for each attachment, as in previous versions of Mac OS X).

   Mail: **SENDING HUGE ATTACHMENTS**

Most e-mail servers have a limit to how large an attachment they'll accept. Most limit an attachment size to 5 MB (some even less) and if you e-mail somebody a 6-MB file, it's probably going to get "kicked back" to you as undeliverable. Want to get around that? Use iChat instead. Once you have an iChat session started with someone, you can go under the Buddies menu and choose Send File. Navigate your way to the file you want to send, click OK, and the file is sent to the person you're chatting with (and a link to download your file appears in their chat window), and no matter how big the file size it, it'll get there.

   Mail: **ABOUT TO E-MAIL? WOULD YOU RATHER CHAT?**

When you open a New Message window and type in the recipient's e-mail address, if you've got iChat running, Mail instantly checks to see if this person is available for an iChat. (After all, who wants to wait for e-mail, when you can instantly talk face-to-face?) If they're available, a little green button appears right before their name, letting you know they're online and ready to talk. Click-and-hold on their name and choose iChat with Person from the pop-up list, and you can invite them to chat with you (at which point, they'll politely decline, but hey—it was worth a try). *Note*: This same "green button for chat" feature is activated in Address Book, so if you go searching there for an e-mail address, you'll see if they're ready to chat).

   Mail: **ADDING CUSTOM MAIL SOUNDS**

If you don't like Apple's built-in mail alert sounds, you can use your own custom sound (I downloaded the AOL classic "You've got mail.aiff"). Once you have got the audio file you want to use for your alert, go to your Home folder, open your Library folder, then open your Sounds folder and drop it in there. Then, go back to Mail, and under the Mail menu, choose Preferences. In the Preferences dialog, click on General, and then in the New Mail Sound pop-up menu, you should see your new sound at the bottom of the list. If not, choose Add/Remove. This opens your Sounds folder, where you'll find the alert sound you put there moments ago. Click on it, then click Done (which adds your sound to the New Mail sound menu). Now that it's in the list, you can choose it as your new mail sound. Dig it.

   Mail: **SEEING MULTIPLE MAILBOXES IN THE SAME WINDOW**

If you want to see the contents of multiple mailboxes displayed in the same window, just click on the first mailbox you want to see, then Command-click on the second mailbox, and you'll get a merged list in the main window. This is really handy for things like looking for an important incoming e-mail when you have multiple e-mail accounts. By Command-clicking on the different accounts, you can see all of your new mail, from all your accounts, in one window at the same time. Think about it. It boggles the mail. Uh…the mind.

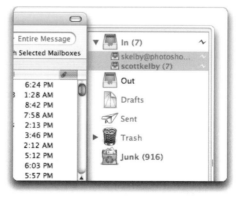

Mail: ADDING A VCARD (OR PHOTO) TO YOUR SIGNATURE

You can attach your vCard (Virtual Businesss Card) to your e-mail signature, but some people prefer to just include a small headshot instead, adding that personal, extremely vain touch. Here's how: Go under the Mail menu, and choose Preferences. Then, in the Preferences dialog, click on the Signatures icon. Click on Add Signature, then type in your info (your name, title, contact info, etc.) Then (without closing this window), go find the JPEG photo you want included with your signature, and drag-and-drop it into this window, then click OK. Oh, one more thing: While you're in the Signatures pane, turn on Show Signature Menu on Compose Window, which adds a pop-up menu where you choose to include your signature when composing your next e-mail.

   Mail: GETTING YOUR SIGNATURE WHERE IT SHOULD BE

If you've used Mail for a while, you've probably noticed the maddening phenomenon that occurs when someone sends you an e-mail, and you reply and decide to attach a signature. If you wrote your reply above their e-mail (like most folks), you were probably surprised to see that Mail added your signature below their original message, instead of at the end of yours. Makes you stop and think, doesn't it? Anyway, in Panther, you can get the signature to appear after your e-mail reply (where it should be) by going under the Mail menu, to Preferences, and clicking on the Signatures icon. When the dialog appears, click on Place Signature Above Quoted Text, and all will be right with the world.

   Address Book: **HIDING YOUR PRIVATES**

If you're sending someone your vCard, depending on who they are, you might want to limit how much info you give them. For example, if this contact is a business contact, you might not want them to have your private e-mail address (these are all the rage right now, thanks to spam), or home phone number (more and more people have one), or credit-card number. Well, luckily, you can decide which fields are saved as your vCard, and which are kept private, by going under the Address Book menu, under Preferences, and then clicking on the vCard icon. Then, click on the Enable Private 'Me' Card checkbox. Now, go back to your vCard in the Address Book; click the Edit button and a series of blue checkboxes appear. The info in any "checked" fields will be included in your vCard, so uncheck any field you want kept private. It's as easy as that.

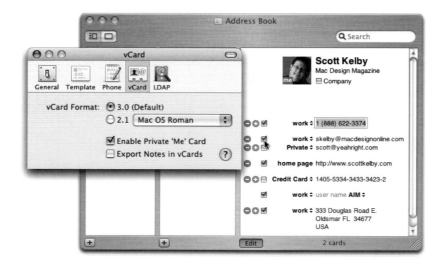

Address Book: **SENIOR-SIZED PHONE NUMBERS**

Okay, the phone numbers in the contact window are pretty small, but don't sweat it, you can make the numbers so large that senior citizens who are standing a good 15 to 20 feet from their monitor could make them out. Just click-and-hold directly on the name of the field for the number you want to read (Work, Home, Mobile, etc.) and choose Large Type from the pop-up menu that appears. The menu item should really read "Huge, gigantic, billboard-like type" because it plasters the number in giant letters across your entire screen. (Try it on an Apple Cinema Display—it's stunning.) To make the huge numbers go away, just click once on them and they disappear, back into a giant cave.

   Address Book: **WAS IT KAL-IB-RA OR KAL-EEB-BRA?**

If you enter a new contact and you're concerned that when you call them again, perhaps months from now, you won't remember how their name is pronounced, Address Book can help. Just go under the Card menu, under Add Field, and choose Phonetic First/Last name. This adds a tiny field right above your contact's name where you can enter the phonetic spelling of their name, so when you do call them back, you sound like a genius (or at least, someone with a good memory).

   Address Book: GETTING VCARDS IN FAST

vCards (Virtual Business Cards) are getting so popular that they now have an "industry standard" format. Luckily, Address Book not only supports them but makes it easy for you to enter vCards. If you're e-mailed a vCard, just drag-and-drop it right into the Address Book Name window and Address Book automatically formats the information into a contact for you.

   Address Book: GETTING VCARDS OUT FAST

Getting a vCard out of Address Book got much easier in Panther. Just go to the contact you want, and when you're there, if you look up in the Address Book's title bar, right before the words "Address Book," you'll see a little rectangular icon. That's a "mini vCard." There are two ways to use it: (1) If you hold the Option key, click on it, wait just a second, then drag it out to your desktop, and it makes a freestanding vCard. You can then attach it to e-mails, send it to friends, etc. (2) If you don't hold the Option key—you just click-and-drag it to your desktop, it just creates an alias to that Address Book contact. Either way, the choice is yours; to option-pause or not to option-pause.

Address Book: **MAKING YOUR OWN VCARD**

I know, I know, you want to be all trendy and hip, so here's how to make your own vCard. (*Note:* The first step in being trendy and hip is not to use the 1970s word "hip.") Here's how: First, set up your own personal card the way you want it, then go under the Card menu and choose Make This My Card. This changes the icon for your personal contact to a silhouette of a person rather than a square photo icon, letting you know which card is "your card." If you've got a lot of contacts and want to get to your card fast, choose Go To My Card from the Card menu.

If you want to e-mail your card to somebody (to show you're trendy and that other thing), first choose Go To My Card from the Card menu, then go under the File menu and choose Export vCard. Save your vCard file (I save mine right to my desktop) then send it as an attachment to any Mail file. You can also drag-and-drop your card's silhouette icon right from Address Book into a New Message window in Apple's Mail app. Or if you're using iChat, you can send your vCard to someone you're chatting with by going under the iChat Buddies menu and choosing Send File.

Address Book: **IS YOUR CONTACT AVAILABLE FOR CHATTING?**

If you're getting ready to send some-body an e-mail, wouldn't it be better to get an answer right away, rather than waiting for them to reply to your e-mail? Address Book can help, because when you go to a contact to get their e-mail address, if they're using iChat and they're available for chatting, you'll see a little green dot next to their picture (consider that a green light for chatting—they're online and available!). All you have to do now is click directly on that little green circle to bring iChat to the front, and

then you can ask them if they will accept a chat from you. They probably won't, but that's an entirely different issue.

   Address Book: **SEEING WHICH GROUPS THEY'RE IN**

If you have a contact that appears in more than one group, you can instantly see which of your groups this individual appears in by simply clicking on their contact, then holding the Option key. When you do this, every group that they appear within becomes highlighted. This is handy if you want to clean up your groups by de-duping people who appear in multiple groups.

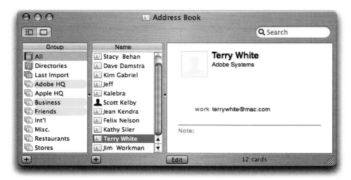

   Address Book: **SENDING AN E-MAIL TO EVERYONE IN YOUR GROUP**

Once you create a group (like friends, or co-workers, or perhaps Total Mac freaks), you can send that entire group an e-mail with just one click. Simply Control-click on the group (in this case, we'll control-click on our group named "Business") and then choose Send email to "Business." It opens Mail and a New Message window, with the word "Business" in the To field. Put in your subject, write your e-mail, and when you click Send, everyone in your "Business" group receives the e-mail. Not bad, eh?

Address Book: **SENDING NOTES WITH YOUR VCARD**

For some freaky reason, when you send someone your vCard, by default, it sends them every single field except the Note field. Why? I have no earthly idea, but it doesn't have to be that way. To send your Note field along with your vCard, go under the Address Book menu, under Preferences, and click on the vCard icon at the top. In the vCard panel, turn on the checkbox for Export Notes in vCards and from then on, your Notes will be sent along as well.

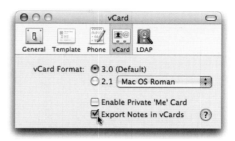

   Address Book: **THE WORLD'S EASIEST BACK-UP PLAN**

If you're not using a .Mac account to sync your Address Book (and if that all sounds very foreign, you're not), you'll definitely want to make a backup copy of your contacts just in case anything unspeakable happens to your Mac (from its being dropped, stolen, confiscated by the FBI, or just a really nasty hard disk crash). And since backup is so incredibly simple, there's no excuse not to—just go under the File menu and choose Back Up Database. This exports a copy of your entire Address Book (you should then put this copy on a removable drive, burn it to a CD, e-mail it to a close family member, etc.) just in case the unimaginable becomes manageable (that doesn't make much sense, but it would make a great tagline for a company "We make the unimaginable manageable").

CHAPTER 10 • Business Apps 187

Address Book: **GETTING DIRECTIONS TO THEIR OFFICE**

Now this is really cool—you can have Address Book automatically get a map and local directions to your contact's physical address. Just click on their address field (not the address itself, the field title before it) and choose Map Of from the pop-up menu that appears. It quickly goes online and gets a map and directions to their location for you. Seriously, how cool is that????

Address Book: **MERGING TWO RECORDS**

If you have two contacts for the same person (it happens more than you'd think—at least to me), you can have Address Book merge the two into one contact. First, press Command-1 to make sure your mode is set to Card and Columns view. Then, use the Search field (in the upper right-hand corner) to find the two redundant contacts. Then, in the Name column, click on the first contact. Hold the Shift key and click on the second to select them both. Then, go under the Card menu and choose Merge Cards, and the two shall become one (like the way I switched writing styles there? "The two shall become one." Hey, if nothing else, I'm versatile). If any of the information is redundant (two of the same phone numbers, etc.), press Command-L to go into Edit mode, highlight the duplicate info, and

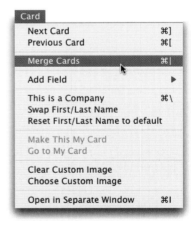

press Delete. When you leave Edit mode, not only will the duplicate info be gone, but the duplicate field will also be deleted.

iCal: ARE YOU "MEETING THEM TO DEATH"?

Want to find out if you're "meeting someone to death"? Just go to the Search field at the bottom of the iCal window and type in their name. A window pops up with a list of all the meetings you have invited them to attend. If you see dozens of listings, you might want to ask yourself, "Do I really need to have them there?" (You might want to ask yourself other questions, like "Do I have a life outside of meetings?" and "Have I become co-dependent on iCal?" Things along those lines.)

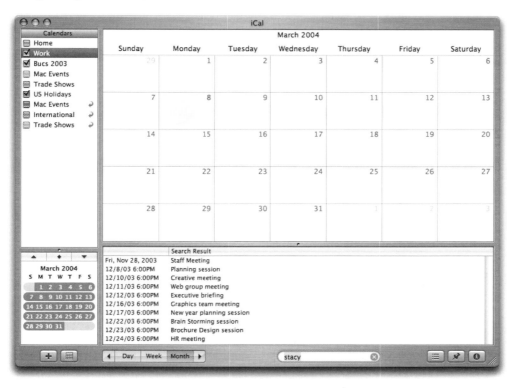

   iCal: **HAVE iCAL CALL YOUR CELL PHONE**

If you're like me, you sometimes need "extra" reminders about things like appointments, birthdays, meetings, etc. If you do, you can actually have iCal send an
e-mail to your cell phone reminding you of that important meeting (provided, of course, that you have a cell
phone that accepts e-mail). The first thing you need to
do is put your phone's e-mail address in your Address
Book (not in iCal—in the Address Book application),
in the card that you have designated as "My Card."
Then, go to iCal and create a new event (something like
"Fight with a PC user: playground @ 10:00 a.m.") and
in iCal's Info panel, click to the immediate right of the

word "Alarm" on the word "None" and a pop-up list of alarm notifcations appears. Choose Email.
Then a new field appears, with a list of e-mail address that you have in (guess where?) your Address Book application in your "My Card" card. Choose your cell phone's e-mail address, choose
how long before the appointment you want that e-mail reminder sent, and you're good to go.
As long as (a) your cell phone's turned on, (b) your Mac is still on, and (c) you have an Internet
connection, it'll do it.

   iCal: **GETTING A LINE BREAK IN YOUR HEADER**

When you're entering a new event in your calendar, you've probably already noticed that hitting the Return key to add a line
break in the Info panel doesn't work—instead, it just thinks you've
finished typing and closes the field (that's because by default, iCal
doesn't allow multiple lines. Go figure). But there's a little-known
keyboard shortcut that lets you create a line break. Instead of
pressing just Return, press Option-Return, and you get that so well-
deserved line break.

iCal: **HAVING A MEETING? LET iCAL DO THE INVITES**

If you're scheduling a meeting, you can have iCal send out an e-mail invitation to the people you want to attend. Start by adding your meeting to your calendar. Then, go under the Window menu and choose Show People. This brings up a dialog with a list of people in your Address Book. Just drag-and-drop the people you want invited right onto your event. As you do this, look in iCal's Info panel, and you'll see their names added as attendees. When you're ready to send your invitations, click on the word "Attendees" and choose Send Invitations from the pop-up, and they're on their way! (*Note*: This only works if you have each attendee's e-mail address in your Address Book, so make sure you do first.)

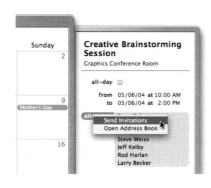

   iCal: **KEEPING TABS ON YOUR LOCAL APPLE STORE**

If you have an Apple Store nearby, you probably already know that it holds lots of free seminars and special events. But how do you know which one is coming up next without going to its Web site to check? It's easy—just go to apple.com/retail, click on the link for your local store, and subscribe to the iCal event calendar. This adds its calendar of upcoming events to your iCal so you can know what's happening next at your local Apple Store. (Did you catch my *What's Happening!!* reference there? It was my small tribute to actor Fred "Rerun" Berry, who passed away this year.)

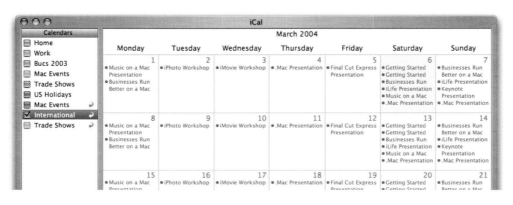

   iCal: ADDING LIVE WEB LINKS TO YOUR CALENDAR

If you're leaving yourself a note to check a Web site, you can imbed a live link to that site right in your iCal header (you could always imbed a URL into a note, but not into the header that appears in the calendar itself). For example, let's say your message would have been "New Toni Braxton CD comes out today. Visit CDNOW.com to order." If you add angle brackets around CDNOW and include the full full Web address like this:

<http://www.cdnow.com>

the link becomes live and you can click on that header from within iCal's main calendar and be taken directly to that Web page. If you look in the capture below, in the main Calendar window, you'll see that the link that appears is clickable and live.

iCal: SETTING YOUR ALARM TO PLAY A SONG

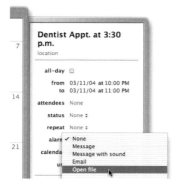

Why just have an annoying alert sound as your iCal alarm, when you can have it play your favorite song as your alarm? It's easy. All you have to do is click on the event you want to set an alarm for, then in the Info panel, click-and-hold on the word "None" that appears to the immediate right of the word "Alarm." In the pop-up menu that appears, choose Open File. This puts the entry "Open file" in that field, but it adds a new field directly below it. Click on that field and choose Other. Then, in the standard Open dialog that appears, navigate to the song you want played as your alarm (I use the 1980s club mix of Kano's "I'm Ready"), then click the Select button. Last, in the bottom field, choose when you want the alarm (the song) to "go off." That's it—when your alarm goes off, you get the jams!

  ## iCal: UNLEASHING THE SCROLL WHEEL'S POWER

If you're using a multi-button mouse with a scroll wheel, it's time to "unleash its power" by taking advantage of using your scroll wheel with iCal, because it lets you jump from field to field in the Info panel simply by moving the scroll wheel back and forth. This makes quick work of entering alarm times, status settings (just about anything in the Info panel) and if you bring up the Go To Date field, you can even scroll through the dates. It's "wheely" great (sorry, that was lame).

   iCal: **CUSTOMIZING YOUR iCAL INVITE MESSAGE**

If you're inviting people to a meeting using iChat, iChat sends them a pretty straightforward, business-sounding e-mail invitation. However, if you'd prefer iCal's invitation to read something like "If you have any hopes of keeping your job, you'd better be at the 4:00 p.m. meeting today," you can do it pretty easily.

STEP ONE: Go into your Applications folder and Control-click on the iCal application's icon. Choose Show Package Contents from the pop-up window that appears. This brings up a folder named Contents. Look inside that folder and you find another folder named Resources. Look inside this folder for a folder named English.lproj, then look inside that folder for a file named iTIP.strings.

STEP TWO: Open this iTIP.strings in TextEdit (you can also open it in Microsoft Word if you like).

STEP THREE: As you look through this file, you see a line that reads "/* Mail body when sending an invitation to an event (IP 56)". Directly below this line, you see the default text that iCal uses when inviting someone to a meeting. This is the text you'll edit. HOWEVER, iCal customizes part of this invitation with the recipient's name, the time you want your meeting, etc., so don't erase any characters that look like this: "%@"—leave those in place, and work around them. For example, the default invitation reads "%@ has invited you to the iCal event %@, scheduled for %@ at %@ (%@)." You could change that to "%@ is warning you to get your lazy butt into gear for my meeting about %@, and if you have any hope of keeping your miserable job, you'd better be there at %@ in the %@."

Now you can close the file, save changes, restart iCal, and scare the hell out of your employees.

Safari: **HIDING YOUR TRACKS**

Let's say that you've been visiting some sites that you don't want other people to know about (like Microsoft.com, Depends.com, etc.). If that's the case, you probably want to hide any tracks that might lead others to learn of your whereabouts. Just choosing Clear History isn't enough. Heck, these days your average middle-school student could trace you back to those sites in about five minutes. If you really want to hide your tracks, go under the Safari menu and choose Reset Safari. This brings up a warning dialog that says, in essence, choosing this is the next best thing to a clean reinstall of your browser. It basically "cleans house," so don't click it unless you're on the run from the CIA (or a crafty middle-school student).

Safari: **ONE-CLICK TABBING**

By default, you have to Command-click to load a particular folder of sites for Tabbed Browsing, but if you find you're loading full folders of sites (rather than just one individual site within the folder), you can change how Safari lets you click. That way, just a simple click loads the folder for Tabbed Browsing and if you want just one particular site in the folder to load, then you Command-click. Surprisingly, this isn't found under Safari's Preferences; instead, click on the Bookmark button up in the Bookmarks Bar and then under Collections, click on the Bookmarks Bar to bring up a list of the sites and folders in your Bookmarks Bar. To make any folder a one-click load, click on the Auto-Tab checkbox (as shown) and now all the sites in that folder load with just one click.

   Safari: OPENING GOOGLE RESULTS IN A SEPARATE WINDOW

By default, when you do a Web search using Safari's built-in Google Toolbar search, the results of your search replace what was currently in your browser window. That's okay unless you're using that search to look up something relating to the page that you were on (which seems to happen, at least to me, more often than not). Here's a way around that: Once you enter your search term in the Google search field, instead of hitting Return (or Enter), press Command-Return, and the Google results open in their own separate window. (*Note:* If you have Tabbed Browsing turned on, it will open the results in a separate tab.)

   Safari: A KEYBOARD SHORTCUT EXTRAVAGANZA

As you might expect, there are dozens of keyboard shortcuts for Safari, and I could include them all in this book; but I don't have to, because believe it or not, they're already on your hard drive (they're pretty much buried, so don't feel bad if you haven't run across them yet). To find this exhaustive list, go to your Applications folder, Control-click on the Safari icon, and choose Show Package Contents from the pop-up menu. This brings up a folder named Contents. Look inside there for a folder named Resources, then look in the Resources folder for a folder named English.lproj. Last, look inside that folder (I told you it was buried) for a file named Shortcuts.html. Double-click this file to see a pretty darn complete list of Safari's keyboard shortcuts.

Safari: **TYPING IN URLS THE FAST WAY**

Before you can type in a new URL (Web address), of course, you have to get rid of the one currently in the address field. Of course, you could drag your cursor over the old address to highlight it, and if you're charging by the hour, I highly recommend doing it that way. However, if you want the fastest one-click method in town, just click on the little Apple icon (or custom site icon) that appears immediately before the address in that field. Doing that instantly highlights the field, and you can type your new URL over the old URL lickety-split (whatever that means. I heard some guy at the General Store say that once).

   ## Safari: **FINDING YOUR DIGITAL BREADCRUMBS**

Like any browser, Safari keeps track of where you've been, page by page. If you want to hop quickly back to a page where you've been recently, just Control-click on the Back button in Safari's toolbar. If you've hopped back, and want to jump ahead, Control-click on the Forward button. (I didn't really have to tell you that Forward button trick, did I?)

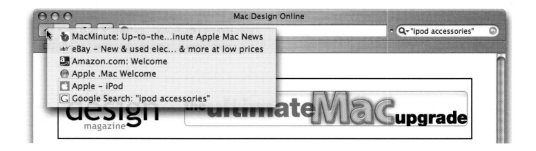

   Safari: **USING GOOGLE'S SEARCH TERM MEMORY**

When you're using the Google Search field in Safari's tool-bar, Safari keeps track of your last 10 searches, just in case you want to re-search using one of those same terms. To access one of your previous search terms, just click on the Magnifying Glass icon within the Google Search field and a pop-up list of recent terms appears.

   Safari: **FINDING YOUR SEARCH TERM ON THE RESULTS PAGE**

Here's a trick for quickly finding your search term in a Google toolbar search's results page. Just press Command-G and Safari instantly highlights the first occurrence of the word. To find other occurrences, just press Command-G again.

  Safari: **A FASTER BOOKMARKS MENU**

If you thought adding your favorite sites to Safari's Bookmarks Bar sped things up, wait till you hear this tip. Once your favorite sites are added, you can have even faster access to those sites than clicking on them. Instead, press Command-1 to load the first site in the Bookmarks Bar. Press Command-2, Command-3, Command-4, and so on to instantly load the sites in order. (*Note*: Sadly, this trick only works with individual sites added to your Bookmarks Bar—it doesn't work with folders on the bar.)

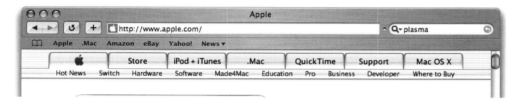

   Safari: **SUPER-FAST WAY TO E-MAIL A URL**

If you run across a cool Web site, and want to e-mail that site to a friend, probably the fastest way is to highlight the Web site name, go under the Safari menu, under Services, under Mail, and choose Send Selection. This opens Mail, and inserts the Web URL into the body of your e-mail. All you have to do now is type in the recipient's name, put "Check this site out" in the Subject line, and click OK. Then, all you have to worry about is their Spam Blocker stopping your e-mail from getting through with such a generic subject in the title. Really don't want it to get there? Add the word "Viagra" somewhere in the title.

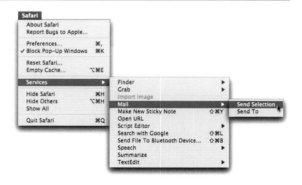

   Safari: **JUMPING FROM TAB TO TAB WHEN TAB BROWSING**

Tabbed browsing is about the coolest single thing in Safari, and jumping quickly from one tab to the next may well be second. To get from tab to tab in a flash, just press Shift-Command-Right Arrow to move right, and press (do I really need to mention how to move left? Didn't think so).

   Safari: **MAKING ONLINE ARTICLES EASIER TO READ**

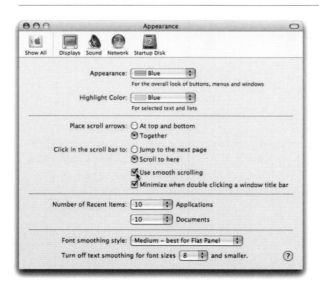

This is a great tip for people who read a lot of articles online, because when you're reading these articles and you come to the bottom of the page, using the scroll bars is a pain and pressing Page Down usually moves too far. However, you can set up Safari to better accommodate reading articles using Smooth Scrolling. To turn it on, go under the Apple menu, under System Preferences, and choose Appearance. Click on the Use Smooth Scrolling button and then when you hit the Page Down button, it moves line by line, rather than page by page.

  ● Safari: **TURN ON THE TABS, BABY!**

This isn't actually a tip, but so few Safari users I run into realize that's it there, I had to include it, because for many people, this will forever change the way they get their info on the Web.

It's called Tabbed Browsing and what it does is let you put a folder of sites you visit daily (like news sites, Apple news sites, graphics sites, sports sites, etc.) up on the Bookmarks Bar. If you Command-click on that folder, it loads every single site in that folder, and puts each one on its own separate tab just under the Bookmarks Bar. It loads the first site in the list first, so while you're reading that page, all the others are loading (in order). So when you click on the second page, it's already loaded (unless you have a really slow Internet connection, of course). While you're looking at the second site, the rest are all still loading, so when you click on the next, and the next, they'll instantly appear (because they're already loaded). It makes you feel as if you're browsing at hyperspeed, and if you try it once, you'll be hooked!

You turn on Tabbed Browsing by going under the Safari menu, under Preferences, and clicking on the Tabs icon, then turning on Enable Tabbed Browsing. Close Preferences. Next, click on the Show All Bookmarks button to bring up all your bookmarked sites. Press Shift-Command-N to add a new Bookmark Folder, and you see a new folder appear in the Collections list on the left side of the Safari window. Give this folder a name (for our example, we'll name it "Sports sites"). Then, click on the collection named Bookmarks Menu to reveal all the bookmarks saved in your pop-down menu. Drag your favorite sports Web sites from this list into the Sport Sites folder in the left column. (Mine has ESPN, CNNsi, and the Buccaneers Home page.)

Once you have all of your sports sites in that folder, click on the Bookmark Bar collection at the top of the Collections list to reveal its contents. Now, just drag your folder into the main window and position it where you want it (to load first, second, etc.). That's it—you've got your first tab. Repeat this process for as many folders as you want (or as can fit in your Browser's Bookmarks Bar), and you're in business. Again, try this once and you'll be hooked on it forever.

  TextEdit: HOW DOES MY LETTER FIT ON A PAGE?

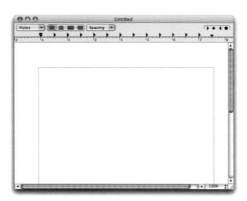

To see TextEdit's page boundaries, press Shift-Command-W (the shortcut for the "Wrap to Page" command) and the page margins appear on screen. Another thing that makes TextEdit behave more like the word processor it really is, is to go under the Format menu and choose Allow Hyphenation, so when a word extends to the page edge, it gets automatically hyphenated and split by syllable to the next line, like you'd expect in a standalone word processor.

   TextEdit: COPYING FONT FORMATS

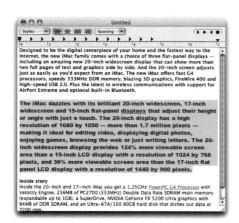

I mentioned this elsewhere in the book, but I thought it needed repeating here because this is such a cool tip and TextEdit totally supports it (not all Mac OS X apps do). If you've got a block of text formatted just the way you want it (font, type style, size, color, etc.), you can copy just that formatting (not the words themselves) by highlighting the text and pressing Option-Command-C. Then, to apply that copied formatting to another block of text that's formatted with different font styles, sizes, etc., just highlight the other text and press Option-Command-V. That text now has the same font formatting as your original text. Big, big timesaver.

TextEdit: COPYING PARAGRAPH FORMATS

Another typography tool usually found in page-layout applications and full-powered word processors is paragraph styles. Instead of the font formatting copying we talked about in the previous tip, in this instance, you copy the paragraph formatting (first line indents, justification, tabs, etc.). To do this, highlight part of the paragraph that has the formatting you want, then press Control-Command-C to copy that formatting. Then, switch to another paragraph, highlight that paragraph, and press Control-Command-V to paste that formatting onto this paragraph.

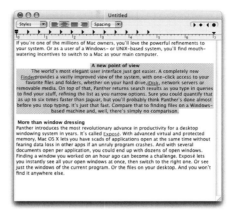

   TextEdit: ADJUSTING THE SPACE BETWEEN LETTERS

Kerning is the act of adjusting the space between letters. (When it's called kerning, that usually refers to adjusting the space between just two letters. If you're adjusting more than two letters at once, it's usually called tracking.) At standard text sizes like 10, 11, and 12, you don't normally worry about kerning, but when you start creating display-sized type (like 72-point type), sometimes wide gaps appear between letters. (The space between a 72-point capital W and the small letter "a" is a perfect example.) To

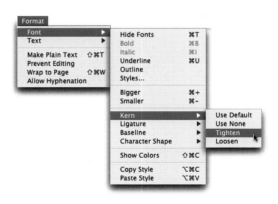

tighten the space between letters, highlight the letters, then go under the Format menu, under Font, under Kern, and choose Tighten. This is a very slight adjustment, so you'll probably have to run it more than once (okay, probably more than five or six times). To loosen the space, choose Loosen as many times as you need.

TextEdit: FONT CONTROL CENTRAL

TextEdit gives you surprisingly robust control over your font formatting. Press Command-T to bring up the Font dialog. You can choose the font family, typeface style (bold, italic, etc.), and point size, and you can see your choice in a large preview at the top of the Font panel (just choose Show Preview from the palette's Action button, in the bottom left-hand corner of the panel. Just under the preview is a toolbar where you'll find everything from controls for colorizing your text to adding drop shadows.

TextEdit: MISS SIMPLETEXT? BRING IT BACK

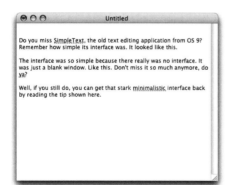

If you miss the clean wide-open "rulerless" look of SimpleText (from the Mac OS 9 era), you can have TextEdit mimic that look. Simply launch TextEdit, and then press Command-R (Show Ruler) to hide the Ruler, buttons, and entry fields that make TextEdit look more like the word processor it really is, and less like its country cousin—the wonderfully bland SimpleText many people grew to love (because of its speed and sheer simplicity).

TextEdit: **CREATING SOFT DROP SHADOWS**

Okay, I know this sounds like a Photoshop technique, but in Panther, the ability to create a soft drop shadow effect behind your type is built into TextEdit. Here's how to "drop it." Create your text (large type sizes work best) and highlight it. Then, press Command-T to bring up the Font panel. At the top of the panel is a button with a large "T" with a slight drop shadow on it. Click on this to turn the shadow feature on. The three sliders to the right of the "T" control the Shadow Opacity (how dark the shadow will be), Amount of Blur (how soft it will be), and Offset (distance the shadow appears from the letter), respectively. To create a soft drop shadow, drag the middle slider (Blur) to the

right (dragging it to the center looks pretty good). You can also control the angle of the light source using the circle to the immediate right of the three sliders. Just drag the small dot in the circle where you want your light source. Cool!

   TextEdit: **POP-UP SPELL CHECKING**

If you want to spell-check your TextEdit document, save yourself a trip to the menu bar. Simply Control-click right within your document and a pop-up menu appears where you can take control of the spell-checking process. This works particularly well if you have a word in question—just highlight that word, Control-click within it, and the proper spelling (if it's misspelled) appears in the pop-up menu. By the way,

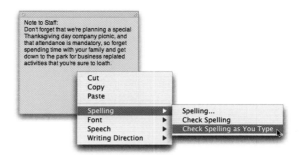

if you prefer to have the Spell Checker check as you type, and flag misspelled words as soon as they're created, go under the TextEdit Preferences, and under Editing, turn on Check Spelling as You Type.

   TextEdit: ALWAYS WRAP TO PAGE

Want to see those page margins every time you create a new document? Go under the TextEdit menu and choose Preferences. In the TextEdit Preferences, under New Document Attributes, check the box marked Wrap to Page and from then on, every new page automatically displays the page margins.

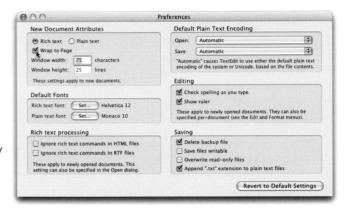

   TextEdit: CHANGING YOUR PAGE COLOR

Want to change the color of the live area of your TextEdit document? No problem—you just do it in a place where you probably won't think to look—in the Font panel. Just press Command-T to bring up the Font panel, and in the toolbar at the top of the panel, the fourth button from the left has a tiny page icon then a square swatch. The swatch is white by default, but you can change your page color by clicking on this button and a Color Picker appears where you can choose the page color of your choice.

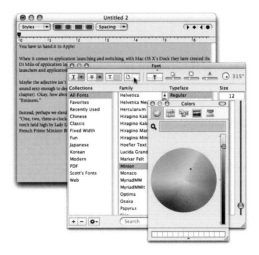

   TextEdit: CAN'T THINK OF THE RIGHT WORD? TRY THIS

In Panther, TextEdit has a very cool feature that can help you out of a word logjam or spelling mishap. As you're typing, when you come to a word you're not sure how to spell, or you can't quite remember the word you want to use, take a stab at it by typing the first few letters, then press F5 on your keyboard. A pop-down menu appears with a list of the words TextEdit thinks you might be trying to conjure up. All you have to do is click on the word that looks right, and it's input in your document.

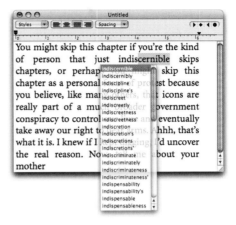

   TextEdit: SAVING FILES AS WORD DOCUMENTS

If you love TextEdit, but routinely send text files to people on other platforms who don't have TextEdit, but surely have Microsoft Word, you can make things easy for them by saving your TextEdit files in Word format so they can easily read them. Here's how: When you go to save your file in the Save As dialog, the default saves your file in Rich Text Format (RTF), but if you click-and-hold on the File Format pop-up menu, you see that you can also save the file in Word format. Choose that, and your worries are over. (Well, you'll still have worries, just not about how other people will open your text files).

   Preview: **CUSTOMIZING PREVIEW'S TOOLBAR**

Like the Finder itself, Preview's toolbar is very customizable and you can easily adjust it so that only the tools you want appear in the toolbar in the order that you want them. You do this by Control-clicking anywhere in Preview's toolbar, and a pop-up menu appears where you can choose Customize Toolbar. A sheet slides down with various tool icons that you can drag right up to the toolbar. If there's a tool you don't want in the toolbar, while this sheet is still open, just click-and-drag it off. Notice that in Panther, there are now buttons for Crop Image, Scale percentage, Zoom to Fit, and Zoom to Selection.

   Preview: **THE NON-MAGNIFYING GLASS TRICK**

If you're used to Photoshop's Magnifying Glass tool, where you drag a selection around the area you want to zoom in on, you're probably frustrated with how the Preview Magnifying Glass works. There's no dragging—you just click on the Zoom in Magnifying Glass and it zooms in. In Panther, you can get the same "drag-a-selection-and-zoom" effect by going under Preview's View menu and choosing Customize Toolbar. When the dialog appears, drag the icon called Zoom to Selection up to the toolbar. Now, to use it, get Preview's selection tool, drag out a selection around the exact area you want to zoom in on, then press the Zoom to Selection button, and that area zooms in and fills your window. Nice.

Preview: **STEPPING THROUGH TOOLBAR VIEWS**

Command-click on the white pill-shaped button in the upper right-hand corner of Preview's title bar, and each time you click, you get another view that's smaller than the default toolbar view (which is large icons and large text). Click once, you get smaller icons. Click again—icons with no text, smaller icons with no text, then just text, and then really small text. Of course, if you don't want the toolbar visible at all, simply click once on the pill-shaped button, and it hides out of view.

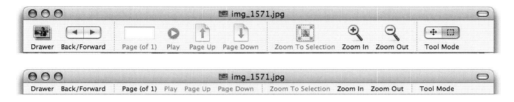

   Preview: **SWITCHING THUMBNAIL SIDES (GO LEFT, NOT RIGHT)**

If you open a PDF file in Preview, you can see thumbnails of the pages in your PDF document by pressing Command-T. A little pane pops out to the right side of Preview's window display-ing tiny thumbnail images of each page. These are clickable and enable you to jump right to the page you want. However, if you'd prefer that this pop-out pane appear on the left side of your screen rather than the right, simply drag your Preview window to the right side of your screen before you press Command-T. Now, it pops out to the left.

  Preview: **KEEPING LINE BREAKS WHEN COPYING TEXT**

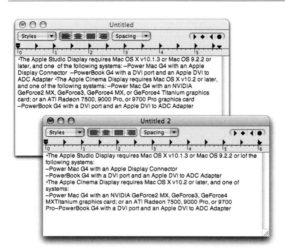

If you're copying text out of a PDF and pasting it into an e-mail (or into TextEdit, etc.), you find that when you paste the copied text, you lose all the line breaks, giving you one contiguous big blob of text. To keep those line breaks intact, just hold the Option key, then drag over the text you want to copy. That way, when you paste the text, the line breaks stay intact. This can also help when copying text in your PDF that appears in two columns.

   Preview: **PRINTING FINDER WINDOWS**

Since Mac OS X doesn't have the ability to print Finder windows (as in previous versions of the OS), here's a popular workaround: Make a screen capture of the window (Shift-Command-4 and drag a marquee around the window), which saves the capture as a PDF file on your desktop. Double-click on your PDF screen capture to open it in Preview, and then you can print the image from within Preview, which produces a printed view of your Finder window (just like in "the old days").

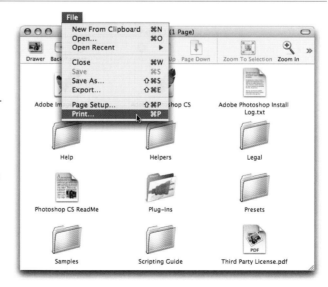

Preview: **CONVERTING TO TIFF, JPEG, OR PHOTOSHOP**

Want to change most any graphic into a Photoshop file? Just open the file in Preview, go under the File menu, and choose Export, where you can export your graphic in Photoshop format. But, you're not limited to Photoshop format—Preview also exports your file as a JPEG, PICT, QuickTime (to open in QuickTime Player), BMP (for sharing files with PC users), PICT, Targa (for video), and more. If the format you're saving in has options (such as quality and compression settings for JPEG and TIFF images), click the Options button in the Export dialog to access those controls.

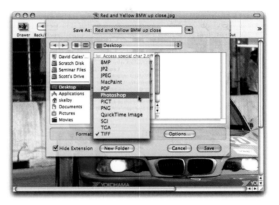

   Preview: **THE TRICK TO PLAYING ANIMATIONS IN PREVIEW**

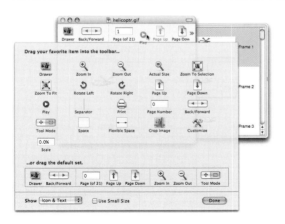

You may have heard that Preview can play .gif animations, but "how?" is the big question because when you open a .gif animation in Preview, it just puts each individual frame of the animation onto a separate page, rather than playing the animation. So what's the trick? Go under Preview's View menu and choose Customize Toolbar. In the Customize Toolbar dialog, you find a Play button. Drag this button up to the toolbar, then click Done. Now when you click the Play button, the animation plays. While it's playing, a dialog appears over the toolbar with a Stop button.

    Sherlock: **STEPPING THROUGH SHERLOCK'S TOOLBAR VIEWS**

Sherlock has a new job in Panther—just Web searches (hard drive searches are now relegated to the Find Command using the shortcut Command-F). Although this has changed, it shares many of the same toolbar controls as other Mac OS X apps. For example, if you Command-click on the white pill-shaped button in the upper right-hand corner of Sherlock's title bar, you get another Icon/Text view that's smaller than the default toolbar view (which is large icons and large text). Click once, you'll get smaller icons. Click again—icons with no text, then smaller icons with no text, then just text, and then just really small text. To hide the toolbar altogether, click once on the white pill-shaped button in the upper right-hand corner, and it hides itself from view. Want to customize its toolbar? Just Control-click anywhere within the toolbar itself and choose Customize Toolbar.

Sherlock: TARGETING CHANNELS THE FAST WAY

Know which Sherlock 3 channel you need next? Don't waste time—jump right to it by Control-clicking on Sherlock's icon in the Dock. A pop-up list of channels appears and you can jump right to the one you need fast. (*Note*: If you quit Sherlock after your last search, this won't work—it has to be running, but it doesn't have to be the active application, meaning that you could be running Adobe InDesign, and jump right to the Sherlock channel you want directly from the Dock.)

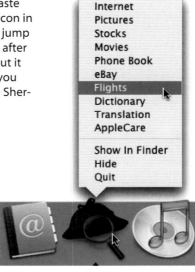

   Sherlock: YOUR CHANNEL JUST ONE CLICK AWAY

If you were thinking, "There's got to be a faster way to get to the channel I need," there is. At least after you do this one thing. Open Sherlock and double-click on the channel you want (so, if you find yourself using the Phone Book a lot, double-click on Phone Book). Then, go under the Channel menu and choose Make a Shortcut. This brings up a Save dialog, and I recommend that you save this file to your desktop (and/or drag it to your Dock).

Once you do that, you can close Sherlock. The next time you want to get to the Phone Book, just double-click this file and Sherlock launches and takes you right to the Phone Book. One click to get right where you want to go.

Sherlock: MOVING THE NAME COLUMN. WHAT??!!

I know what you're thinking—moving the Name column—it can't be done. Mac OS X just doesn't let you do that. Oh sure, you can click, hold, and drag to reorder columns in any Finder window, and many other applications, but as a rule, Mac OS X never lets you move the Name column out of its safe, comfy home at "first column on the left." Well, that age-old rule is broken in Sherlock where you're actually allowed to click-and-drag directly on the first column and drag it to a different location. Do it once, just because you can.

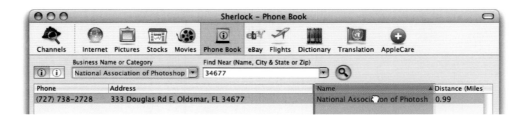

Sherlock: SAVE THAT SITE FOR LATER

If Sherlock finds a site that you think you might want to save for later (kind of like a Favorite), just click on it (in the results window) and drag it right to your Desktop. It creates a file that you can use (by double-clicking) to get back to that Web page any time.

Sherlock: **REMOVING CHANNELS**

If there's a channel that you just don't ever see yourself using, you can Command-click on it and drag it right off the toolbar, and it disappears in a puff of smoke (an Apple-approved, fully animated puff, with accompanying sound effect).

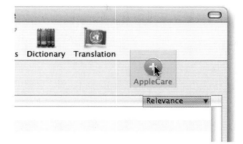

⬤ ⬤ ⬤ Sherlock: **PERFORMING MULTIPLE SEARCHES**

Let's say that while you're checking on the details of an arriving flight, you also need to find out what time *Shrek 2* is playing at the local AMC, and you need to be simultaneously searching for "Think Different" posters on eBay. How do you pull off this "miracle of multiple searches?" It's easier than you'd think. Just start one search in motion, then choose New from the File menu to bring up another search while the previous one's still chuggin' away. I told you it was easy.

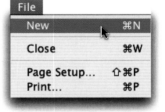

Stickies: **STICKIES WILL SPELL IT FOR YOU**

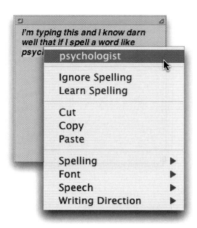

If you're working in Stickies and you're not sure you've spelled a word correctly, just Control-click on the word, and a pop-up menu appears. At the top of this menu are choices for what it believes to be the proper spelling of that word (if it's actually misspelled and it recognizes the word in the first place). If you agree, just move your cursor over that word, release your mouse button, and your misspelled word is replaced. Mighty handy.

   Stickies: **KEEPING YOUR NOTE UP FRONT**

You probably already know how frustrating it can be if you have to toggle back and forth between an open Sticky and another application (let's say you're copying some text from a Web site into Stickies). Well, now the toggling is finally over: Just press Command-Option-F (the command for Floating Window), and this makes your current Sticky note float above your current application. That way, you can clearly see your note while working in another application (like Safari) because it'll be floating above it. Try

this once, and you'll be using it daily. Provided, of course, that you use Stickies daily. And use your Macintosh daily. And that you use Stickies with another application daily. And that you bathe daily. (I just threw that last one in as a subtle personal hygiene reminder. See, I care.)

Stickies: SEE-THROUGH NOTES

One of my favorite Panther Stickies features is the ability to make a sticky translucent. Just click on a Sticky and press Command-Option-T (Translucent Window). Then, you can see right through your Sticky to the items behind it. This is really handy if you want to see items in Finder windows that would normally be covered by any open Stickies. To turn off the transparency (pardon me, translucency), just press the shortcut again.

   Stickies: SAVING YOUR TEXT COLORS

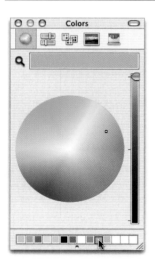

You've been able to colorize text in Stickies since at least Mac OS 10.1, but did you know that you can save your favorite colors and apply them with just one click? (Obviously, I'm hoping you didn't or it really kills this tip.) To do so, just highlight a word, then go under the Font menu and choose Show Colors. When the Colors dialog appears, choose the color you'd like. Then, click-and-hold in the horizontal color bar up top (where the color you've created is displayed), and a tiny square appears under your cursor. Just drag-and-drop this square on one of the white square boxes at the bottom of the Colors dialog. This saves that color for future use, so when you want it, all you have to do is click once on that square (no more messing with the color wheel). This is a great place to save commonly used colors like red, solid black, white, etc.

   Stickies: **PUTTING STICKIES IN MOTION**

Actually, this tip really should be called "Motion in Stickies" because believe it or not, you can put a QuickTime movie into a Sticky. Just locate the QuickTime movie you want (don't open the movie, just find it on your drive), and then open Stickies. Drag out your Sticky's window so it's big enough to accommodate the physical dimensions of your movie, and then drag-and-drop your movie right from the Finder window (or desktop) into your sticky note. You'll get a dialog asking if you want to actually copy it, or just place an alias of it there. Choose Copy, and within a few moments, it appears within your Sticky with a standard embedded-style QuickTime player bar beneath it. Click the Play button, and your QuickTime movie plays from right within your Sticky note. Why would you want to do this? I have no idea.

   Stickies: **JOTTING DOWN A QUICK NOTE ANY TIME**

Working in the Finder and need to jot something down real quick? Just press Shift-Command-Y and Stickies instantly launches and opens a new sticky for you. It's super-fast and pretty darn handy.

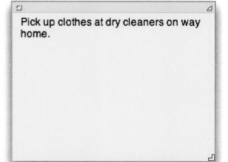

Stickies: **SETTING FONT, STYLE, SIZE, AND COLOR DEFAULTS**

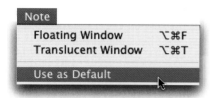

If you have a favorite font, font size, Sticky size, and color you like to use for your Stickies, you can quickly change the defaults so every new Sticky uses your favorites. Just open a new Sticky, press Command-T to bring up the Font Panel, and set your font, type style, and size, just the way you like it. Choose which color you'd like for your default Sticky by going under the Color menu and choosing a color. Then, go under the Note menu and choose Use as Default. Now, when you open a new Sticky, it uses your new custom default settings.

   Stickies: **FROM STICKY TO TEXTEDIT IN ONE CLICK**

If you get carried away in a Sticky and you wind up writing more than you expected, you can instantly convert your Sticky note into a TextEdit document by selecting all of your text and then going under the Stickies menu, under Services, under TextEdit, and choosing New Window Containing Selection. This immediately launches TextEdit and opens a new document with the contents of your Sticky within it. You can now save your file in TextEdit format and use all of TextEdit's features as if your file had been created in TextEdit to begin with.

CHAPTER 10 • Business Apps   **219**

   Stickies: **TURNING YOUR SELECTION INTO A STICKY**

If you've selected some text in a Mac OS X application such as TextEdit (a phone number, Web address, etc.), you can turn that selected text into a Sticky in one click. Just go under the TextEdit menu, under Services, and choose Make New Sticky Note. Stickies launches and opens a new note with your selected text. The keyboard shortcut for this automation is Shift-Command-Y.

   Stickies: **THE ONE PLACE WINDOW SHADE STILL LIVES**

In Mac OS X, Apple did away with the popular Window Shade feature that appeared in previous versions of the OS, where you could double-click on a window's title bar and it would roll up like a window shade, leaving just the title bar visible. But in Stickies, a Window Shade feature still exists—just double-click the Sticky's title bar (or press Command-M) and the current sticky rolls up—just like a window shade.

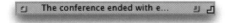

Font Panel: **FINDING WHERE THE © AND ™ SYMBOLS LIVE**

Since nearly the beginning of Mac-dom, when you wanted to find out which key combination produced a font's special characters (stuff like ©, ™, £, ¢, ‰, ƒ, etc.), you used a utility called KeyCaps. More than a decade later, KeyCaps is still a part of Mac OS, but a better better way to access these special characters is through the Character Palette. You can access it two ways: (1) from within Mac OS X business apps like Mail, TextEdit, Stickies, etc.), just go under Edit and choose Special Characters or click on the Action tab at the bottom of the Font Panel and choose Characters; (2) add Character Palette access to your menu bar, so you can access it when you're working in other applications (like Word or Adobe InDesign). You do this by going to the System Preferences, to International, and clicking on the Input menu. Turn on the Checkbox for Character Palette and it appears in the menu bar, after the last menu in your current application. Either way you open it, here's how you use it: When you open the Character Palette, click on the By Category tab. The left column shows a list of special character categories

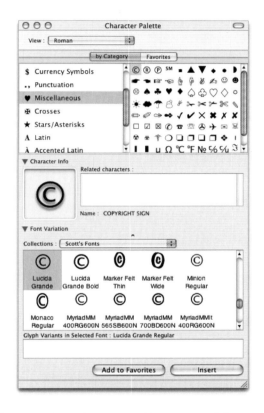

and the right column shows the individual characters in each category. To get one of these characters into your text document, just click on the character and press the Insert button in the bottom right-hand corner of the dialog. If you find yourself using the same special characters over and over (like ©, ™, etc.), you can add these to your Favorites list, and access them from the Favorites tab in the Character Palette. To see which fonts contain certain characters (they don't all share the same special characters), expand the Character Palette by clicking on the down-facing arrow on the bottom left side of the palette. This brings up another panel where you can choose different fonts. You can also ask that this list show only fonts that support the character you have highlighted.

   Font Panel: **ACCESSING SPECIAL CHARACTERS FROM THE MENU BAR**

If you need a quick special character (such as é, or °, or ˆ) but don't know which keyboard combination you need to create it, you can have the Character Palette (a list of every character) added to your menu bar. Here's how: Go under the Apple menu, and choose System Prefer- ences. Click on the Inter- national icon. When its pane appears, click on the Input Menu tab, and turn on the checkbox for Character Palette. This adds a little icon to the right of the Help icon in the Finder, where you can quickly choose Character Palette without going through the Font Panel.

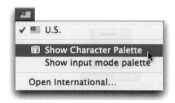

   Font Panel: **SEEING YOUR FONTS BEFORE YOU USE THEM**

Apple has heard your plaintive cries, and finally they've included a preview of your fonts so you can actually see what they look like before you decide which one to use. You access this new wonder of modern science in any application that uses Mac OS X's built-in Font Panel (apps such as TextEdit, Stickies, Mail, etc.). Press Command-T to bring up the Font Panel. When it appears, click on the Ac- tion button at the bottom of the panel and choose Show Preview. A font preview pane appears at the top of the dialog, and as you click on different fonts, their previews appear in that pane. It also works for both type style and font sizes.

PDF: THE SMALLER PDF SECRET CONTROL

This is another one of those "secret, buried-in-a-vault" killer tips that address something Mac OS X users have complained about: The file sizes of PDFs that Mac OS X creates are sometimes too big (vs. Adobe's Acrobat PDFs). Believe it or not, there's a way to get smaller PDFs; it's just buried under 40 tons of clay. Here's how to "unearth" this control. Launch TextEdit, then choose Print from the File menu. From the second pop-up menu under Presets, choose ColorSync. From the Quartz Filter menu that appears, choose Add Filters. Click on the Filter named Reduce File Size, then click the Duplicate button. This creates an unlocked filter you can edit. At the bottom of the dialog, under the Details button, change the pop-up menu from Color to Images. From the next menu down, choose Compression, and you see the magic slider that lets you control the amount of JPEG compression your PDF images receive. For smaller file sizes, drag the Quality slider toward Least. Click the Apply button (in the middle), go back to TextEdit, and in the Print dialog, choose Save As PDF. That's it. (Whew!)

jukebox
hero

iTUNES TIPS

Okay, why does iTunes get its own entire chapter, when applications like iDVD, iMovie, and iPhoto are all covered in the same

Jukebox Hero
iTunes tips

chapter? Well, Bunky, there's more than just one reason, and like many lists in life, we'll start with #1: Everybody digs music (even bad people), and everybody loves iTunes (probably even Bill Gates). But iDVD and iMovie have a much smaller audience. For example, if you don't have a digital video camcorder, you probably don't use iMovie; in which case, you probably don't use iDVD either. If you're not shooting digital photos, you're probably not using iPhoto (though you could); so again, it's not a ubiquitous thing like music. Reason #2: I use iTunes a lot, and I've got so many really cool iTunes tips that they take up an entire chapter. But perhaps the real reason is (#3) after watching iTunes' built-in visual effects for a few hours one day, in a sudden moment of total clarity, I realized that it had become my master, and it told me it needed its own space. Then it asked me to sell my car and give it the proceeds. Yes, master.

  YOUR "TOP 10" PLAYLIST, AUTOMATICALLY

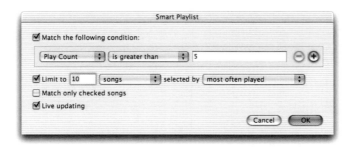

In iTunes, you can create a custom Top-10 playlist that automatically updates. Here's how: Go under the File menu and choose New Smart Playlist. Then, from the first pop-up menu, choose Play Count; from the second menu, choose Is Greater Than, and then type "5" in the Info field. Then, in the Limit To field, enter 10 (so you'll only wind up with 10 songs—your top 10). For Selected By, choose Most Often Played, and make sure Live Updating is checked. Click OK and you have a new playlist made up of your top 10 most-played songs, in the order you most play them, and it updates automatically.

   HOW TO KILL A LONG, BORING INTRO

If you've got a song with a really long, boring intro (like the incredibly long intro to Aldo Nova's "Fantasy," an otherwise way-cool song), you can trim away that intro, and get right to the "good part" from right within iTunes. You start by finding out exactly when the "good part" starts (look up top for the time readout), then click on the song in your playlist and press Command-I. When the Info window appears, click on the Options tab. You see a field for Start Time. Turn on the Start Time checkbox, enter the time when the good part starts

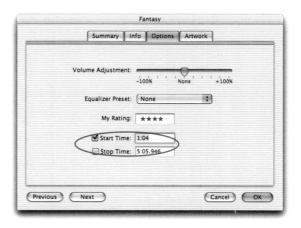

(for "Fantasy," it's 1:04), and you're set—the long boring intro is long gone. BTW: Europe's "The Final Countdown" needs a good intro trim, too!

SAVING TIME WHEN IMPORTING A BUNCH OF SONGS

If you're importing a number of different CDs into iTunes, there's a preference setting that can make the process much easier (and much more automated). Go under the iTunes menu, under Preferences, and click on the General icon. Under the preference On CD Insert, change the pop-up menu from Show Songs to Import Songs and Eject. Now, you just insert the audio CD, and iTunes automatically imports all the songs on the CD and ejects the disc so you can pop in the next one. It's like a "Batch Import" function, and it saves loads of time over doing it all manually.

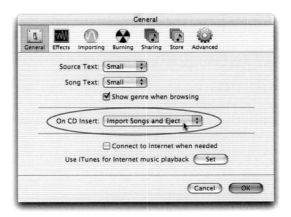

WANT TO SEND THAT MUSIC STORE LINK TO A FRIEND?

If you find a song in the iTunes Music Store that you think a friend might like, you can send your friend right to that song by clicking on the album cover and dragging that cover into a new e-mail message in Mail (the album won't appear, but the link to the song within iTunes Music Store will). When your friend gets your e-mail, he'll be able to click on the link and launch his copy of iTunes to take him right to the song. That's viral marketing at its best, baby!

   SAVING YOUR OWN CUSTOM EQ SETTINGS

iTunes has a built-in graphic equalizer (EQ) for adjusting the audio frequency (the tone quality) of your music to get the best quality sound from your speakers. This is particularly important to Power-Book and iBook users whose computers have such tiny little speakers that they possess a flat-tone quality enjoyed only by desert squirrels. To bring up the iTunes EQ, press Command-2. You can adjust the sliders manually (bass sliders on the left, midrange in the middle, and highs on the right) or use the built-in presets from the pop-up menu. If you've come up with a custom EQ setting that you want to save for future use, just choose Make Preset from the top of the built-in presets pop-up menu. It lets you name your preset,

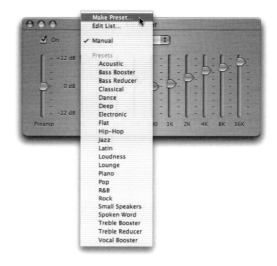

and then your named custom preset is added to the pop-up menu alphabetically.

   HOW TO SET A CUSTOM EQ FOR ANY INDIVIDUAL SONG

Okay, now you know how to EQ your overall system, but if your playlist contains jazz, hip hop, rock, R&B and classical, you'll find that having just one overall EQ setting ain't gonna cut it. Luckily, if you know this little-known tip, you can set a custom EQ for each song individually. Here's how: Press Command-J to bring up the View Options dialog, then click on the checkbox for Equalizer. When you click OK, it adds an Equalizer column on the right side of your playlist, and you can choose which custom EQ preset you want for each song from this pop-up list.

CONTROLLING ITUNES FROM THE DOCK

I covered this in the chapter on using the Dock, but since you might have turned right to this chapter, I wanted to make sure you didn't miss one of the most convenient iTunes features—the ability to control iTunes while it's minimized to the Dock. Just Control-click on its icon in the Dock and a pop-up list of controls (including the name and artist of the current song) appears, so you can start, stop, and change iTunes songs without having to bring iTunes to the front.

   THE ITUNES MUSIC STORE WISH LIST TRICK

The iTunes Music Store doesn't have a "wish list" feature (like Amazon.com) yet, but you can create your own using this little trick. First, start by creating a new folder on your desktop called "iTunes Wish List." Then, if you're browsing through the Music Store, and you run across a song (or album) you think you might want later, just click directly on the song's album cover and drag it into your iTunes Wish List folder. This creates a file that's a direct link to that song (or album) and you can get right back to that spot by simply double-clicking on it.

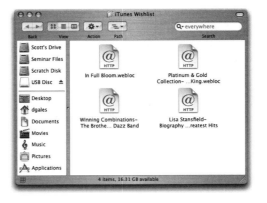

   GROOVIN' ON THE METERS

When you're playing a song in iTunes, the names of the current artist, song, and album slowly cycle in the status display at the top center of

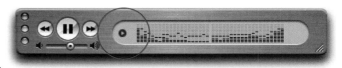

the iTunes window (provided that this info is included with your audio file, in the Tags section of the iTunes info palette). You can click once directly on the current item being displayed and it instantly changes to the next item in the list. In the left center of this status display is a tiny gray circle with a right-facing triangle in the center. Click on this tiny button, and the name of the song is replaced by a digital EQ meter. Having the EQ meters displayed is important because…uh…it's important because…uh…. Okay, they're not really important, but they look cool, and that should be reason enough to display them in appropriate social situations.

   ALL OF YOUR FAVORITE SONGS, IN ONE PLAYLIST, INSTANTLY

If you use iTune's rating system to rank how much you like each song (by assigning them one to five stars), you're just one click away from having iTunes create a playlist of just your absolute favorite songs. Here's how: Go under iTunes' File menu and choose New Smart Playlist. Then, in the Smart Playlist

dialog, change the first pop-up menu to My Rating. The second pop-up menu automatically changes to "is," and the Info field shows five rating stars. Click OK and a new playlist appears in your playlist (Source) column (ready for you to name) made up of nothing but your five-star-rated songs.

TIME WON'T LET ME WAIT

By default, the status display shows you
the elapsed time of the current song
(if you've played 30 seconds of your
song, it displays 0:30). However, if
you'd prefer it to show remaining time

(if you've played 30 seconds of a 3-minute song, it displays 2:30), click directly on the Elapsed
Time display and it switches to Remaining Time. Click again, and it shows the total time of the
entire song.

  STOPPING THE SONG INFO OVERLOAD

The song list window gives you so much
info, sometimes it seems a bit overwhelming
(especially if you're new to iTunes). But you
don't have to live with this "information overload," because you can tell iTunes which fields
you want visible by pressing Command-J to
bring up its View Options. When the View
Options pane appears, make sure only the
fields you want visible are checked (for example, I show only Song Name, Time, and Artist
in my song list).

  HOW TO PLAY DJ BY BROWSING

iTunes has a slick built-in song-sorting tool that lets you find songs by artist, by album, by genre, and more. So, if you're in the mood for nothing but Blink 182, you can have your song list display just their tunes. Once you do that, if you just want to hear their songs from a particular album, you can do that too. Or, in a broader sense, if you want to hear just jazz songs, you can have only the songs that you've tagged as jazz appear in the song list. You do this by first clicking on the Library button (in the Source list on the left), then the Browse button appears (it's the eye icon at the top right of the iTunes window.) When you click it, rather than giving you a long scrolling list view of all the songs in your library, it gives you something more like the Column view of a Finder window, with different category panes sorted by info you've entered (or that was embedded) in your music files. If you don't see the Genre column, go to the Preferences, under the iTunes menu, click on General, and then turn on Show Genre When Browsing.

   ORGANIZING SONGS ON YOUR HARD DISK

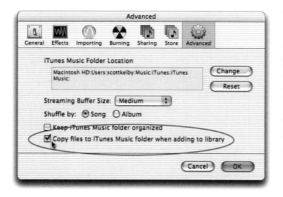

When you play a song that's on your hard disk, iTunes simply creates an alias to the original song file and places that alias in your iTunes music folder. So basically, the original songs can be scattered all over your hard disk, in different folders, etc. However, if you want to bring some order to your music world, iTunes can instead copy the songs into your iTunes folder (rather than just making aliases), which keeps all of your original song files organized in one central location. To do this, go under the iTunes menu, under Preferences, and choose Advanced at the top right of the dialog. Then, turn on the checkbox for Copy Files to iTunes Music Folder when Adding to Library.

GETTING "BETTER-THAN-MP3" QUALITY

MP3 is a great format for compressing audio to create smaller file sizes, but there's a trade-off—smaller file sizes mean a loss of quality due to compression. Although MP3 is the Web standard, when you're importing songs from a CD, you're not on the Web, so you can use a higher quality format, which gives you a much "closer to CD quality" audio encoding than MP3 provides. It's called AAC encoding, and you turn it on by going under the iTunes menu, choosing Preferences, and then clicking on the Importing icon. From the Import Using pop-up menu, choose AAC Encoder, and from that point on, all your songs imported from CD will use the highest quality encoding.

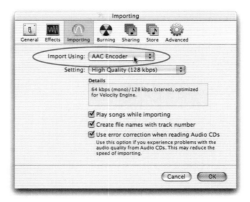

   GETTING ALL OF YOUR SONGS IN ONE PLACE

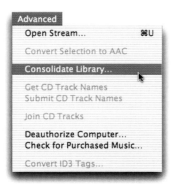

If, like most people, you have your songs in a dozen different places on your hard drive, you can bring instant order to your music world by going under the iTunes Advanced menu and choosing Consolidate Library. This copies all of your audio files from their current scattered locations into one central folder (your iTunes music folder), bringing an eerie sense of peace to your high-tech world.

   EDITING JUST ONE FIELD

If you don't want to enter scads of song info, and you only want to edit one item (like the band's name, song title, etc.), you don't need to go to the Get Info dialog—you can just click on the song you want to edit, then click once right on the field you want to edit in the Song Name list window. The name becomes highlighted and you can edit it right there. Press the Return key when you're done.

   "GOTCHAS" WHEN REARRANGING SONGS

Rearranging the order in which your songs play is easy—just click on a song and drag it to the position where you want it to appear—but there are three little catches (gotchas!) that might trip you up: (1) You have to be in a playlist—you can't change their order in the main Library window. (2) Once you're in a playlist (rather than the Library), to be able to rearrange their order by dragging, you must have your playlist sorted by track number (rather than by song, artist, album, etc.). To sort by track number, just click at the very top of the first column from the left (it's the only blank field header), and then you can drag songs into any order you'd like. (3) The third "gotcha" is that you can't do any of this if you have the Shuffle (random play) button turned on under the Controls menu, so turn that off before you begin sorting.

TREATING THE SONG WINDOW LIKE A FINDER WINDOW

You can pretty much think of the iTunes window like a Finder window set to List view, because they play by a lot of the same rules: You can stretch the window; you can change the order of the columns (except for the Song Name column—just like a Finder window); clicking on a column header

sorts by that field (by default, columns sort from A—Z, first to last, top to bottom, etc.—clicking the little arrow in the column header reverses the sort order [Z—A, last to first, etc.]); you change column width by clicking-and-dragging between headers, etc.

   WHICH SONG IS PLAYING RIGHT NOW?

To have iTunes highlight the song that's playing right now, just press Command-L.

   CRANKING IT UP/TURN IT DOWN

If you like, you can adjust iTunes' volume control from the keyboard. Press Command-Up Arrow to crank it, or Command-Down Arrow when the neighbors bang on the wall. Press Option-Command-Down Arrow to mute iTunes if the cops arrive, and press Command-H to hide your stash before you answer the door (kidding. Kind of).

   GETTING GEEKY WITH YOUR PLAYLIST

If you really want to put on a propeller beanie and have an iTunes geek-fest, go under the File menu and choose Export Song List. This exports a tab-delineated text file of your entire iTunes Library and playlists that you can open in your favorite spreadsheet or database, with all the song info sorted into fields. If you do this immediately after watching a *Star Trek TNG* repeat, a "Sad Social Life" extraction team is immediately dispatched to your home and they forcibly take you to the nearest rave.

GETTING PLUGGED IN TO THE VISUALIZER

If you're totally sucked in by the whole Visualizer thing (I know I joke about it, but it's really pretty cool), there are people out there creating their own iTunes visuals and you can download them from the Web (many are free) and import them into your copy of iTunes. Go to your Home folder and open your Library folder. Inside your Library folder, open the iTunes folder, and there you'll find a folder called iTunes Plug-ins. Drop your downloaded Visualizer plug-ins in there, and then relaunch iTunes. These new

Visualizer plug-ins now appear at the bottom of your Visualizer menu. Now, it's time to sit back, turn on the visuals, and fire up a fatty (again, just a joke).

   ## ITUNES FONT SIZING

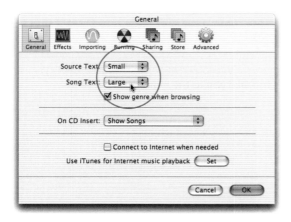

If the font in the iTunes song list appears too small to you, you can increase the font size by going under the iTunes menu, under Preferences, and clicking on the General icon. In the General preference pane, choose Large from the Song Text pop-up menu.

   THE PSYCHEDELIC BUTTON

If you're using iTunes and want to see what life was like for your parents when they were young, press Command-T (or click on the center button on the bottom right of the iTunes window). This turns on iTunes' Visualizer—a sync'd-to-music onscreen display that you'd expect to see projected behind bands like Cream and Jefferson Airplane during concerts back when people smoked anything that wasn't tied down. These visual effects make an LSD trip look relatively mild in comparison (at least, that's what my older brother Jeff says, and he should know). Personally, I like this psychedelic blast-from-the-past, and sometimes, I turn it on simply as a form of personal punishment. But as best as I can tell, the reason this mind-bending visual display is included in iTunes is that at some point, Apple must figure that all Mac users will grab a giant party bong and subsequently want to then (a) stare at some freaky colors for long periods of time, or (b) call Pizza Hut delivery. So far, I've done the "b" part quite a number of times, but I still haven't tried the "a" part. However, if I stare at those visuals long enough, if nothing else, it makes me want to burn my draft card.

   EXPANDING YOUR PSYCHEDELIA

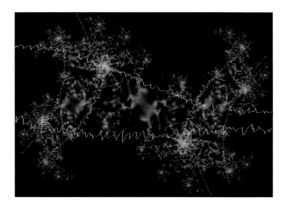

Watching the psychedelic visuals from within the iTunes window is somewhat interesting, but if you really want to get the full mushroom-induced effect, press Command-T, then Command-F, and the effect then takes over your entire screen (and perhaps your entire life).

SELLOUT TO THE GIANT CORPORATIONS

Want to really "mess" with people's heads while they're sucked into the endless vortex of iTunes' psychedelic visuals? Just press the letter "b" while it's turned on and the corporate logo of a giant Fortune 500 company will appear in the center of the visuals and stay there, reminding you that the world is really run by giant corporations and we're powerless to do anything but send them more money and follow their orders. (Okay, pressing "b" really just brings up a white Apple logo at center screen, but it sounds much more Orwellian to call it the corporate logo of a giant Fortune 500 company.)

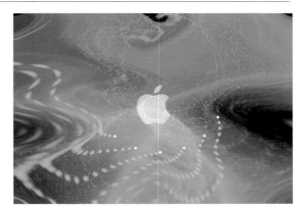

   ### PRETEND THE VISUALIZER MATTERS

Let's pretend for a moment that these cool visual effects are important. If they were, they'd need a set of options to control various aspects of their playback, right? Well, sadly, there are options for the Visualizer—and when they're running within the iTunes window, their Options button appears where the old "Browse" button used to be (in the upper right-hand corner of the window). They probably figure you don't need the Browse button because if you're watching the visuals, you're probably too stoned to start sorting your music

files, right? (Kidding. Just a joke, etc.) These options include adjusting the playback frame rate and displaying the frame rate—you know, critical stuff like that.

DUDE, WHO DID THIS SONG AGAIN?

Want to see not only the visual effects but also the song name and artist that you're zoning out to? They appear on screen for a few moments when you first start the Visualizer, but then they fade away. If you're busy ordering/eating your munchies and can't remember who did the song, or even its name (this is quite common), once the visuals are running, click on the Options button and in the Visualizer Options, turn on the checkbox for Always Display Song Info. Even cooler—if you add album art, that's displayed along with the name.

HELP FOR THE VISUALLY CHALLENGED

If you're really serious about iTunes' Visualizer (perhaps you're a dealer or own a head shop), you might as well learn how to make this puppy really jump through some hoops. While the Visualizer is running, press "?" (the question mark key) on your keyboard to bring up "Basic Visualizer Help"—a list of one-button shortcuts for various other features you can control. I know what you're thinking—"If it says 'Basic Help,' then somewhere there must be an 'Advanced Help,' right?" Right! Just press the "?" button again, and another screen appears that lists more one-button controls.

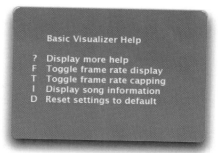

CONTROLLING YOUR EXPERIENCE

Are the colors you see during your Visualizer experience displeasing you? Is it, in effect, creating a "bad
trip?" If so, the next time you're running the Visualizer,
try mashing a few keys. Depending on which keys you
press, the color combinations and effects change in real
time, while they're happening on screen. For example,
if you press the letter "z," it steps you through different color combinations, but better yet—it displays the
names of these color schemes on screen. Seeing what

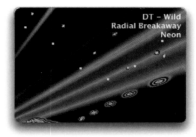

the Apple engineers named these color schemes gives an eerie sense of credibility to my
"drug-related" gag comments. For example, one color scheme is called "Electric Acid." Another
is called "Sunchemicals From a Queen Bee." Somebody call the cops! If you press the letter
"q," it changes the wireframe lines that dance to your music. Pressing the letter "a" changes
something (I know it's changing, because I see its name changing in the display, but I've yet to
figure out quite what it is; but I know after watching it for just a short time, I get a craving for a
bag of Cheetos™).

SAVING YOUR EXPERIENCE

If you use the keys in the previous tip to create your
own custom Visualizer and you come across just the
right combination to induce a momentary total loss of
equilibrium, you might want to save that combination
for future use (perhaps, as a party trick at Rick James'
house). Just hold the Shift key and choose a number key
where you want to save your custom preset. (You can
save up to 10 presets, using the numbers 0 through 9.)
Then, when you want to play "Tri-Cycle Directix Expand
X," just press Shift and the number where you saved it
and that visual appears on screen (e.g., Shift-2).

SUPER-FAST COLUMN VIEWS

The quickest way to choose which columns you want visible in the Song list window is to Control-click on any of the headers (such as Song Name, Time, Artist, etc.), and a pop-up list appears of all the different columns available for viewing. Just check the ones you want displayed.

   A PERFECTLY SIZED ITUNES WINDOW

Wouldn't it be nice if you could have iTunes resize itself to the perfect size—with no extra empty space at the bottom of your Song list, and just wide enough to show the columns you've chosen to be visible? Well, it can (I know, it's not much of a surprise after that lead-in). Just Option-click on the green Zoom button (in the upper left-hand corner of the iTunes window), and

it resizes to "the perfect size" (i.e., if your current playlist has only six songs, the player window will be only six songs deep).

TAGGIN' YOUR TUNES

All the background info for your iTunes music is stored in the Info pane. If you download MP3s from the Web, you already know how often song names, artists, and album information is partially or totally wrong (and, like this book, they're rife with typos). You can edit these "tags" by clicking on a song in your list, pressing Command-I, and clicking on the Info button. There, you can type in the right name (if necessary) and any other supporting info you want access to (artist, album title, genre, CD track number, and your own personal comments).

   AUTO-TAG—YOU'RE IT!

If you're not the type to go in and enter all the tag info manually, you can have iTunes automatically go the Web, research the song info (at the CDDB Internet audio database), and enter it into the Song Information Tag's field for you. (How cool is that?) There are only two catches: (1) It only works when you're importing songs from an audio CD in your Mac's CD drive, and (2) of course, you have to have an active Internet connection. To set up iTunes to do this automatic search, press Command-Y to bring up iTunes Preferences, click on the General icon at the top, and then click on the checkbox for Connect to Internet When Needed. If you prefer to do this manually every time you're importing a CD, go under the Advanced menu and choose Get CD Track Names from the Advanced menu, and it'll do its Internet thing.

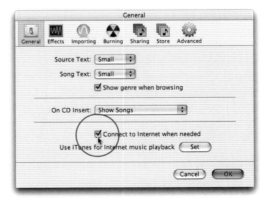

   OPENING ANY PLAYLIST IN ITS OWN WINDOW

If you'd like to have multiple playlists open at one time, or if you'd just like to have your playlist open in a separate window, double-click directly on the playlist's tiny icon (rather than single-clicking its name as usual).

   BALANCING YOUR VOLUME

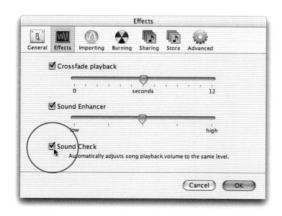

Have you ever had a situation (and I'll bet you have) where you set the volume to just the right level while playing one song, but another song comes on and is either way too loud or way too soft? Luckily, iTunes lets you balance the volume between songs with a simple preference setting: Just press Command-Y to bring up iTunes preferences, then click on the Effects icon. When the Effects pane appears, turn on the checkbox for Sound Check which, according to the dialog, "Automatically adjusts song playback volume to the same level."

SHORTCUT FOR CREATING SMART PLAYLISTS

Clicking on the Plus Sign button at the bottom-left corner of the iTunes window lets you create new playlists, but if you hold the Option key, you'll notice that the button changes to a "gear" icon, which gives you a quick way to create a Smart Playlist instead.

  SETTING YOUR ITUNES MUSIC STORE BUDGET

Afraid you might spend too much at the iTunes Music Store? (Hey, it's easy to get carried away with one-click downloads for only 99¢ a pop. Before you know it, you've got a $600 Visa bill.) Then, you might want to turn on the Shopping Cart feature, which puts all the songs that you want to purchase into a shopping cart that appears in your Source list on the left (rather than instantly downloading and charging as you go). That way, you can see a list of all of your songs before you buy any, and decide if you've gone over your budget (or, if you can add a few more because you're under budget). Just go under the iTunes menu, under Preferences, and click on the

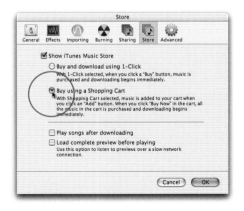

Store button. Then, turn on Buy Using a Shopping Cart and then at the Music Store, you'll notice that the Buy buttons beside each song have changed to Add. When you check out, all of your added songs appear in your shopping cart, and they don't get charged or downloaded until you click the Buy Now button.

LIKE THIS SONG? RATE IT FROM THE DOCK

If you're playing a song and decide you want to add or
change its rating (how much you like it based on a one- to
five-star ranking system), just Control-click on the iTunes
icon in the Dock and under My Rating, choose your rating.
It doesn't get much easier or faster than that!

   LISTENING TO SONGS WITHOUT COPYING THEM

By default, when you drag an audio file from
your desktop (or other Finder window) and
drop it into iTunes, it copies that entire file onto
your hard disk. However, if you just want to play
the song without making a permanent copy
on your drive (maybe it's an MP3 on a CD, on a
server, or on a removable FireWire drive), just
hold the Option key before you drag. That way,
it just points to the original audio file (like an
alias) rather than copying it.

GIVING 'EM A TASTE OF YOUR TASTE

If you're on a network with other users, you can set up iTunes so they can see and play music from your playlists, and best of all, you can choose which of your playlists they can access from their iTunes Source list. Since you control which playlists are "shared" with other users on the network, you can create a fake playlist with a bunch of critically acclaimed music, so they'll think, "Hey, this guy's pretty heady" while your real "un-shared" playlists are full of Britney Spears and *NSYNC. To share selected playlists, go under the iTunes menu, under Preferences, and click on the Sharing button. Then, turn

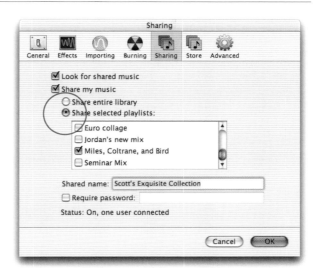

on the Share My Music checkbox, and below that, choose Share Selected Playlists then choose which playlists you want to share (like Miles, Coltrane, and Bird rather than Britney, Justin, and Hanson). Also, it's really helpful if you rank your songs so other users know which ones to start with.

I SHALL CALL IT...MINI-TUNES

If you don't need all the bells and whistles that the screen real-estate–hogging iTunes interface offers, you can request a much more compact version that I call "Mini-tunes" (I shall call it... "Mini-tunes"). You create the Mini-tunes version of iTunes by click-ing once on the Zoom control button (the green one) in the upper

left-hand corner of the iTunes window, which shrinks the iTunes interface down to just a horizontal bar. Then, drag the bottom right-hand corner of the Mini-tunes window to the left. This hides the small status display and leaves only the Rewind, Play, and Fast Forward buttons. If you feel that it still takes up too much space, seriously—it's time to buy a big-ger monitor.

   BETTER SONG PREVIEWS FOR DIAL-UP USERS

One of the absolutes coolest and most useful features of the iTunes Music Store is the 30-second song preview you can play. It makes finding the right song infinitely easier, and it's fun. That is, unless you're using the Music Store with a dial-up Internet connection: A little bit of the preview downloads, you play that little bit, then it stops as the next chunk downloads. If you're using dial-up, you can change one preference setting that will do away with this. Go under the iTunes menu, under Preferences, and choose Store. In the Store prefs, choose Load

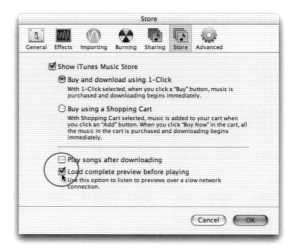

Complete Preview before Playing. That way, after just a few seconds, you'll get the full uninterrupted preview.

   FROM CD TO PLAYLIST IN ONE CLICK

When you're importing songs from a CD, generally the process goes like this: You import the song into your Library, and from there, you decide which songs go in which playlists. Well, you can go straight from the CD right into the playlist you want (saving a step) just as easily. Just insert the CD, then click on a song on the CD, and drag it straight to the playlist where you want it to appear. It is then imported right into that playlist (with the original appearing in the Library automatically).

THE DANGER OF ADDING ALBUM ARTWORK

You can add the artwork from the album the original song came from, but I don't recommend doing this, unless you're retired, or you're in college with a really easy schedule, because once you start—you can't stop. I killed an entire weekend adding album artwork to all my songs, and now when I import a new song, I go searching all over to find the album artwork (much of which is obscure disco club hits from the late '70s and early '80s). Before I tell you how, just remember: I warned you what an intense productivity killer this will become. Start by pressing Command-G (which is the shortcut for "Show Artwork"). Then, go to the Web and track down the artwork for your song. You can start at CDNOW.com, or try AllMusic.com. When (if) you find the album cover, just drag

it straight from the Web page onto iTunes' Artwork area, and iTunes automatically scales it down to fit. Now you can kiss your weekend goodbye.

   CLEANING UP BAD AUDIO WHEN IMPORTING

If you're importing music from scratched or otherwise trauma-ridden CDs, iTunes can sometimes help hide the pain. Go under the iTunes menu, under Preferences, and click on the Importing button. Then, turn on Use Error Correction when Importing Audio CDs. iTunes then tries importing at a higher quality, using a slower method of importing, but if it works and cleans up the track, the extra time spent is worth it.

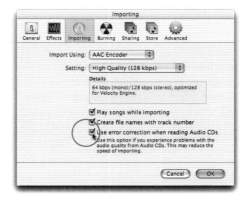

   KEEPING RELATED SONGS TOGETHER WHEN IMPORTING

Let's say you're importing songs from Boston's Greatest Hits, and although the song "Long Time" was released as a single, on the album there's a pre-song called (aptly enough) "Foreplay." These two songs are really one big song with just a brief moment of silence between them (as a transition between "movements," if you will). However, when they get imported into iTunes, they could come in as two separate tracks with a big gap, ruining an important moment in classic rock history. To keep two "related" tracks together as one track when you're importing them, before you import them, Command-click on both tracks, then go under the Advanced menu, and choose Join CD Tracks. A little join icon appears between the two songs, and they'll now import as one song. If you decide later that "Foreplay/Long Time" should be two separate songs, you can choose Unjoin CD Tracks (but you'll feel somewhat guilty).

   THE "ALMOST-AN-IPOD-IN-YOUR-CAR" TRICK

If you don't have a cassette player in your car, there's no simple way to connect your iPod to your car's stereo. But my buddy Terry White (a certified iPod freak) came up with the next best thing. Here's his plan: You create a giant playlist with all your favorite songs (let's say it's 340 songs, and if you're like Terry, it's mostly Spice Girls, Hanson, and 98º).

Instead of putting the 340 songs on your iPod, click on your playlist, hit the Shuffle button, then press the Burn Disc button. Now, I know what you're thinking, "Scott, you're not going to fit 340 songs on a CD." That's right, unless they're very, very short songs and that's the secret (kidding). No, iTunes creates a series of CDs. When the first one is full, it will eject it—you pop in another, and it'll keep burning CD after CD until all 340 songs are burned. Now, you can listen to your iTunes playlist in your car without your Mac or an iPod.

electric avenue

DIGITAL HUB APPLICATIONS

When you hear the word "multimedia," what does it really mean? Isn't "multimedia" one of those buzz words that are now so

Electric Avenue

the ilife applications and other digital stuff

"mid-'90s" that they belong with other lame mid-'90s terms like "information super highway" and "cyberspace?" Absolutely. When I think of the word "multimedia," I think of someone using a slide projector and a cassette player. (Say it to yourself, "Get ready for my multimedia presentation!" It just sounds so 1996.) That's why I chose to use Apple's way cooler made-up term "Digital Hub" for this chapter. Wait a minute? Isn't iTunes (which selfishly has its own separate chapter) considered one of the "Digital Hub" applications? Well…yes. So, if you want to pretend, just for the sake of this exercise, that the iTunes chapter and this Digital Hub chapter are really just one big chapter, that's perfectly fine by me. Yes, but couldn't you lump the two chapters together and use the all-encompassing term "Multimedia Applications" as a chapter head? No. Were you even listening at the beginning of this intro?

   iMovie 3: **SHUTTLING THROUGH YOUR MOVIE**

The Rewind button in iMovie 3 takes you all the way back to the beginning of your movie, but if you just want to back up a little bit, there's a keyboard shortcut that gives you a live rewind (and by that, I mean it will play your movie in reverse) until you get to the spot where you want to be. Just press Command-[(Left Bracket) to start the backward playback, then press it again to stop: once to start the Playhead in motion, and press it once again to stop. For a live fast forward, press Command-] (Right Bracket).

   iMovie 3: **THE CLIP VIEWER'S VISUAL CUES**

If you've adjusted the speed or direction of a clip, the Clip Viewer gives you a visual cue with tiny black icons just above the clip itself (in the upper-right corner of the clip's "slide mount"), to let you know just what you did. Two right-facing arrows show that you sped the clip up. A vertical line with one right-facing arrow lets you know the clip has been slowed down (for a slow-motion effect). A left-facing arrow tells you you've reversed the clip (it plays backward). If you've added a built-in iMovie effect (like Black & White, Sepia Tone, etc.), a little checkerboard pattern appears. If you add a title to your clip, expect a "T" to appear.

iMovie 3: UNDO, UNDO, UNDO, UNDO, UNDO, UNDO +4

If you realize you've made a mistake while in iMovie, as long as you catch your mistake fairly quickly (and before you empty the Trash), you may be in luck. That's because iMovie gives you 10 undos. Just press Command-Z again and again until you come to your mistake, or you reach the 10th undo (which ironically is usually just one step before your mistake). (*Note*: In Panther, the undos seem to be actually unlimited, but if you get to 10 and it stops, you didn't hear that from me.)

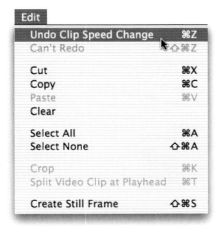

  iMovie 3: GETTING BACK CROPPED-OUT SCENES

When you crop a clip in iMovie, the cropped portion is put in the Trash and you can't access those cropped-away areas. That is, unless you know this little secret—if you need to get back to the original clip you imported, perfectly intact, believe it or not you can, as long as you haven't emptied the Trash. Just click on the cropped clip in the Timeline or Clip Viewer, then go under the Advanced menu and choose Restore Clip. A dialog appears, telling you how much you'll get back, and asking you to OK the process. Click Restore, and the original clip is back in its entirety. This even works on title screens created, and then cropped, right from within iMovie 3.

   iMovie 3: LOCKING YOUR SOUND FX INTO PLACE

If you've meticulously added sound effects to your movie, and you've sync'd them to events in your clips, you might think twice about inserting a clip in your movie because it would slide all the video clips that come after your insertion point down to accommodate this new clip—making your movie longer—but leaving all of your audio clips in their original spots. Now all of your sound fx will be out of sync by the amount of time your imported clip takes. To get around this, before you import your clip, Shift-click on each sound effect in your audio track, then press Command-L to "lock" your audio clips to your video clips. That way, when you insert your new clip, and all the video clips move over to accommodate the new track, all the sound fx clips move right along with them.

   iMovie 3: MOVING CROP MARKERS WITH PRECISION

Once you have Crop Markers in place, you can be very precise in their placement by using the Arrow keys on your keyboard to position them right where you want them.

iMovie 3: **MULTIPLE CLIPS IN THE SAME MOVIE**

If you want the same clip to appear in multiple places within the same movie, here's a quick trick to make it fast and easy. Click on the clip in the Clip viewer, then press Command-C to copy the clip into memory. Then go up to the Clips pane, click on any random clip up there, and press Command-V (Paste). Don't worry—it doesn't paste over that clip, instead it pastes a copy of the clip right beside it. (In the example shown here, I copied Clip 05 from the Clip viewer, then I clicked on Clip 47 in the Clips pane, and hit Paste.) Now, you can drag this copy down to your Clip viewer. If you need more copies, use the same trick.

 iMovie 3: **PRECISE NAVIGATION**

To fast forward one frame at a time, press the Right Arrow key. To rewind one frame at a time, press the Left Arrow key. To move 10 frames at a time, just add the Shift key.

   iMovie 3: CONTROLLING AUDIO FADE INS/FADE OUTS

In iMovie 3, if you want to fade in (or out) your background audio track, you've got pretty decent control over exactly when, and how long it takes, for that fade-in/out to happen. The first step is to click on the Edit Volume checkbox just below the Timeline viewer. When you do this, a line appears in the center of your audio tracks. This line represents the volume of your audio track, so to create a fade-in, click once at the point where you want the audio to be at full volume (and a point is added at that spot along with a tiny red square at its left, as shown below). Drag the little red square to where you want the fade-in to begin, and then click at the beginning of your audio track and drag straight downward. The length of time between the beginning of your audio track and the little yellow point is how long your fade-in will be. If you want a longer fade-in, drag the yellow point to the right.

   iMovie 3: CONTROLLING SOUND FX VOLUMES

If you import sound effects (or use the built-in sound effects), you can control the volume of each sound effect individually. Just click directly on the sound effect you want to adjust (in the Timeline viewer), then move the main volume slider to the level you'd like the effect to play. iMovie keeps track of each sound effect's individual volume and adjusts them accordingly as your movie plays.

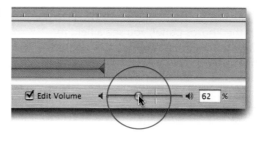

iMovie 3: **SENDING IMPORTED CLIPS STRAIGHT TO THE TIMELINE**

By default, imported clips appear on the Clips pane, and then once imported, you can drag them individually to the Timeline viewer. However, if you'd like, you can change one preference setting and iMovie 3 sends your clips straight to the Timeline viewer instead. You do this by going under the iMovie menu, under Preferences. In the Import section, under New Clips Go To, choose Movie Timeline, and from now on, all imported clips appear in the Timeline viewer, rather than the Clips pane.

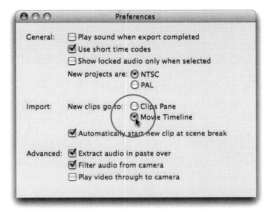

 iMovie 3: **CONTROLLING HOW LONG STILLS STAY ON SCREEN**

When you import a still image into iMovie 3 (from Photoshop, a scanned image, a screen capture, etc.), you can determine how long the still image stays on screen. Just click on the image in the Timeline or Clip viewer, and then click on the Photos button right above the Timeline, and in the upper portion of the Photos panel, you see a field for Duration. Highlight that field and type in any duration you'd like. You can also determine how much you'd like to zoom in on the photo. After you enter the amount of time and zoom you

want, click on either the Apply or Update button (it's Apply the first time you make a change to a photo). When you're there, you can turn off the Ken Burns effect for that still (if you like) using the checkbox at the top of the Photos panel. From now on when you import a still, it comes in at that duration and zoom. You can easily change the settings by going back to the Photos panel.

   iMovie 3: **VISUAL TRANSITION CUES**

Once you drag a Transition into your Timeline or Clip viewer, the icon of the Transition can sometimes give you a visual cue as to which Transition you dragged. Just look at the little arrows in the square window in the center of the Transition icon for a hint. To see the name of the Transition, click on it. If the default name doesn't help you (like the name "Push"), double-click on the Transition and enter a new name (like "1st clip slides 2nd clip over").

   iMovie 3: **GETTING MORE AUDIO TRACKS**

In the Timeline, there are three tracks where audio can go: The top timeline where the video clips are located also supports any audio from your digital camcorder's microphone that was captured when you shot your clips. The second track is usually used for sound effects or a narrator track. The third is usually used for background music. So you'd think you'd be limited to three tracks; but actually, iMovie 3 lets you continue to import and lay multiple audio tracks right over one another. For example, if you have a music score on the bottom track and you import a sound effect, you notice that its little bar icon appears right on top of your score track's icon. It also plays right over it—not knocking it out—but playing right along with it. This enables you to use more than just the three tracks it appears you're limited to.

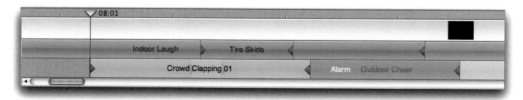

iMovie 3: BEATING THE SORTING SLUDGE

If you've got a movie with a lot of different clips in your Clip viewer, dragging a clip from one end of your movie to the other can take what seems like forever, while you sludge through clip after clip dragging your way down to where you want it. But there's a much faster way—instead, drag the clip out of the clip viewer and drop it on an empty space up in the Clips pane. Then, use the scroll bar below your Clip viewer to move quickly to the spot where you want your clip to appear. Now, you can simply drag-and-drop your clip from the Clips pane back down to the Clip viewer, right where you want it in less than half the time.

   ## iMovie 3: MUTING YOUR CAMERA'S AUDIO TRACK

If you're putting a music track behind your movie and you don't want to hear the audio that was captured by your digital camcorder's built-in microphone, you can turn off the audio track for your camera clips. Just go to the Timeline viewer, and at the far right of the viewer, uncheck the top checkbox.

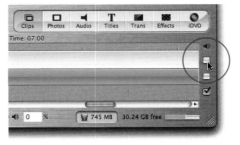

   iPhoto: **GETTING A MINI SLIDESHOW**

You already know that if you create a slideshow in iPhoto, it takes over your full screen, but there's a little-known trick that lets you create a smaller slideshow in its own floating window. Just click on the Album you want for your slideshow, then click on the Slideshow button. This brings up a window where you pick the song that goes with your slideshow. Pick your song, hold the Control-key, then click on the Play Slideshow button. Now, your slideshow appears in its own floating window.

   iPhoto: **PHOTOGRAPHER'S BASIC BLACK**

There's a background that's very popular with photographers for organizing their photos. It's basic black. Using black as your background gives you that "artsy photographer" look that artsy photographers love. To get that look, go under the iPhoto menu and choose Preferences. Drag the Background slider to the far left (to black), then it's up to you whether you want your thumbnails to appear with a white border (choose Border) or without (choose No Border).

iPhoto: **MAKING SLIDESHOW MOVIES**

This is one of my favorite iPhoto tips because it lets you create a self-contained QuickTime movie slideshow, complete with music and a dissolve transition, and the file size of this movie is surprisingly small, making it great for posting slideshows on the Web. Here's how it's done: Just click on the album you want for your movie slideshow, then click on the Slideshow button. When the music window appears, choose your music but don't click Play. Instead, click Save Settings (this closes the window). Then, go under the File menu and choose Export. In the Export window, click on the QuickTime button. Set the options for how you'd like your movie to look (size, how long each slide appears, background color, etc.),

then click Export. That's it—you've got a QuickTime movie slideshow with music.

   iPhoto: **LISTING YOUR MOST RECENT PHOTOS FIRST**

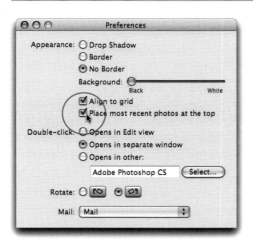

For some reason I can't figure out, by default, iPhoto displays the thumbnails of your oldest photos at the top of the main Organize window, so to get to the most recent photos you imported, you have to scroll all the way to the bottom. If you'd like the convenience of having your most recent photos at the top, go under the iPhoto menu, under Preferences, and click on Place Most Recent Photos at the Top.

iPhoto: DUMPING THE SHADOW

You know that little drop shadow that appears behind your thumbnail images in the Photo Viewing Area? If it gets on your nerves, you can ditch it by pressing Command–, to bring up iPhoto's Preferences. In the Preferences dialog, under Appearance, click on the Drop Shadow button and the shadow effect is removed and replaced by a thin white border around the thumbnail of your photo. While you're there, you can change the background color behind your thumbnails from white to any shade of gray or solid black by using the Background slider in the Appearance section.

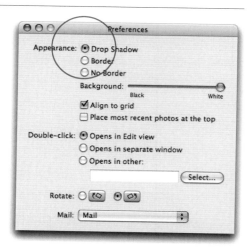

   iPhoto: EDITING IPHOTO IMAGES IN PHOTOSHOP

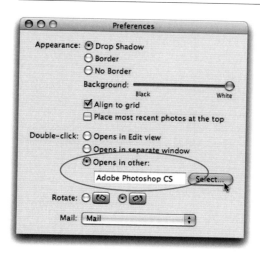

iPhoto lets you adjust a variety of aspects of your image, from tonal adjustments to removing red eye, in iPhoto's built-in image editor. However, if you prefer to edit your images in another application (such as Adobe Photoshop or Photoshop Elements), you can configure iPhoto to launch the editing application of your choice when you double-click on the image inside iPhoto. You do this by pressing Command–, to bring up iPhoto's Preferences dialog. In the Prefs dialog, where it says Double-Click, click on the Open in Other button, navigate to the application you want to designate as your editing app, and then click OK. Now when you double-click a photo, your photo opens in your designated image-editing application.

iPhoto: **GETTING PHOTOS FROM YOUR DRIVE INTO IPHOTO**

If you're new to iPhoto and you want to import photos from your hard drive, the natural thing to do is click on the Import button at the bottom of the Photo Viewing area, right? The Import toolbar appears, but unless you have a digital camera connected to your Mac, the Import button is gray. To get those images from your hard drive right into iPhoto, skip the Import button and instead go under the File menu and choose Import. A standard Open dialog appears so you can navigate to the folder of images you want to import. Of course, there's an even faster way—just drag and drop the photos right into iPhoto's Album pane.

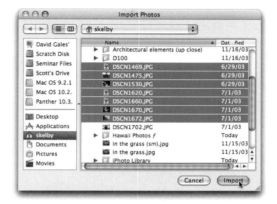

   iPhoto: **SKIPPING THE NEW ALBUM BUTTON**

If you want to start a new album, skip the New Album button. You can save time by just selecting one (or more) images that you want in your new album, and then dragging them over to the Album pane—a new album is created for you automatically.

 iPhoto: **WHAT TO DO WHEN ALL GOES WRONG**

If you've edited, cropped, and otherwise adjusted an image in iPhoto and, after looking at the results, you wish you really hadn't, you can actually start over—from scratch—and get back your clean un-retouched original image. You do this by selecting the image, going under the File menu, and choosing Revert to Original. Okay, but what if you set up iPhoto to let you edit your image in another application, such as Photoshop? Believe it or not—Revert to Original still works.

 iPhoto: **ROTATING IN THE OPPOSITE DIRECTION**

When you press the Rotate Image button, by default, it rotates your image counterclockwise. If you want to rotate your image clockwise, hold the Option key before you click the Rotate button.

iPhoto: **DEALING WITH LONG COMMENTS**

iPhoto lets you add comments to your photos, and you can use these comments to help you sort, categorize, or just make notes about a particular photo. These comments are entered in the Comments field, which appears in a field below the Info panel. (If you don't see the Info panel, click on the button with the little "i" on it on the bottom left-hand side.) If you add a long comment for a particular photo, iPhoto accommodates you, but you won't be able to scroll down and see your entire comment because the Comments field doesn't have scroll bars. There's only one way to see your entire comment—and that's to click on the little circle at the top of the Info panel and drag upward to make more of your comment visible.

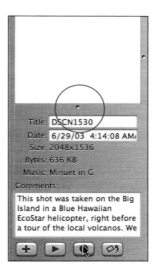

iPhoto: **PUTTING YOUR COVER SHOT INSIDE THE BOOK**

There will be times when you want the photo you chose for the cover to also appear inside your book (perhaps because you want to add a different caption, or you want to pair it with another photo inside, or maybe you want to show it without a caption at all). To

do this, all you have to do is duplicate the photo. You do this by going back to the Organize window, clicking on the photo you want to duplicate and pressing Command-D. This creates a duplicate and when you go to Book, you see your cover shot, and a duplicate in your book's layout.

  iPhoto: **CHANGING FONTS IN BOOK MODE**

If you're creating a book in Book mode, you can edit the font used in any page by highlighting the text and then Control-clicking on it. Click on Font, Show Fonts on the pop-up menu that appears, and now you can set the font, size, type style, and type color of your choice.

   iPhoto: **CUSTOMIZING THE EDIT TOOLBAR**

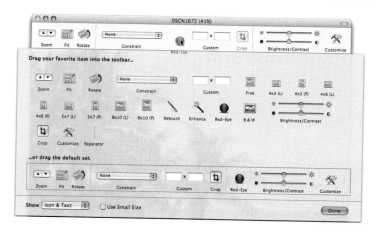

If you want more control over editing your images in iPhoto, press Command–, to bring up the Preferences window, and where it says Double-Click, choose Separate Window. Then, when you double-click a photo to edit it, your image opens into a different environment, giving you more control over your editing process, including the ability to customize the toolbar that appears at the top of the window. Just Control-click on the toolbar, and a pop-up menu appears where you can choose Customize Toolbar. This brings up a large sheet full of different tools for different tasks, and it works very much like customizing the toolbar in Finder windows—just drag the icons you want in your toolbar up to it. To reorder the tools, just drag their icons, and to remove a tool, just drag it off the bar.

iPhoto: **EDITING IN PHOTOSHOP WITHOUT SETTING PREFS**

Earlier, we showed how to set up iPhoto to let you edit your photos in a separate image-editing application (such as Photoshop) by changing your iPhoto Preferences. But here's a great tip if you only occasionally want to edit your photos in a separate application: Just drag the thumbnail of your photo right from the Photo Viewing area onto the Photoshop icon right in the Dock, and your image opens in Photoshop (or of course, you can drag it to any other image-editing program just as easily, but really, why would you?).

   iPhoto: **SUPERSIZING THAT PHOTO**

If you want to quickly see a photo from your Photo Viewing area at a very large size, just click on the Organize tab, and then in the toolbar at the bottom, click on the Desktop button. Your selected image is set as your desktop image and takes over the entire screen (and it's huge!).

iChat AV: GETTING A TRANSCRIPT OF YOUR CHAT

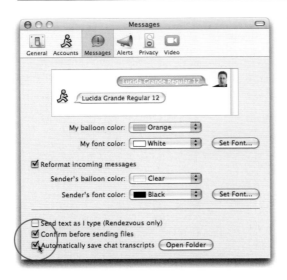

There are a dozen reasons why you might want a written log of your text chats; maybe someone gave you instructions, a recipe, or just typed a bunch of stuff that cracks you up. Well, luckily, you can ask iChat to keep a running log of your text chats—go under the iChat menu, to Preferences, then click on the Messages icon, and turn on Automatically Save Chat Transcripts.

iChat AV: A BUDDY IN YOUR DOCK

This is one of those things that just make you smile—if you're chatting with someone and you minimize their chat window to the Dock (maybe they're taking a break for a moment, for a snack, etc.), their buddy photo shows up in your Dock as a Dock icon (as shown top left, where my good friend Terry White is killing some time in my Dock). When your chat buddy comes back and sends you a message, a tiny iChat AV icon slowly blinks on and off to get your attention (as shown in the bottom capture).

iChat AV: **KEEPING YOUR CAMERA FROM GOING TO SLEEP**

I picked up this great tip from Scott Sheppard over at OSXFAQ.com and it's for people who don't use iChat AV with Apple's iSight, but instead use their own digital camcorder. The problem: After about five minutes, most commercial camcorders go to sleep automatically to preserve battery life. The solution: Remove the DV tape from the camcorder and it stops the camera from ever going to sleep. I never would have thought of that. Thanks, Mr. Sheppard.

   iChat AV: **AVOIDING UNWANTED CHATS**

If you have a lot of buddies in your Buddy List, you can wind up with a lot of incoming chats, which is cool if you're sitting around doing nothing; but if you're trying to get some work done, it can drive you crazy. Here's how to narrow the list of who can get through (so you can get some work done). Press Command-, (comma key) to bring up iChat's Preferences, then click on the Privacy icon at the top. You can go one of two ways: (1) Click on Allow Specific People, then click the Edit List button. Going this route,

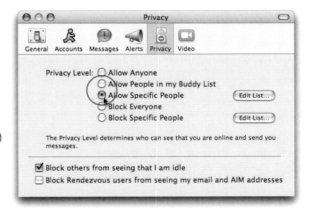

in the Edit List window, you enter the e-mail names of only the people you want to know you're online. To the rest of the people in your Buddy List (and the rest of the world), you're offline. Or (2) Choose Block Specific People, and click the Edit List button to enter the people who, if they chatted with you, would drive you crazy. Either way, only the people you want to know you're online will know.

iChat AV: **BEATING THE 5-MB E-MAIL LIMIT**

If you're sending someone an e-mail with an attachment that's larger than 5 MB, you can almost bet that it's going to get bounced back because their server has a 5-MB limit for incoming e-mails. So, how do you get around this? Use iChat AV to send the file, since it has no file size limits. Start a chat with the person you want to e-mail, then simply drag-and-drop the file you want to send right onto their photo in your Buddy List. How cool is that!

iChat AV: **IGNORING THE FREAKS**

If you're in a public chat with several people, and one of them starts to really get on your nerves (in other words, they're a PC user), you can ask iChat to completely ignore their comments by going to the list of participants (in the Sidebar), clicking on their name, and then going under the Buddies menu and choosing Ignore. From that point on, their comments will no longer appear in the chat window. In short: You dissed them (by using "dissed," I picked up incredible street cred with people still stuck in the '90s).

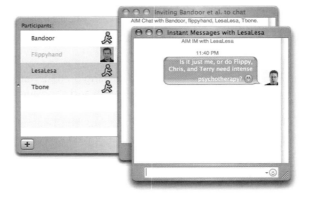 iChat AV: **SENDING YOUR HOME MOVIES VIA ICHAT**

If you're using your own DV camcorder with iChat AV, you can use
it to play pre-recorded video tapes
to the person you're chatting with
(perfect for sharing home movies).
Just switch your DV camcorder from
Camera to Video Playback; put in
the DV tape you want them to see,
and press the play button on your
camcorder. The smaller inset preview displays the video tape you're
playing, while you'll see the person's
reaction to the video in the main
window (as shown here).

   iChat AV: **PULLING SOMEONE INTO A PRIVATE CHAT**

If you've got a group chat going,
and you want to pull someone aside
into a private chat (so you can make
fun of someone else in the chat),
make sure you have the Participant
pane open by going under the View
menu to Show Chat Participants.
Then, just double-click on their
name in the list and they'll be
invited to a private chat outside the
current chat. You can also double-
click on their name in the Buddy List
to invite them to a private chat.

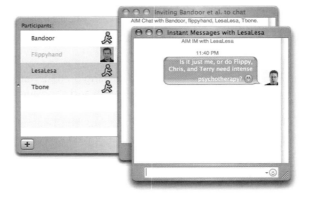

   iChat AV: AVOIDING LATE-NITE AUDIO CHATS

If you're working late at night and the spouse and kids are in bed, you may not want one of your buddies calling you for an audio chat. If that's the case, go under the Audio menu and turn off Microphone Enabled. Now, when they look at you in their Buddy List, the green Audio Chat button is hidden, and if they want you, they'll have to text chat.

   iChat AV: ADDING A BUDDY FAST (WITHOUT ALL THE EXTRA INFO)

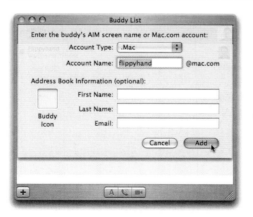

When you add a buddy to your Buddy List, it looks like you have to enter all of their Address Book info, but in reality, that's totally optional. To add a buddy quickly, just click on the Plus Sign at the bottom-left corner of the Buddy List, and when the Address Book dialog appears, just click New Person. When the Add a Buddy window appears, just enter their chat address and click OK; you can skip all the other info.

iChat AV: **THE TRICK TO GETTING LINE BREAKS**

When you're doing a text chat, if you're typing and press Return, it doesn't give you a line break—it sends your message. If you want a line break, just press Option-Return instead.

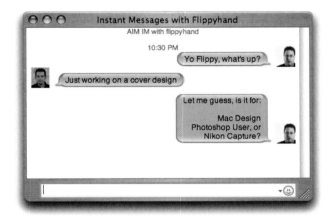

iChat AV: **QUICK WAY TO CUSTOMIZE YOUR BACKGROUND**

Want to put a background photo behind your chat window in iChat? Just drag-and-drop the photo you'd like as a background right into your message window and it appears behind your text. If the photo is smaller than the window, the photo will tile (repeat) automatically, just as in a Web browser. To delete it (if it's too busy—like the one shown here), go under the View menu and choose Clear Background.

iChat AV: POPPING THE BALLOONS (QUICK VIEW CHANGE)

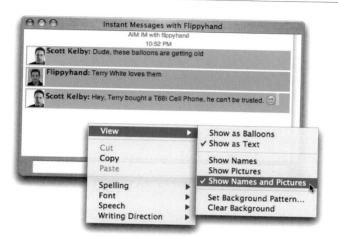

Want to view just text, just photos, both at the same time, or toggle back and forth? Just Control-click within your message window (where the bubbles appear). A pop-up menu appears, and under the View submenu, you can choose how you'd like your chat messages displayed.

iChat AV: A BUBBLE OF A DIFFERENT COLOR

Don't like the default color of your "dialog bubble?" You can change it by going under the iChat menu, and choosing Preferences. When the Preferences window appears, click on the Messages icon and in that pane, choose your desired color from the My Balloon Color pop-up menu. While you're there, why not pick a cooler font for your chat, and even your font color? You can also change the color of incoming chat balloons so they color-coordinate with yours. Be sure to tell your therapist about this aspect of your chat life. It will answer a lot of questions.

iChat AV: **PUTTING LIVE LINKS INTO YOUR CHAT**

In previous versions of iChat, if you wanted to put a live link into your chat messages, you had to bring up a special screen. Now, all you have to do is type in the address of the site you want them to click on (you don't even have to add the "http://" to the address). When they see the link, they can click on it and it launches their browser and load that site.

   iChat AV: **GETTING YOUR MESSAGES ONCE YOU'VE QUIT ICHAT**

One of the coolest things about iChat AV is that you don't have to have it up and running to get instant messages. Start by lauching iChat AV, then go under the iChat menu, choose Preferences, and click on the General icon. When the General pane appears, turn on Show Status Bar in Menu Bar to add an iChat pop-down menu to your menu bar. In this menu, choose Available as your status. Back in the iChat Preferences, click on the Alerts icon, then under Event,

choose Message Received. That way, iChat notifies you when you receive a message, so you can close it. Now, how will it alert you that a new message has been received? That's where the fun begins. Click the Speak Text checkbox and iChat verbally tells you you've got a message (there's even a field for you to type in what you want it to say). If you're afraid that won't get your attention, click on the checkbox for Bounce Icon in the Dock. If that's still not enough no-tification, click the checkbox for Send Repetitive 110-Volt Electric Shocks Via Keyboard. (Okay, that last one isn't really in iChat, but don't ya think it should be?)

   DVD Player: **THE SUBTLE CONTROL DIFFERENCES**

It seems that it would make sense for Apple's DVD player to share the same keyboard shortcuts as the QuickTime player, since they're both motion-graphics players, and they're both from Apple. Ah, if life were only that simple. While the Up/Down Arrow keys work for controlling the volume in the QuickTime player, you have to press Command-Up/Down Arrow to control the volume in the DVD player (the same volume shortcuts as iTunes). And while you mute the QuickTime player by pressing Option-Down Arrow, you have to press Option-Command-Down Arrow to mute the DVD player. Thankfully, one important command is the same no matter which player you're using—pressing the Spacebar starts or pauses movies in the DVD player.

   DVD Player: **GETTING TO THE MAIN MENU DURING THE MOVIE**

One of the most important keyboard shortcuts to me is the ability to get back to the main DVD menu while the DVD is already playing. To get there, just press Command-~ (the key just above the Tab key), and it cycles you back to the DVD's main menu.

DVD Player: **CONTROLLER MAXIMUS (THE HIDDEN CONTROLS)**

If you're wondering whether the DVD player is missing some DVD functionality, you're only half right. It does have the ability to access DVD controls, such as slow motion, subtitling, camera angles, language, etc., but for the sake of space considerations, they're tucked away. To bring these buttons into view, double-click on the little gray lines on the right center of the Player and the Player expands to show two additional rows of buttons.

   DVD Player: **GOING VERTICAL**

Tired of the boring horizontal player? Maybe it's time to get vertical. Just press Option-Command-C and a vertical version of the player appears. To return to the horizontal player, press the same shortcut.

   DVD Player: **BOOKMARKING YOUR SPOT**

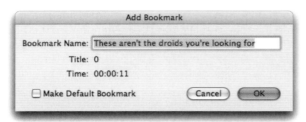

One of the coolest things Apple added to the DVD player in Panther is the ability to bookmark your spot while you watch a DVD and if you have to stop, or eject the DVD, when you re-insert the disc, it gives you the option of starting from the beginning or starting where you bookmarked. To bookmark a particular spot while a DVD is playing, just press Command-= (equals key) and that spot is bookmarked. A dialog appears asking you to name your bookmark. Click OK, and when you insert that DVD again, you'll have the option to start from your bookmarked spot.

   DVD Player: **USING AND EDITING BOOKMARKS**

You can actually set more than one bookmark, and there's even a bookmarks submenu, so you can set multiple bookmarks and jump to your favorite bookmarks any time. Once you've saved some bookmarks, to use them, just go the DVD player's Go menu, under Bookmarks, and choose the bookmark you want. You can also edit and manage your bookmarks by going under the Controls menu and choosing Edit Bookmarks. This brings up a window where you can rename, delete, and choose one bookmark as your default, so when you reinsert the DVD, you have the choice of jumping to that default bookmark.

DVD Player: **PUTTING CAPTIONS IN THEIR OWN WINDOW**

Imagine having the ability to put captions in their own separate windows. Then, imagine why in the world anyone would want to do this? Not coming up with anything? Me either. Nevertheless, here's how to do it: Go under the Controls menu, under Closed Captioning,

and choose Turn On (if it's not already on), then under the same Closed Captioning menu, choose Separate Window.

   DVD Player: **CONFIGURING THE PLAYER FOR DVD TRAINING USE**

If you use your Mac's DVD player mostly for educational purposes, (like watching Photoshop-training DVDs from PhotoshopVideos.com, hint, hint), you probably want to be able to jump back and forth between the DVD and whichever application you're learning, so you can watch a technique and then try it yourself. If that's the case, you can configure your DVD player so it doesn't go "full screen," but instead displays the video in a floating window, so you can easily jump back and forth between it and any open applications. To set up this mode as the default, go under the DVD player menu, choose Preferences, click on the Player icon, and where it says "When DVD Player opens," turn off "Enter Full Screen mode" (it's on by default). Then, the next time you insert a training DVD, it appears in a floating window.

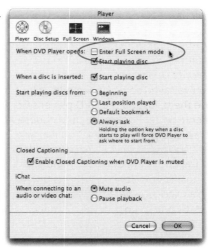

   iDVD 3: **CREATING YOUR OWN THEMES**

No doubt, iDVD comes with some fairly cool background themes, but you can also create your own (using a program like Adobe Photoshop). Just create a new document in Photoshop at 640x480 pixels, and design your new theme. Save your theme as a Photoshop file. Go to iDVD, click on the Customize button to make the Customize Drawer visible. Click the Settings button in the Customize Drawer, and then drag-and-drop your Photoshop file onto the Background Image/Movie well and it becomes the current background theme. If you don't have Photoshop, just drag a picture from your iPhoto Library.

   iDVD 3: **STOPPING THAT INFERNAL MUSIC LOOP**

If you've used iDVD at all, you already know how short a time it takes before the looping music track that plays over, and over, and over again starts to drive you mad. If only there were a way to stop it. Thankfully, there is: Click the Motion button (of all things) to stop the infernal music loop until you want it on again (it's hard to imagine that time will ever come, but it will). Then, you'll press the Motion button again.

iDVD 3: **BREAKING THE 60-MINUTE DVD LIMIT**

If you go to the Customize Drawer and click on the Status icon, it shows a DVD with a 60-minute status by default, and you'd figure that's the limit, but if you compile enough content that it exceeds 60 minutes, a dialog appears letting you know you've passed 60 minutes, and that you can continue, up to 90 minutes, but the quality may suffer a bit. Hey, at least they warn you, eh?

iDVD 3: **CREATING THEMES THAT WORK ON TV**

If you're creating your own custom iDVD themes, you have to be careful not to get your buttons or any other content too close to the edges, or when your DVD is played on a TV screen, the edges will be cropped off (that's just the way TV works). However, you can make certain that you don't enter this "no man's land" area (called the NTSC title safe area by the video crowd) by going under the Advanced menu and choosing Show TV Safe Area. This puts a backscreened border around the outside edges of your theme, indicating which areas to steer clear of.

   iDVD 3: SETTING THE TRACK ORDER

This one throws a lot of people, because moving the clips around in the iDVD menu doesn't actually change the Track List Order on the DVD. To put the clips in the order that you want them to appear on the DVD (so you can bypass the menu altogether and just shuttle from one track to the next), drag each clip (one at a time) to the iDVD window. Double-check the order by clicking Theme to open the Themes drawer and then click Status.

   iDVD 3: WHICH SETTINGS WORK BEST FOR IMPORTING

iDVD 3 supports most of the same video and image file formats that QuickTime does, so if your video-editing app can export to QuickTime, you can probably use these movies in your iDVD project. To get the best results, here are some QuickTime export settings you can try: Choose DV/DVCPRO-NTSC with a frame rate of 29.97 (if you're creating video that will be viewed outside the U.S., use PAL-DV with a frame rate of 25). For audio, choose No Compression and set the rate to 48 KHz. Also, for best quality on screen, don't use QuickTime movies that are smaller than the DVD standard size of 720x480 pixels.

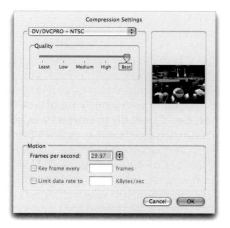

iDVD 3: GETTING RID OF THE APPLE LOGO WATERMARK

I'm never one to deny Apple its props, and I love the Apple logo (in fact, I have an Apple logo sticker on my car and at least one-third of my clothing), but the one place I don't want it to appear is on my iDVD projects (where it appears by default as a watermark). If you're like me and want it to go away, just go under the iDVD menu, under Preferences, click on the General icon, and turn off the Show Apple Logo Watermark checkbox.

iDVD 3: MOVING YOUR IDVD 3 PROJECT TO ANOTHER MAC

If you're thinking of moving your iDVD project from your Mac to another Mac, make sure you move all the source files (both still images and movies) you used in your project right along with it. You'll need to, because iDVD references those files, and without them, you're pretty much out of luck. Your best bet is probably to store all your source files in the same folder as your iDVD project file, that way (a) you won't forget them when copying, and (b) you don't have to worry about iDVD going to search for them—they're right there.

iDVD 3: BEATING THE SLIDESHOW LIMIT

While it's true that iDVD limits your slide-show to 99 slides, iDVD does allow you to have multiple slide shows on the same disc, so your only real limitation is that it can show only 99 at a time.

   iDVD 3: THE MOTION MENUS MISSING FROM BURNED DVDS

If you burn a DVD and you don't get the motion menus or motion backgrounds, here's an easy fix: Before you burn your DVD, make sure you have the Motion button checked (turned on), or the motion menus, buttons, and audio won't be available when you try to play your disc.

I smell trouble

TROUBLE-SHOOTING TIPS

If Mac OS X is the most stable operating system in the world, why do we need a troubleshooting chapter? Well, this chapter

I Smell T-r-o-u-b-l-e
troubleshooting tips

really isn't about system crashes—it's more about dealing with applications that freeze up and stuff like that. In fact, Mac OS X is so amazingly stable I'm not sure you could write an entire chapter on system crashes. In fact, I know many Mac OS X users who have never had even one system crash—it works all day, every day, flawlessly. Outside of Mac OS X users, you'd be hard-pressed to find anyone else on this entire planet who's never experienced Microsoft Windows' "blue screen of death." Okay, admittedly, I did once hear about a man in Walpole, Massachusetts (a retired CPA), who only uses his PC for writing letters to his brother in Novi, Michigan (a retired airline pilot). They don't get along all that well, so he only writes him two or three times a year, and then mostly to complain about a pustulated bunion on his left foot that's the size of a Titleist Pro V1. Thus far, his PC hasn't crashed. But it's comin'. Oh yes, bunion man—it's a-comin'.

   SOMETHING'S WRONG: TRY THIS FIRST

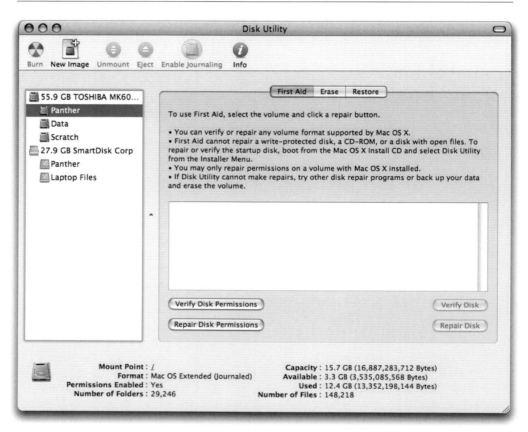

If your Mac starts acting funky, it's time to reach for Disk First Aid. In Mac OS X, Disk First Aid is part of Disk Utility—a free utility program that comes with Mac OS X, and it's the first place I go when things get hairy. Because Disk First Aid won't (can't, refuses to) repair your startup disk, you'll have to start up from your Mac OS X install disk (just restart and hold the letter "c" while the system is booting to start up from the CD, rather than the system on your hard drive). Once restarted from your CD, click on the Installer menu, then choose Disk Utility. Once Disk Utility opens, click on the First Aid button, then click on the drive you want to repair and click the Repair Disk button.

MAC MESSED UP? TRY THIS NEXT

If Disk First Aid doesn't fix your Mac's "wonkyness," you should probably try the age-old Mac repair trick known as "Zapping the PRAM." (This resets the battery-powered memory that retains all of your Mac preferences after you've shut down your Mac. Zapping it resets everything back to the factory default settings.) Restart your Mac and hold Option-Command-P-R (that's the letter "p" and the letter "r"—hold them both down, along with Option-Command). Keep holding these down and your Mac will "bong" and restart over and over again. Let it go through this "bonging and restarting thing" at least three times, then release the keys you've been holding down, and let your Mac go through its regular startup routine. This can fix a number of your Mac's ills. (*Note*: Don't be surprised if one of the preferences it resets is your startup disk back to OS 9.)

   **IN AN EMERGENCY, THEY BREAK THE GLASS**

I said on the back cover and in the introduction that I wasn't going to include any UNIX, and in keeping with that promise, I'm not going to even open the Terminal window (your Mac's evil gateway into its UNIX soul, where really scary command line stuff takes place). However, I'm going to just mention, in passing, a great Mac OS X repair technique used by some UNIX-savvy people. Now, because I'm simply relating a story about how other people use a UNIX-y repair trick, instead of telling you how to do it, I'm not really teaching you UNIX. Hey, if you wind up learning something by my simply relating their story, that's not my fault, right? Well, here's what those UNIX hooligans do—they restart their Macs, but on restart, they hold the Command key and the "s" key. Soon, a list of scary-looking commands appears on their screen, then they type "fsck -y" (*note*: after the "k," type a space, the minus sign, and then the letter "y"), then press the Return key. This invokes some sort of freaky UNIX ritual in which line after line of UNIX mumbo-jumbo starts scrolling up their screen in white reversed text on a black background. If their Mac is okay, it'll say so—"The volume appears to be OK." If that's the case, they just type "reboot" and go on with their lives. However, if a problem is found on their machine, it reads "File System Modified," which means "uh-oh!" If they get the "File System Modified" message, it seems that they repeat the process of typing in "fsck -y" and then hitting the Return key, again and again, until "The volume appears to be OK" finally appears (which they say, usually takes just a few tries). *Then* they can type "reboot" and their Macs restart as usual. These people reportedly then go on to live otherwise productive lives knowing that they cheated death, used UNIX, and lived to fight another day.

   DEALING WITH PROBLEMS IN CLASSIC MODE

If you run into problems while in Classic mode, you can use many of the old pre-OS X trouble-shooting tips (disabling the Extensions from loading, bringing up the Extensions Manager on startup, rebuilding the desktop, etc.). The great thing is, you don't have to remember all those keyboard shortcuts, because Mac OS X lets you choose which Classic startup tweaks you want to do in Classic, while you're still in Mac OS X. Just go to the System Preferences and click on the Classic icon.

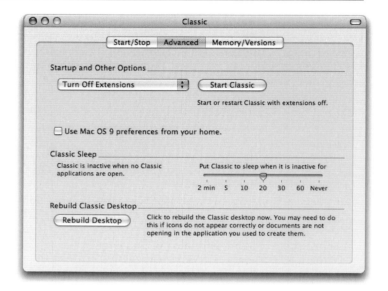

In the Classic pane, click on the Advanced button. You'll see a pop-up menu and a Start/Restart button where you can choose to have Classic boot with all extensions turned off or open the Extension Manager. There's even a button for rebuilding the desktop.

   DEALING WITH EL CRASHO GRANDE

If Mac OS X has such a momentous crash that it disables your whole machine (this has only happened to me twice), all you can really do is shut down and restart. If you're sure you've really crashed and all hope is lost, you can usually restart by pressing Shift-Option-Command and the Power On Button (if your keyboard has one—Apple's latest keyboard sadly doesn't have one and that tweaks me to no end). If you don't have a Power On button on the keyboard, press-and-hold the one on your Mac itself and after a few seconds, it should shut down. Then, you can restart by simply pushing the Power On key again.

WHEN FILES DON'T WANT TO BE TRASHED

If you have a file that clearly has a burning will to live on, because it won't let you drag it into the Trash, here are a couple of things to help you shorten its life span:

(1) If you see a little lock icon at the lower-left corner of the file's icon, that means it's locked. Click on the stubborn file, press Command-I to open its Info window, and turn off the Locked checkbox. It should now accept its new life in the ol' dump-a-roo.

(2) If the reluctant document is in a folder (or if it's a folder itself), click on the folder, then press Command-I to open its Info window. Click on the right-facing gray triangle to the left of the words "Ownership & Permissions" to reveal that pane. Assuming you're the administrator (or assuming that this is your Mac and you're its only user), in the pop-up menu for Owner, change from Read Only to Read & Write. Now, you should be able to move your document/folder into the Trash.

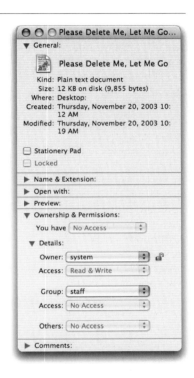

   UN-FORGETTING YOUR PASSWORD

What do you do if you forget your administrator password? Believe it or not, you're not SOL (Suddenly Out of Luck. Okay, we both know that word isn't suddenly, but for the sake of my editors, let's pretend it is). To get around your forgotten password, you need your original Mac OS X installer disc. Put it in your CD-ROM drive, restart your Mac, and as soon as it begins to restart, hold down the letter "c" on your keyboard (this tells your Mac to boot from the CD, rather than the system on your drive). Go to the Installer menu, and then choose Reset Password. When the dialog appears, choose which disk you want to access, then type in a new user name and password. Click the Save button, and quit the Reset Password dialog, then quit the Installer program. That's it. When you restart your Mac, you can use your new user name and password. I know what you're thinking—shouldn't this have been in the Mac OS Pranks chapter? Probably, but I just didn't have the heart.

   WHEN YOUR APPLICATION FREEZES UP

It happens: You're working along, not doing anything earth-shattering (you're not splitting atoms, reanalyzing the national debt, etc.), and your current application just freezes. The good news is—this freeze affects only your current application—all other running applications and the system itself are just fine. The bad news—you'll have to force quit, so any unsaved documents are, well, unsaved. To force quit, press Option-Command-Esc to bring up the Force Quit dialog (or Option-Control-click on the frozen application's icon in the Dock and choose Force Quit from the pop-up).

   CHICKENING OUT OF A FORCE QUIT

When you go to force quit an application, the Force Quit window appears, where you can choose which application you want to force quit. If this window is open and you decide force quitting is not what you wanted to do (in other words, you "chicken out"), instead of clicking the Force Quit button (which force quits the highlighted application) just press Command-W (or click the red button) to close the window, and you've effectively "chickened out."

WHEN THE MAC WON'T LET YOU INSTALL A PROGRAM

This happens sometimes, even if you're the administrator. You double-click on an installer to install an application, and a large dialog appears, telling you, "You need an Administrator's Password to install the software," but then it doesn't ask you for a password. What's the deal? All you have to do is click on the little lock icon at the bottom left-hand side of the dialog, where it says "Click the lock to make changes" and the password dialog appears (I know, it doesn't make much sense, but that's the way it works). Once it appears, just enter your admin password, and then you can install the program. That is, if you're the administrator (if you're a single user, and not sharing your machine with other users, or across a network, you're automatically the administrator).

   WHEN IT COMES TO TROUBLESHOOTING, YOU'RE NOT ALONE

One of the most amazing and gratifying things about Mac OS X is that it's so stable that there's just not much troubleshooting stuff necessary. Needless to say though, there's more to troubleshooting a computer than I can fit into this chapter; but you're not out of luck. That's because Apple has created a huge database of Macintosh problems and their solutions (called the Apple Knowledge Base) that you can access via their Web site at http:// kbase.info.apple.com.

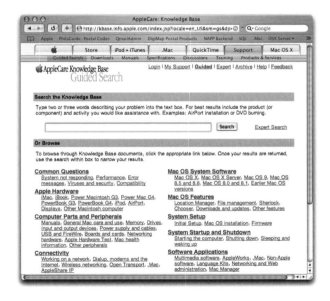

WHEN ALL ELSE FAILS, REINSTALL

If you've tried just about everything and your Mac is still acting up, there comes a point when you realize that you're going to have to do a full reinstall. This isn't a bad thing—you're not reinstalling Windows. And luckily, this doesn't reformat your drive—it doesn't erase or uninstall your applications—in fact, it doesn't mess with your Home folder at all—it just reinstalls your System stuff (that's the technical term: "System stuff"). To do a reinstall, insert your Mac OS CD, restart holding the "c" key down (to start up off the CD), and then run the

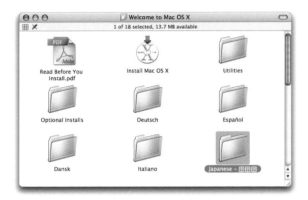

installer. It sounds like a lot of trouble, but it's really not, and doing a reinstall usually fixes all that ails your Mac. It's like the "Magic Fix-it Potion," and now that it's so easy, you don't have to fear a reinstall any more.

PANIC ROOM

Now don't panic, but there's a chance that one day you will—panic, that is. That's right—a full-fledged "running down the halls screaming" total freak-out type of panic. This will occur should you, or a loved one, encounter the dreaded "Kernel Panic." (This is the same term used to describe a situation that happened back in the 1970s at local KFCs if they thought the restaurant's namesake was going to drop by unannounced [okay, that was bad. Sorry]). Actually, a Kernel Panic appears without warning, right in the middle of your work, as a black screen packed with frightening UNIX code. The fix? Just restart right away, and chances are the panic will immediately subside (the Mac's—not yours). It will probably never rear its ugly head again. If for some reason, restarting doesn't do the trick (get this), just restart again. Okay, does it seem like simply restarting one's Mac cures just about everything? Yup—it sure seems like that.

TRASHIN' THE PREFS

If you have an application that keeps crashing for some unexplained reason, it may be because its preferences file has become corrupt. This is more common than you might think, and luckily, fixing it is easier than you might think. Just go to your Home folder, into your Library folder, into your Preferences folder, locate the preferences file for the application, and drag it to the Trash (the file might be in a folder with the application's name). Restarting your application rebuilds a new factory-fresh set of preferences, and this often takes care of your problem. A good hint that a corrupt preferences file is the root of the problem is if something looks wrong within the application itself. For example, in Photoshop, I've seen tools missing, menu commands suddenly missing, and handles missing from bounding boxes. Trashing Photoshop's preferences file fixed all these problems in just seconds.

   WHEN TRASHIN' THE PREFS DOESN'T WORK

If deleting the preferences file doesn't fix your application's problems, it might be time for (you guessed it) a reinstall of your application. Before you do, make sure you trash the preferences file (as detailed in the previous tip) and delete the application by dragging it into the Trash. Then, put your application install disc in the CD-ROM drive, and get to it.

FROZEN IN THE DOCK

This particular problem (freezing a Dock icon in its magnified view, or the whole Dock itself just freezes up) usually happens to me when I'm toggling back and forth between an application running in Classic mode and one running in Mac OS X. Luckily, fixing the problem usually just requires force quitting the Dock. You do this by going to your Applications folder, into the Utilities folder, and double-clicking on a utility called Activity Monitor. Once it launches, you see a list of

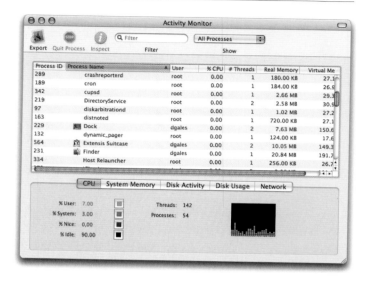

the currently running processes, including the Dock. To force quit it, just click once on its name to highlight it, then click the Stop sign at the top of the window.

 AVOIDING THE CRASHING BLUES

If you want to bring on problems—bad stuff like Kernel Panics, crashes, freezes, bronchitis, etc.—a sure way to bring them about is to delete or rename files or folders that Mac OS X needs to do its thing. Some of these are invisible files (I know, if I can't see them, how can I delete them? They become visible when you're accessing your machine across a network, or if you boot from Mac OS 9), and some are files and folders on the root directory. If you rename them, that freaks the OS out. The real danger of this happening is when you have booted in Mac OS 9, because when you do, the OS no longer protects these files and folders (they're locked and protected in Mac OS X). So basically, if you've booted in Mac OS 9, don't go messin' with stuff that looks strange to you (in other words, hands off anything you're not absolutely sure about—don't change its name, don't move it, and for sure don't delete it).

Index

Symbols

A

privileges, changing, 168
programs. *See* applications
progress bars in Dock, 124

Q-R

question mark icons, 42
QuickTime
   converting Preview images to, 211
   Hot Picks, disabling, 97
   updates, disabling, 97
QuickTime movies. *See also* **movies**
   in Dock, 47
   playing from Stickies, 218
   previewing in Column view, 11
QuickTime Pro, tweaking video, 142
quitting
   applications, 45, 103, 130, 148
   Classic mode, 117

rating system (iTunes), 246
   top-rated songs playlists, 230
rebuilding the desktop, 111
reducing
   icon size, Mail Drawer, 174
   intros to songs (iTunes), 226
reinstalling
   applications, 297
   Mac OS X, 296
remaining time, displaying for songs
   (iTunes), 231
reminders (iCal), sending to cell phone,
   190. *See also* **alarms (iCal)**
removing. *See also* **hiding**
   channels from Sherlock, 215
   color from monitor, 166
   File Extension dialog, 156
   hard disk icon from desktop, 167
   icons in Menu Extras feature, 85
   Preview column, 8
   shadows, 264
renaming. *See also* **file names;
   names of icons**
   icons
     in Column view, 75
     copying file names for, 75
   labels in Color Labels feature, 63
resizing
   columns in Column view, 12
   Dock, 46, 55
   icons, 70
   song list window (iTunes), 242
restarting
   Classic mode
     with keyboard shortcuts, 119
     manually, 118
   computer, 292
restoring cropped out scenes in
   iMovies, 255
restricted characters, file names, 76

Revert to Original, 266
Rewind button, 254
right-click menus. *See* **contextual menus**
rotating images, 266
rulers, hiding in TextEdit, 204

S

Safari
   backtracking to visited sites, 197
   Bookmarks Bar, keyboard
     shortcuts, 199
   emailing URLs, 199
   Google searches
     accessing previous searches, 198
     finding search term on results
       page, 198
     opening in separate window, 196
   hiding sites visited, 195
   keyboard shortcuts, 196
   Smooth Scrolling feature, 200
   Tabbed Browsing, 201
     one-click loading, 195
     switching between tabs, 200
   typing URLs, 197
Save As dialog box
   expanding, 87
   keyboard shortcuts, 129
Save dialog box, 88
saving
   files, 86, 125, 137
     with existing file name, 80
     expanding Save As dialog box, 87
     with file extensions, 89
     keyboard shortcuts for Save As
       dialog box, 129
     when quitting Classic mode, 117
     Save dialog box, 88
     in Word format, 207
   text colors in Stickies, 217
   Visualizer plug-in color
     combinations, 241
   Web sites in Sherlock, 214
Scale effect, 58
   enabling, 101
screen captures
   creating of one window, 140
   shortcuts to creating, 153
screen savers
   hot corners, disabling, 104
   passwords, 165
Scripts, assigning Folder Actions to
   folders, 64
scroll bars
   customizing, 22
   keyboard shortcuts for, 22
scroll wheels, iCal usage, 193
Search field in toolbars, narrowing
   searches, 37
Search Results window, closing, 126

searches. *See also* **finding**
   by color, 62
   Google searches
     accessing previous searches, 198
     finding search term on results
       page, 198
   Mail, 175
   meetings by attendee name, 189
   multiple searches in Sherlock, 215
   narrowing, 37
Secure Empty Trash, 83
security, 151
Security icon, 151
see-through notes (Stickies),
   creating, 217
selecting
   files in Icon view, 132
   multiple icons, 72, 74
selections
   converting to Stickies, 220
   in Preview, zooming to, 208
sending
   imported clips straight to the
     timeline, 259
   movies via iChat, 273
separate windows, opening
   folders in, 14-15
   Google in, 196
   Sidebar items in, 127
separator bars, inserting in toolbars, 7
shadows, removing, 264
sharing
   files, changing permissions, 96
   playlists (iTunes), 247
Sherlock
   channels
     navigating, 213
     removing, 215
   multiple searches, 215
   Name column, moving, 214
   toolbar, customizing, 212
   Web sites, saving, 214
Shopping Cart feature, iTunes Music
   Store, 245
shortcuts. *See also* **keyboard shortcuts**
   to applications, 140
   for creating screen captures, 153
Show Item Info feature, 73
shutting down computer, 103, 133
   without warning dialog box, 105
shuttling through movies, 254
Sidebar
   customizing, 8, 17, 18
   ejecting disks, 73
   Favorites folder, inserting, 9
   folders, inserting, 80
   hiding, 9
   Icon view, 7
   launching applications, 129

COLOPHON

This book was produced by the authors and their design team using all Macintosh computers, including a Power Mac G4 450-MHz, a Power Mac G4 500-MHz, a Power Mac G4 Dual Processor 1.25-GHz, a Power Mac G4 733-MHz, a Power Mac G4 933-MHz, and an iMac. We use LaCie, Sony, and Apple Studio Display monitors.

Page layout was done using Adobe InDesign 2.0. Our graphics server is a Power Mac G3, with a 60-GB LaCie external drive, and we burn our CDs to a TDK veloCD 32X CD-RW.

The headers for each technique are set in Adobe MyriadMM_565 SB 600 NO at 11 on 12.5 leading, with the Horizontal Scaling set to 100%. Body copy is set using Adobe MyriadMM_400 RG 600 NO at 9.5 points on 11.5 leading, with the Horizontal Scaling set to 100%.

Screen captures were made with Snapz Pro X and were placed and sized within Adobe InDesign 2.0. This book was output at 150 line screen, and all in-house printing was done using a Tektronix Phaser 7700 by Xerox.

ADDITIONAL RESOURCES

ScottKelbyBooks.com
For information on Scott's other Macintosh and graphics-related books, visit his book site. For background info on Scott, visit www.scottkelby.com.

http://www.scottkelbybooks.com

Mac Design Magazine
Scott is Editor-in-Chief of *Mac Design Magazine*, "The Graphics Magazine for Macintosh Users." It's a tutorial-based print magazine with how-to columns on Photoshop, Illustrator, QuarkXPress, Dreamweaver, GoLive, Flash, Final Cut Pro, and more. It's also packed with tips, tricks, and shortcuts for your favorite graphics applications.

http://www.macdesignonline.com

National Association of Photoshop Professionals (NAPP)
The industry trade association for Adobe® Photoshop® users and the world's leading resource for Photoshop training, education, and news.

http://www.photoshopuser.com

KW Computer Training Videos
Scott Kelby is featured in a series of more than 20 Photoshop training videos and DVDs, each on a particular Photoshop topic, available from KW Computer Training. Visit the Web site or call 813-433-5000 for orders or more information.

http://www.photoshopvideos.com

Photoshop Down & Dirty Tricks
Scott is also author of the best-selling book *Photoshop CS Down & Dirty Tricks*, and the book's companion Web site has all the info on the book, which is available at bookstores around the country.

http://www.downanddirtytricks.com

Adobe Photoshop Seminar Tour
See Scott live at the Adobe Photoshop Seminar Tour, the nation's most popular Photoshop seminars. For upcoming tour dates and class schedules, visit the tour Web site.

http://www.photoshopseminars.com

PhotoshopWorld
The convention for Adobe Photoshop users has now become the largest Photoshop-only event in the world. Scott Kelby is technical chair and education director for the event, as well as one of the instructors.

http://www.photoshopworld.com

Photoshop CS for Digital Photographers
This book cuts through the bull and shows you step by step the exact techniques used by today's cutting-edge digital photographers, and it shows you which settings to use, when to use them, and why.

http://www.scottkelbybooks.com

Photoshop Hall of Fame
Created to honor and recognize those individuals whose contributions to the art and business of Adobe Photoshop have had a major impact on the application or the Photoshop community itself.

http://www.photoshophalloffame.com